D0906378

COMPUTERS AND EDUCATION SERIES
Keith A. Hall, Editor

READING

A·N·D

COMPUTERS

Issues for Theory and Practice

Edited by
DAVID REINKING

Foreword by
GEORGE E. MASON

TEACHERS COLLEGE PRESS

Teachers College
Columbia University
New York and London

Published by Teachers College Press, 1234 Amsterdam Avenue,
New York, NY 10027

Library of Congress Cataloging-in-Publication Data

Reading and computers.

(Computers and education series)
Bibliography: p.
Includes index.
1. Reading—Computer-assisted instruction.
I. Reinking, David. II. Series.
LB1050.37.R42 1987   428.4'07'8   87-10053

ISBN 0-8077-2866-7

Manufactured in the United States of America

92 91 90 89 88 87 1 2 3 4 5 6

Contents

    of Reading Diagnosticians   127
        John F. Vinsonhaler, Annette B. Weinshank,
        Christian C. Wagner, and Ruth M. Polin

9. Using Computer-Simulated Instruction to Study
    Preservice Teachers' Thought Processes   141
        Donna Alvermann

10. Computer Speech in Reading Instruction   156
        Richard K. Olson and Barbara Wise

11. Using Computers as an Integral Aspect
    of Elementary Language Arts Instruction:
    Paradoxes, Problems, and Promise   178
        Larry Miller and J. Dale Burnett

    About the Contributors   193
    Index   197

Foreword

This is a different book than most of its predecessors. Rather than explaining how computers may be used in today's reading instruction, the authors of this book present their views and their reasoning about how computers *should be used and may be used in the future*. They do it very well.

Throughout this excellent book two themes are constant. One is that the computer can become an even more exciting instructional tool than it is today. The other is that the research necessary for developing the potential of this tool is now underway.

Among the topics presented are a method for arranging computer drills so that they can actually teach generalizations inductively, a tested plan for using computer simulations to improve teachers' skills in reading diagnosis, and a description of a computer-controlled video-tape simulation for teaching reading diagnosis. Also included are a thought-provoking description of the many kinds of research projects now underway, a description of new computer-generated measures of writing that are helping us learn more about the general principles guiding writers at various levels of proficiency, and an in-depth analysis of the effect that teacher beliefs and methodological preferences exert on their selection and evaluation of reading instructional software.

However, the most provocative chapters in this work are those that address the computer's ability to change texts and graphic displays and/or to speak in response to requests for help by readers. The authors sketch numerous possibilities for text and graphic presentations by computer. They point out that various text presentations can be made contingent upon eye movements as well as upon direct requests for help or the missing of a test item. Moreover, they describe not only programs that prompt readers by pronouncing words that readers don't recognize when encountered on the screen, but also research aimed at determining whether a particular reader should hear the whole word pronounced or hear it syllable by syllable.

This is a forward-looking book, one that will help all of us concerned with the teaching of reading to better understand the issues to be confronted if the computer is to help us achieve the goal of universal literacy. The writing is skillful and generally straightforward, so that even those with little computer knowledge should be able to follow the reasoning and gain much of the excitement shared with the reader by the authors. I recommend it strongly.

George E. Mason
University of Georgia
December 30, 1986

Preface

Over the past several years I have been approached by a number of graduate students who were considering similar dissertation topics. Each was interested in investigating the use of computers in some aspect of reading instruction. Although they enthusiastically presented their ideas for research, I suspect that most left my office with less enthusiasm for the topic. This change of heart was due, I think, to the fact that I pressed them to consider questions like the following: What characteristics of the computer make a difference for reading and reading instruction? What are the hypothesized effects of these characteristics and how will you isolate them for study? What literature will you review? What orientation, theoretical or otherwise, will you adopt to explain findings? My intent in asking these questions was not to discourage research in this area, because I feel that there are reasonable answers that could be the basis for important research. Yet, the difficulty students had in responding reflects in microcosm the difficulty faced by many in the field of reading who are trying to understand how computer technology interacts with reading and reading instruction. Professionals in reading, from educational researchers to classroom teachers, are struggling to discover the rightful place of the computer in their activities.

This book, then, is aimed at those graduate students and others like them who are interested in examining seriously the topic of reading and computers but who may be unaware of scholarship and research applicable to the topic. In the chapters that follow the reader will not find definitive answers to questions about computers and reading, but important issues are raised and interesting new applications are presented. The purpose of this book is to stimulate thought, not make specific recommendations. This was my primary motivation for inviting recognized scholars to share their insights, technological expertise, research, and innovative applications of computer technology in the area of reading.

Collectively the chapters indicate that activities involving the computer in the field of reading extend considerably farther than the commercial software frequently associated with computers and reading. A disproportionate amount of the existing literature is linked to the use of computers for developmental reading instruction and frequently is limited to testimonials, reviews of commercial software, and a few studies from which it is difficult to make generalizations. This literature provides little guidance for research and mixed messages for practice. In contrast the chapters that follow examine a broad range of applications and draw on current research and theory in reading and related fields. The ideas presented by these authors should give direction to research as well as stimulate more divergent thinking about how computers might be applied to reading. In short, I feel that the chapters in this book are convincing evidence that the computer deserves the attention of serious scholars and researchers who are interested in reading and reading instruction.

The organization of the book reflects an attempt to achieve a balanced consideration of issues that range from theory to practice. Thus, the book has been divided into three sections: theoretical issues, research issues, and instructional issues. Those interested primarily in research will find that many of the chapters suggest empirical questions, testable hypotheses, and new methodologies for research. Practitioners will be exposed to perspectives for instructional uses of the computer and will get a glimpse of applications that may dramatically affect instruction in the future. Those interested in exploring new applications of the computer will find ideas and useful insights for the development of computer-based products.

The diversity of topics addressed in each section is due to the authors' varied backgrounds and experiences. All of the authors are practicing scholars in reading or a related field (e.g., educational psychology), and all have had experience working with computers in some aspect of their professional work. Yet, each has followed a different path to arrive at an interest in computers in reading. Their experiences to a varying degree include research involving the computer, development of instructional software, and publication of articles about computers in scholarly journals. Significantly, several of the authors are widely recognized for their scholarship in aspects of reading and reading instruction that are not directly related to the computer. This background gives them a broad perspective for considering how computer technology interacts with reading.

Despite the diversity of topics and the varying backgrounds of the authors, several dominant themes emerge across the chapters. First, the computer makes possible new and potentially powerful alternatives for the display and manipulation of written text, a feature that both suggests interesting new possibilities for reading and reading instruction and also leads to new questions for research. Second, computer technology promises to enhance reading research. The computer has already helped researchers conduct more sophisticated analyses of data, but it also makes possible new methods for gathering new kinds of data concerning readers and texts. Finally, these chapters accentuate the need to look more divergently at how the computer may contribute to reading instruction. The instructional applications described in several of the chapters point to an unprecedented array of new options for instruction.

I wish to thank the contributing authors for their effort in bringing this volume to fruition. It is difficult to maintain a spirit of teamwork and unity via phone calls and letters. Nonetheless, the authors of these chapters performed admirably. They are all busy professionals, yet each dedicated considerable time to this project. They were especially gracious in accepting constructive criticism of their work. For this cooperation and confidence I am grateful.

READING

A·N·D

COMPUTERS

Issues for Theory and Practice

Part I
THEORETICAL ISSUES

Adopting a theoretical position, even a rudimentary one, is a mark of maturity in the study of a phenomenon or in the use of a technology. The authors in this section begin to explore theoretical frameworks that might be used to think about computers and reading. Their consideration of how computers, reading, and theory interact is important because there have been few attempts to examine closely the differences between reading with a computer and reading without one. Until such differences can be clarified, it will be difficult to consider appropriate uses of the computer in the field of reading. The nature of reading when text is displayed by a computer also promises to become an increasingly important issue as more reading takes place on a computer screen.

In the first chapter Reinking proposes that the display of text controlled by a computer should be considered a new medium of written communication. To justify this point of view he draws on recent theories of instructional media. He argues that the computer can manipulate text in ways that are significantly different from text displayed on the printed page. These differences have implications for reading comprehension because the internal processing necessary for comprehension can be more directly affected when managing the display of text is controlled by a computer. For example, a computer program can be employed to control what a reader attends to during reading by limiting the reader's access to text. Writers in the field of reading frequently refer to a reader interacting with text. Reinking argues that, unlike the printed page, a computer can respond to the needs of an individual reader, thus creating the possibility of a true interaction between reader and text.

Likewise, Daniel and Reinking highlight the differences between reading text on the printed page and reading it on a computer screen. However, they start by focusing on the physical features of how the text is displayed. They compare factors associated with legibility on the printed page and in electronic text. In so doing they review research on legibility of printed texts. Characteristics of print like font size and spacing, which

were investigated in these early studies, have not been dominant variables in recent research, but these may need to be reconsidered in light
of the differences between a page and a computer screen. Daniel and
Reinking also specify new factors associated with electronic texts that
might influence reading. They categorize these factors as concerns of
dynamic and interactive legibility. These categories draw attention to
the fact that electronic texts can be continually printed on the same
surface to simulate movement. Consequently, *when* the text is presented
to a reader becomes as important as *where* it is displayed. The capability of the computer to make reading interactive is also an important issue
discussed in this chapter.

Finally, Balajthy takes a different tack. He points out that many
instructional programs require an exact match between user input and a
narrowly defined variable in the program. He argues that this type of
programming limits the way the computer can be used in reading
instruction. As an alternative he suggests programs that permit open-
ended responses and discusses some of the programming techniques
that can be used to accomplish this. He also points out the relevance of
artificial intelligence research and theory for guiding the development of
computer applications in reading. An important implication of looking at
the use of computers in reading from an artificial intelligence perspective is that designing "intelligent" programs may lead to a better understanding of covert cognitive processes simulated by these programs.

A unifying feature of these chapters is the search for new metaphors
and terminology that can be used to talk about the use of computers in
reading. Reinking offers two new terms, "computer-mediated text" and
"interactive text," and attempts to define them. Daniel and Reinking
introduce the terms "dynamic" and "interactive" legibility, which are
derived from earlier conceptions of "static" legibility. Balajthy compares
"exact-match" and "open-ended" program designs and their impact on
reading instruction. These attempts to create new terminology are in-
dicative of efforts to impose order on our thinking about how reading
with a computer may be different from reading without one.

1
Computers, Reading, and a New Technology of Print

David Reinking

Old ideas give way slowly; for they are more than abstract logical forms and categories. They are habits, predispositions, deeply ingrained attitudes of aversion and preference.

John Dewey, 1909

New technologies usually precipitate a reformulation of ideas. The internal combustion and jet engines reshaped ideas about transportation just as today the artificial heart confronts us with new definitions of health care. In this chapter I propose that the computer makes available a new technology that may require us to rethink commonly held notions about reading and learning from text.

As Dewey's observation suggests, however, new ideas emerge slowly because they require that we abandon old ideas that have become deeply ingrained and familiar. Likewise, pondering the relationship of computers to language processes may be hampered by our familiarity with conventionally printed text. For thousands of years the dominant medium for written communication has been the written or printed page. Consequently, the technological characteristics and limitations of the printed page are so completely ingrained in our corporate psyche that we may not fully see or appreciate the implications of a medium that significantly expands options for displaying and organizing text. The computer is such a medium and for that reason deserves our attention. Unlike conventionally printed text, which is subject to the technological limitations of the page, text mediated by a computer represents a technology that approaches the flexibility and complexity of human information processing.

The potential significance of this difference can be seen by comparing concepts evolved from the technology of the printed page with newer concepts of written discourse made possible by a computer. Concepts like "page," "book," "illustration," "index," "periodical," and so forth reflect adaptations to a conventional technology of print. Although each of these terms has or could have a counterpart in text mediated by the computer, this is true only when some of the prominent technological attributes of the computer are ignored. For example, it is more appropriate to think of a window or frame of text on a computer screen than it is to think in terms of pages. Similarly, it is difficult to conceive of a traditional index on a computer without thinking of an automatic word search function being carried out by the computer. Given the networking capabilities of the computer and the potential of electronic bulletin board systems, personal correspondence as well as the means for rapidly disseminating written information may be subject to new protocols. At a number of levels, therefore, the conceptual categories associated with conventional text are not adequate when considering how text could be mediated by a computer.

The purpose of these comparisons is not to argue that all of the functions of the printed page will one day become obsolete and be replaced by computer-mediated text. Instead, these examples simply suggest that there can be something unique about written text when it is brought under the control of a computer. This realization may be a stimulus for new ideas for those interested in written language processes—ideas that are foreign until new conceptions of written discourse can be formulated. For example, a computer might be able to control the presentation of text in ways that could uniquely influence a reader's processing of text, especially during independent reading and study. Cognitive strategies typically employed to acquire meaning from text on a printed page may need to be transformed when an alternate medium like the computer can be used to manipulate the organization and display of text. Similarly, the computer may permit certain reading skills to be modeled or practiced in ways that are not possible or feasible on printed pages. It is difficult to consider these possibilities without first considering how computer technology expands options for mediating text.

The purpose of this chapter is to confront these possibilities within a framework which highlights the differences between conventional text and text mediated by a computer. First, I will identify some limitations of conventionally printed text for conveying meaning and suggest some ways the computer might circumvent these limitations. Second, I will suggest the possibility that the computer could be considered a new medium of written communication and identify the conditions that would qualify it as such. Finally, I will introduce and define two terms—"computer-mediated text" and "interactive text"—that may be useful in conceptualizing and researching differences between conventional text and text mediated by a computer. These terms will also be applied to existing research as well as potential applications involving the computer and reading.

CONSIDERING THE LIMITATIONS OF CONVENTIONALLY PRINTED TEXTS

Until the advent of the computer there has been little need to consider the limitations of text on the printed page. Previously, no other medium could match, let alone exceed, the flexibility of the printed page in displaying and organizing text. Although text can be displayed using motion picture film, for example, film has limited utility for mediating written text from either a practical or a theoretical standpoint. The limitations of the printed page become evident, however, by examining previous attempts to influence comprehension by manipulating text and comparing these to manipulations made possible by the computer.

For example, there has been an interest in studying the effects of varying the display of conventionally printed texts even though there is a relatively narrow range of logical possibilities. Early researchers focused on readily varied display factors like typography (see Daniel & Reinking, chapter 2 of this volume). Results of this research were inconclusive or difficult to interpret because these studies did not proceed from a theoretical base. There continues to be little reason to suspect that even gross variations in type fonts or line spacing have significant implications for semantic processing.

This does not mean that cognitive processing is immune to variations in the display of text on the printed page. Cromer (1970), for example, found that chunking text by expanding the space between phrase boundaries improved the comprehension of poorer readers. Likewise, others have explored the use of various typographical cues to manage the reader's attention during the reading of conventional texts (e.g., see Glynn & DiVesta, 1979; Glynn, Britton, Tillman, & Muth, 1984).

Technological improvements within the printing industry have also expanded the options available for influencing the processing of text-based information. Under certain conditions, for example, the inclusion of a picture or illustration may influence the processing of text (see Samuels, 1970; Schallert, 1980). Although printed graphics still are relatively expensive and labor intensive to produce, their presence in concert with written text is much more likely today than in the early days of printing. Newer technologies continue to expand this potential. For example, holographic techniques have recently made possible the representation of three dimensional images on two dimensional surfaces.

These examples suggest that it is reasonable to consider the cognitive consequences of alternate textual displays despite the relatively limited choices available on the printed page. Logically any extension of these alternatives made possible by the computer should be considered an important subset of these considerations. In fact, computer technology suggests unprecedented increases in the range of options available for manipulating, controlling, and displaying textual information. In this regard there are two levels at which computer technology expands textual displays: (1) enabling novel manipulations not possible on the printed page, and (2) increasing the feasibility of existing but impractical displays. In the first category are examples like cuing textual information by flashing (Daniel & Reinking, chapter 2 of this volume), animating graphical displays, and providing immediate alterations of the text itself (L'Allier, 1980; Reinking, 1985). An example of the second category would be Geoffrion and Geoffrion's (1983) description of how comprehension of technical information like that found in an automobile repair manual might be enhanced by using a computer to display the text in thought units with appropriate highlighting of key actions. This type of display is possible on the printed page, but the expense and the bulk of the resulting materials is often prohibitive.

The effectiveness of generic manipulations of the content and structure of text itself has also been constrained by the limitations of the printed page. Adjunct study aids like advance organizers (Ausubel, 1963), inserted questions (see Anderson & Biddle, 1975), and adjacent-to-text glosses (Otto, 1980) are examples of explicit attempts to reshape and enhance semantic processing by manipulating structural and organizational features of printed text. Adjunct reading and study aids are also subject to the constraints of the printed page, however. For example, in typical reading and study contexts these manipulations must intrude in some fashion on the text targeted for understanding. Their presence is no doubt useful for some readers under certain conditions, but they can also be superfluous or cumbersome for other readers who may be more effective in managing their own reading and study. Inserted questions, for example, have been shown to have a deleterious effect on the recall of information not addressed in the questions (R. C. Anderson & Biddle, 1975; Hartley & Davies, 1976). Furthermore, there is no reasonable way to guide a particular reader's use of these aids during independent reading or study. Also, a general admonition to use these textual manipulations may or may not be heeded by a reader. These limitations are a direct result of the constraints imposed on print displayed on pages and the resulting contingencies of normal reading and study.

Evidence that these are serious limitations is found in the mixed results found across studies investigating the effectiveness of adjunct study aids (see reviews by R. C. Anderson & Biddle, 1975; Barnes & Clawson, 1975; Hamilton, 1985; Hartley & Davies, 1976). Perhaps a more serious limitation is that there is no reason to believe that adjunct study aids have any long-term effect on reading and study behavior. Because adjunct aids are a static component of the text and cannot confront the needs of any particular reader, they may lead readers to only a superficial consideration of their own comprehension. In reviewing reading comprehension research, including adjunct study aids, Tierney and Cunningham (1984) concluded that one of the difficulties in obtaining consistently positive findings is the complex interactions among readers, texts, and tasks. One of the obvious limitations of conventionally printed text is the relatively limited range of textual manipulations that can be employed to accommodate this complexity in any one text. The interactive characteristics of the computer, on the other hand, might be used to deal with a wider range of readers and tasks within a particular text.

An example of how computer technology might alter the contingencies of reading and learning from conventional texts can be found in a study by T. H. Anderson, Anderson, Dalgaard, Biddle, Surber, and Alessi (1974). College students in an economics course were given reading assignments on a computer. After completing a 15- to 20-min reading assignment, students were required to answer several multiple-choice comprehension questions. Students who failed to achieve a criterion score of 75% were signed off the computer for a period of time until they had an opportunity to reread the assignment, after which they would again attempt a set of comprehension questions. New reading assignments were deferred until students had demonstrated mastery of the content as measured by the comprehension questions. Students in three economics courses whose reading was monitored by the computer in this fashion scored significantly higher on final exams than did students reading and studying on their own. These findings are noteworthy in light of the difficulty in obtaining significant achievement differences when college students' grades are at stake (Dubin & Taveggia, 1968).

Although this one study does not permit strong generalizations, it does provide a straightforward example of how a new, computer-based technology of print could overcome a fundamental limitation imposed by conventional texts. Moreover, it demonstrates one way the computer could regulate the presentation of text in a fashion not readily duplicated when students are asked to read and learn from a textbook on their own.

THE PAGE AND COMPUTER AS ALTERNATIVE MEDIA

One way to conceptualize differences between the page and the computer is to consider each a different medium for conveying information. Considering this distinction is important for two reasons. First, different media may require different cognitive skills for successful extraction of information. Second, identifying the attributes of media that affect cognitive processing provides a theoretical basis for generating testable hypotheses. If attributes of the computer and the printed page vary enough to affect the reader's processing of printed text in predictable ways, then it may be useful to consider them as separate media. This perspective would be a significant departure from the more commonly held notion that the comprehension of printed text is essentially the same process regardless of the medium used to display it.

Recently, educational psychologists have attempted to distinguish instructional media on the basis of factors that may affect cognitive processing (e.g., see Olson, 1974; Olson, 1976; Salomon, 1979; Salomon & Clark, 1977). In this perspective, learning is a function of the interactions among attributes of a medium, the nature of the learning task, and characteristics of the learner (Salomon, 1979). Thus, Salomon (1979) has argued that a view of media in a sociocultural sense (e.g., television versus newspapers) is not adequate for psychological or educational comparisons. Instead, more subtle distinctions based on specific media attributes must be addressed. He identifies four classes of these attributes that cut across various media: content; symbol systems; technologies for gathering, encoding, and conveying contents; and situations in which the media are used.

Although Salomon preferred to focus on symbol systems as the category of most consequence for distinguishing instructional media, he acknowledged that "if we exchange one major technology for another, the whole medium changes its nature" (p. 19). This is because new technologies often expand the number of symbol systems that can be used to represent meaning. Thus, technological attributes and their interaction with symbol systems can under certain circumstances play a significant role in distinguishing media on a psychological level. The computer, for example, can be used to simulate the presentation of text much like the printed page; on the other hand, by employing the computer's unique technological attributes, text might be displayed and organized using a wider range of symbolic elements including those involving sound, time-space relationships, and new options for seeking out the meaning of a particular text. In short, using the computer to mediate text may bring to bear a wider range of semiotic functions that may influence how a reader acquires meaning from text.

Salomon's remaining two categories for distinguishing media— content and situation—are usually only correlates of a medium rather than defining attributes. Reading a textbook to study for an exam and reading a recipe to cook a meal do not involve different media. Presumably the same mental skills required to extract meaning from the text are employed in both situations. Acquiring the same content from a film or demonstration, however, presumably requires a different set of skills because technologies and their related symbol systems vary significantly. Thus, in a psychological sense, a film, a lecture/ demonstration, and a written text can be considered different media. Since computer technology makes available a number of previously unavailable manipulations of text that in turn may lead to the use of a different set of mental skills to acquire meaning, the computer may qualify as a different medium of written communication. Such a difference is more than a matter of semantics because it has the potential to broaden thinking about the computer's potential to influence the acquisition of meaning from written discourse.

Another reason that the technological attributes of a medium are directly related to cognitive processing is that they vary as to how readily they permit an external modeling or supplanting of the skills needed to extract meaning (Salomon, 1979). One example is the capability of the computer to animate displays in such a way that the learner does not have to mentally manipulate certain information. Media may also be distinguished, therefore, by the degree to which they permit the modeling of relevant cognitive processing and/or relieve the processing burden placed upon the learner.

Distinctions made on this basis can be employed in evaluating the printed page and the computer as potentially different media for written communication. The content of written text is infinitely varied, as are the situations in which it may be read. Rather than improving the odds for effecting learning from text, these contingencies decrease them greatly. The ability to assist a learner's interaction with the information encoded in print is further limited by the technology associated with the printed page. Text as it may appear on the printed page does not readily permit a modeling or supplanting of the relevant skills or background information necessary for reading and understanding a particular text. During independent reading, readers must rely primarily on their current knowledge, and this knowledge must be sufficient to meet the author's assumptions about the audience if comprehension is to occur. Despite the fact that the visual display of conventionally printed text can be manipulated to affect reading processes, the printed page permits only a limited range of options for either affecting or modeling necessary cognitive activity once the message has been encoded into print.

The bases on which the printed page and the computer might be considered different media should now become clearer: Text mediated by the printed page and text mediated by a computer can be considered different instructional media if the technological attributes of each vary enough to produce variation in the cognitive skills required to extract meaning from them and/or if the degree to which those skills can be modeled or supplanted varies noticeably. The greater flexibility of display and organization afforded the presentation of text by computer technology suggests that such a distinction may be worth investigating. Thinking in these terms may provide researchers with a useful perspective when considering how computer technology interacts with reading and learning from text. Examples of how this perspective might be translated into empirical questions and new variables for study will be provided in the remaining sections of this chapter.

COMPUTER-MEDIATED TEXT

Since the theory of media outlined above is relatively abstract and since the differences between text mediated by a computer or by the printed page may not be intuitively obvious, an operational definition is necessary to establish a clear-cut difference between the two. To that end, the following definition is proposed for the phrase "computer-mediated text": any display of connected, written text that is under the immediate control of a computer program.

There are several advantages in adopting such a definition. First, the full range of computer applications in reading and studying textual information can be included. There are no limitations due to the type or size of the computer, where the text is displayed (paper, video display screen, etc.), the nature of the program or programming language, and so forth. For example, the study of students in an economics course cited earlier (T. H. Anderson et al., 1974) can be considered an example of computer-mediated text even though subjects read the text offline. Another advantage is that this definition makes a clear distinction between conventional texts and those made possible by the computer. Computer programs and the technology that makes them viable are easily identified when compared to the display of text without them.

Research and Instructional Applications Involving Computer-Mediated Text

Currently, research involving computers in reading is not focused on exploring differences between conventional text and computer-mediated text as it has been defined here. Instead, researchers have explored applications of the computer which have arisen largely from reading on printed pages. Research has been focused on using computers to dispense a new or supplemental reading curriculum (e.g., Atkinson, 1974), on comparing the computer to more traditional modes of teaching reading skills (e.g., Easterling, 1982), and on using the computer as a tool to control the presentation of text in psychological experiments (e.g., Just & Carpenter, 1976; McConkie & Zola, chapter 6 of this volume).

Although almost all of the studies in these categories employ computer-mediated text as defined above, they do so incidentally. Systematic comparisons focusing on information-processing variables that may interact with computer technology and media differences are absent in most of the existing research.

Reviewing this research also leads to an ambivalence about the importance of the computer in reading and learning from print. There is the suspicion that computers can or should have a significant and unique impact on reading and learning from text, but taken as a whole, existing research provides little guidance as to the nature or extent of this difference. Until more research can be carried out that systematically confronts the differences between reading with and without a computer, we will be less likely to move forward in our understanding of how the computer expands options for reading and learning from text.

A few efforts run contrary to current trends, however. Some investigators have begun to consider how the attributes of the computer enable unique textual manipulations that may affect the comprehension of printed material. Although not all of these efforts are guided by the theoretical perspective outlined here, they are representative of the kinds of applications and research it would generate.

L'Allier (1980), for example, attempted to increase reading comprehension by using a computer program that could lower the readability estimates of expository text and revise passage structure. Subjects read passages on a computer screen in one of several conditions. An algorithm that took into account reading time and incorrect responses to comprehension probes was used to give one experimental group a revised version of a passage when one or both factors reached a critical value. The revised version of the passage had been rewritten based on a hierarchical analysis of text structure. In two other treatments subjects read the original version of the passages with no adaptations or read only the revised version. High school subjects obtained significantly higher posttest comprehension scores in the adaptive condition. Low-ability readers in the adaptive condition scored as well as high-ability readers reading the nonadaptive, unrevised passages.

This study demonstrates how computer-mediated text can carry out online diagnoses that enable text to be adapted to the needs of a particular reader. One could also imagine the computer gathering data on how certain text structures affect identifiable categories of readers (see Frase, chapter 5 of this volume). These possibilities are feasible only because computer technology makes available a greater number of options for displaying and manipulating text.

McConkie (1983; see also McConkie & Zola, chapter 6 of this volume) has also reported a preliminary evaluation of a computer-aided reading program for nonliterate adults. The computer makes it possible for beginning readers to read above their instructional level by providing the pronunciation of an unfamiliar word when it is touched on the computer screen. Interestingly, adults exposed to this technique did not appear to become overly dependent on the computer. Observations indicated that words chosen by a reader were selected less frequently in later text. Beginning readers exposed to this type of text may more quickly become sensitive to characteristics of written text with which they are unfamiliar simply because they have not learned to read. The computer could also be made to store the words selected to form a personal word list that could be used later for individualized instruction. Readers continually selecting words containing a vowel digraph, for example, could be provided with an appropriate tutorial using the words selected and the contexts in which they were found. This blend of active, purposeful reading and individualized instruction would be difficult to duplicate on the printed page alone.

This use of computer-mediated text parallels similar but less sophisticated devices sold in some toy stores. By moving a special pen across "supermarket-type" bar codes printed below the text, children can hear the words printed on the page. Computer speech connected with printed text may blur the usual distinctions between oral and written language processes (see Rubin, 1980a). Rapid improvements in synthesized or digitized speech produced by a computer will no doubt continue to bring about interesting new applications in reading (see Olson & Wise, chapter 10 of this volume).

Wilkinson (1983), in a report on the use of a program entitled READINTIME, has cited the ability of the computer to regulate the framing, pacing, and allocation of control as important variables when comparing the computer and printed page. One function of the program is to display the words found in connected text in a variety of formats, ranging from a segment of the text under reader control to single words under program control. Although this application appears to mimic some of the characteristics of controlled reading devices, the computer can be used to exercise a wider range of control over the presentation of text. When combined with other attributes of the computer, the number of text formats and contingencies that can be brought under control of the computer or shared by the reader is almost limitless.

Dealing with language processes at a cognitive level via computer technology has not been limited to reading text. Those interested in the writing process have also begun to see how the computer may uniquely affect written communication (Bridwell, Nancarrow, & Ross, 1984). Word processing has become a firmly entrenched computer application that has changed conceptions of the writing process and how writing is taught. In fact, the definition of computer-mediated text proposed here does not exclude the use of computers to write texts.

Burns (1979), for example, conducted a study that had college students work with an open-ended computer program that modeled three heuristic strategies for generating ideas for a composition. Both the quantity and the quality of ideas were significantly greater in the computer group than in the control group receiving traditional rhetoric instruction. Although there was no evidence that the heuristic strategies were internalized, students did strongly agree that the computer-induced modeling helped them think more systematically about their own writing. These results are interesting because they suggest that the computer can be used to uniquely engage a learner in language processes.

Instructional applications that use computer technology to model processes associated with mature reading are also beginning to appear. Rubin (1980b) has described a computer program that may allow young readers to become more sensitive to the structure of stories. The computer periodically asks the reader to select from several alternatives to determine how the events of a story are to proceed. Later a reader is given a story goal and must select an appropriate alternative in order to have the story end in a manner consistent with the goal. Finally, students use the computer to construct their own stories and alternatives for other students to use.

Burnett and Miller (1984) have described another instructional program that encourages readers to make predictions while reading. After reading a segment of text on the computer screen, the reader must make at least one prediction prior to seeing a new segment. The reader's predictions center around attempts to answer a general question that is not explicitly answered in the text. Each segment provides new information that allows the reader to confirm or disconfirm predictions made earlier. By controlling the presentation of text and encouraging the reader to make predictions, the computer can model a normally covert reading strategy used by successful readers.

Interactive Text

One of the distinctive characteristics of the computer is the potential it offers to create interactive learning experiences. The range of intriguing possibilities suggested by this characteristic is probably what most accounts for the general interest and enthusiasm concerning computers in education. Other media do not typically permit much interaction between the source of information and the learner, at least during independent learning. With conventionally printed text, for example, it is not possible to monitor and react to the needs of an individual reader trying to understand a particular text. In fact, the lack of such opportunities may on occasion lead even mature readers to the conclusion that further attempts to extract meaning are fruitless because their background knowledge is inadequate for understanding. The limitations of conventional text have made the option of interactive text both functional and necessary.

A subset of computer applications in reading, therefore, might be created by making possible an interaction between the reader and the text. (Although many in the field of reading talk about an interaction between reader and text, in the literal sense this is impossible because conventional texts are inert.) When a reader experiences a failure to understand, for example, the computer could be used to adjust the text in specified ways. Interactive text is any computer-mediated text that can be manipulated to facilitate a reader's comprehension while she or he is reading. Manipulations of the text may be requested by the reader or initiated by the computer in response to its monitoring of a reader's performance.

Given our current understandings of the reading process, the ability to enhance a reader's interaction with text is an important difference between conventional and computer-mediated text. Successful reading requires active readers who can bring to bear relevant background knowledge and strategies for managing their own comprehension. Conventional print does not offer many options for influencing these processes during independent reading. The capability of computers to make reading and learning interactive may overcome this limitation. Drawing an analogy between the user of a typical computer program and the reader of an expository text may make this distinction clearer.

First, consider the user of a computer program that has been designed to carry out some specific task. The successful use of the program to accomplish the task depends to a certain degree on the expertise of the user. Familiarity with the program, awareness of the syntax to which the computer will respond, knowledge of the parameters that govern the task, and so forth all interact to determine the user's efficient use of the program.

Good computer programmers realize that these factors can be taken into account in the program. Consequently, in the programmer's vernacular programs are frequently evaluated on the basis of how "user-friendly" they are. This phrase refers to the degree to which a computer program is sensitive to the knowledge and skill of the user. For the more expert user the program permits easy access to the tools, techniques, or information provided by the program. Unnecessary prompts or directions are avoided and a great deal of knowledge on the part of the user is presumed in the execution of the program. For the novice or uninformed user, however, the same program provides a great deal of information that would be superfluous to the expert user. Providing help options and using error-trapping routines are examples of how this would typically be accomplished in writing a computer program.

To make a program user-friendly the programmer tries to anticipate those characteristics of the program and its expected use that are most likely to cause the novice user to falter. In the same program the programmer endeavors to meet the needs of a broad range of possible users. Of course, the programmer's success in creating a truly user-friendly program is predicated on his or her ability to understand and anticipate those characteristics of the program or task that are most likely to cause difficulty for different users.

Now consider a reader about to read some expository text. The essential elements of the task of reading are quite similar to those of using a computer program. Presumably, the reader's goal is to understand what is about to be read (although this appears to not necessarily be the case for certain categories of readers; see Brown, 1980). The author, like the programmer, has written the text to accomplish a particular purpose—presumably to communicate a well-defined message to the reader. A good author will also be sensitive to the knowledge and expertise of the reader. Choice of vocabulary, syntax, and subject matter is no doubt influenced by the intended audience. There are even methods, albeit limited ones, that allow the text to be more user-friendly. For example, many textbooks contain glossaries, adjunct study aids, diagrams, and the like. These may be used to accommodate a wider audience of readers.

At this point the analogy breaks down, however. The computer programmer may write the program in such a fashion that a man-machine-task dialogue is possible. Use of the computer program can be dynamic and require overt interaction. The user can directly observe the relevant task variables as defined by the programmer and can use this awareness to request and obtain immediate assistance. The program can in turn monitor the user's performance, offer help, or make recommendations based on that performance. In this process the user can also be actively engaged in evaluating the usefulness of these strategies relative to how successfully the task has been accomplished. The user-friendly program can act as an intermediary aid to externalize the factors that separate the novice and expert user and to bring those factors within the reach of the novice.

On the other hand, text on the printed page, taken by itself, provides few opportunities for constructive interaction outside the reader's head. In effect, the writer has done his or her best to write cogently on behalf of an anticipated reader. Readers are left to their own devices to acquire the author's intended meaning. Overt interaction with the source of the message or the task variables inherent in acquiring meaning from the text is difficult, if not impossible, on the printed page. More expert readers usually have well-developed and sophisticated strategies for deriving meaning from text and can successfully employ these strategies even when they possess little background about the content being read. They invoke their own error-checking routines and heuristics to resolve comprehension difficulty. In general, however, these strategies are necessarily abilities the reader brings to the task, not aids that can be supplied by the text itself. In short, experienced readers have adapted well to the contingencies of acquiring meaning from the printed page. It is only when the problems facing the novice reader or the mature reader reading far-afield are considered that the limitations of traditional print become readily apparent.

There is another point at which the analogy between using a computer program and reading text breaks down. Computer programs can be written so that the kinds of errors made and/or information requested by the user in using the program are recorded for future reference. Although this option is rarely exercised, it is nonetheless a possibility. A programmer could use this information to find out about users, the program, and the interaction between the two. This information might be used to improve the program's overall "friendliness" or to counsel certain categories of users concerning pitfalls they may encounter while using the program. The choices made and the actions taken by users would in effect give the programmer a picture of users' attempts to deal meaningfully with the task and the program.

During independent reading, on the other hand, an outside observer has great difficulty in determining what strategies are being employed by the reader because the interactions between the reader and text are normally internal. To gain insight into the reader's cognitive activity while reading, researchers have had to rely on methods that either are indirect or make significant intrusions into normal reading and study. Recording eye movements would be an example of the former and collecting verbal protocols an example of the latter. Both of these options have proved to be problematic in metacognitive research (see Belmont & Butterfield, 1977; Brown, 1980). If the interactions with text could be made more external as are the interactions with a computer program, it would be possible to obtain reliable, concurrent data that reflect covert processes. For a fuller discussion of this advantage see Reinking (1985, 1986).

An Example of Interactive Text

Applying the interactive capabilities of the computer to the reading and studying of text suggests some interesting possibilities that could change the way we think about learning from text. Some of the limitations imposed by the printed page might be overcome if reading could become more interactive. An example of how this could be accomplished can be found in a program developed by Reinking and Schreiner (1985). In this program short expository passages are displayed on a computer screen. After reading a passage, readers may request the computer to provide a number of textual manipulations to assist them in understanding what they have read.

For example, one passage gives a technical description of how the layers on a piece of photographic film each serve a specific function. In reading the passage a reader encounters the phrase "antihalation coating" to describe one of the layers. Contextual clues are minimal and one would not expect the average reader to know the meaning of the term "antihalation." The computer program, however, allows the reader to easily identify this word which is then immediately defined in the context of the passage. Should the reader decide that the passage is too technical, the computer will also provide a less technical version of it. Some readers may also determine that they possess inadequate background knowledge about the content of the passage. By pressing the appropriate key, a reader can request supplemental information about the topic. An animated graphical representation or illustration could also be given to demonstrate a key concept, relationship, or procedure. Finally, the reader may have difficulty forming a gist from text containing unfamiliar content. In this case the computer program provides the main idea of each paragraph in the passage.

Readers using this program are required to respond to a number of comprehension items after each passage and must achieve a criterion score on these items before they are permitted to see more text. Readers not attaining the criterion score are asked to read and study the passage again, making use of any textual manipulations they feel may be useful. This aspect of the program employs the computer's capability to more closely monitor a reader's comprehension during independent reading and to encourage readers to examine factors that hinder their comprehension. One of the obvious advantages of interactive text, then, could be that it instigates the application of active comprehension monitoring.

This version of interactive text also supplies the interested observer with information about a reader's reading and study behavior during independent reading. The program records not only a reader's performance on the comprehension items but also those manipulations selected during reading. For example, a teacher or researcher could determine which readers requested the definition of the word "antihalation" while reading the passage about film. This can be done after the reader has finished reading the passage, thus avoiding any intrusion on the reader's processing of the information. In fact, the reader is unaware that his or her selections are being monitored. Data gathered in this manner represent reliable, concurrent information that could give unique insights into the strategies used by a reader reading a particular text.

This capability adds a new dimension to reading research and the acquisition of data concerning how readers, texts, and instruction interact. For example, the effects of certain instructional approaches or emphases on independent reading could be measured by changes in the quantity or quality of manipulations selected. Alternatively, selection data could be used to empirically validate revisions in existing texts. If a majority of readers from a certain population repeatedly selected the same textual manipulation while reading a particular passage, this could be interpreted as evidence that the original version of the text should be revised to make the manipulation unnecessary.

Exposing readers to interactive text could be expected to produce benefits at a number of levels. First, comprehension of expository text could be expected to increase because of the wider range of information immediately available to the reader. Similarly, the text would be accessible to a wider range of readers because greater variations in background knowledge, reading skill, and processing strategies could be accommodated. At another level, making textual manipulations available may stimulate more active processing of the text on the part of the reader, especially when the program assists in monitoring the reader's comprehension. Readers known to be deficient in these skills might become more active in monitoring their own comprehension after exposure to interactive text.

Reinking and Schreiner (1985) investigated these possibilities by having intermediate-grade readers use the program described above. In this study good and poor readers read three high-difficulty and three low-difficulty expository passages in one of four treatment conditions: The first group was given the interactive text; the second group read the same passages on the computer, but was not given the opportunity to select textual manipulations; the third group read the same passages on printed pages; and the fourth group was required to view all of the available manipulations prior to using the computer to select manipulations on their own. Results indicated that readers will freely select textual manipulations when given the opportunity to do so and that across the six passages these readers requested supplemental background information significantly more often than the other options.

Although comprehension scores were difficult to interpret because of an unanticipated interaction between treatment and passage difficulty, readers having access to textual manipulations scored significantly higher than readers reading passages on the computer without textual manipulations. The data also suggested that interactive text may be more useful for high-difficulty passages but that intermediate-grade readers may also need time to adjust to using interactive text in their reading and study. The consistently higher comprehension scores of readers required by the computer to view all of the textual manipulations prior to selecting their own manipulations also led to the conclusion that computer control of study behavior may be more beneficial for intermediate-grade readers.

Blohm (1982) has also reported the results of a study in which readers could request the computer to provide information while reading a technical passage. This technique could be classified as interactive text by the definition used here. College students having access to the computer-aided glossing recalled significantly more idea units from the experimental passages than did students reading the passages on the computer without the glosses. Apparently interactive text increased learning from expository text under the conditions outlined in this study.

In sum, interactive text could relieve the processing burden placed upon the reader and at the same time model active comprehension strategies. These possibilities point to the advantages of conceptualizing computer-mediated text as a new technology of print: The technological characteristics of the printed page impose limitations both on the range of strategies that are useful and on how these strategies may be influenced. To think of text mediated by the computer as being subject to the same limitations denies the technological advantages of the computer. Recognizing the distinction between two technologies for representing text, on the other hand, may lead researchers to explore previously unavailable opportunities to influence reading and learning from text.

REFERENCES

Anderson, R. C., & Biddle, B. W. (1975). On asking people questions about what they read. *The Psychology of Learning and Motivation, 9,* 89–132.

Anderson, T. H., Anderson, R. C., Dalgaard, B. R., Biddle, W. B., Surber, J. R., & Allessi, S. M. (1974). An experimental evaluation of a computer based study management system. *Educational Psychologist, 11,* 189–190.

Atkinson, R. C. (1974). Teaching children to read using a computer. *American Psychologist, 29,* 169–178.

Ausubel, D. P. (1963). *The psychology of meaningful verbal learning.* New York: Grune and Stratton.

Barnes, B. R., & Clawson, E. U. (1975). Do advance organizers facilitate learning: Recommendations for further research based on the analysis of 32 studies. *Review of Educational Research, 45,* 637–659.

Belmont, J. M., & Butterfield, E. C. (1977). The instructional approach to developmental cognitive research. In R. V. Kail & J. W. Hagen (Eds.), *Perspectives on the development of memory and cognition* (pp. 437–481). Hillsdale, NJ: Lawrence Erlbaum.

Blohm, P. (1982). Computer-aided glossing and facilitated learning in prose recall. In J. A. Niles & L. A. Harris (Eds.). *New inquiries in reading research and instruction* (pp. 24–28). Thirty-first Yearbook of the National Reading Conference. Rochester, NY: The National Reading Conference.

Bridwell, L. S., Nancarrow, P. R., & Ross, D. (1984). The writing process and the writing machine: Current research on word processors relevant to the teaching of composition. In R. Beach & L. Bridwell (Eds.), *New directions in composition research* (pp. 381–398). New York: Guilford Press.

Brown, A. L. (1980). Metacognitive development and reading. In R. T. Sprio, B. C. Bruce, & W. F. Brewer (Eds.), *Theoretical issues in reading comprehension* (pp. 453–481). Hillsdale, NJ: Lawrence Erlbaum.

Burnett, J. D., & Miller, L. (1984). Computer-assisted learning and reading: Developing the product or fostering the process? *Computer Education, 8,* 145–150.

Burns, H. L. (1979). *Stimulating rhetorical invention in English composition through computer assisted instruction.* Unpublished doctoral dissertation, The University of Texas at Austin.

Cromer, W. (1970). The difference model: A new explanation for some reading difficulties. *Journal of Educational Psychology, 61,* 471–483.

Dubin, R., & Taveggia, T. (1968). *The teaching-learning paradox: A comparative analysis of college teaching methods.* Center for the Advanced Study of Educational Administration, University of Oregon, Eugene, OR.

Easterling, B. A. (1982). *The effects of computer assisted instruction as a supplement to classroom instruction in reading comprehension and arithmetic.* Unpublished doctoral dissertation, North Texas State University.

Geoffrion, L. D., & Geoffrion, O. P. (1983). *Computers and reading instruction.* Reading, MA: Addison-Wesley.

Glynn, S. M., & DiVesta, F. J. (1979). Control of prose processing via instructional and typographical cues. *Journal of Educational Psychology, 71,* 595–603.

Glynn, S. M., Britton, B. K., Tillman, M. H., & Muth, K. D. (1984, April). *Typographical cues in text: Management of the reader's attention.* Paper presented at the meeting of the American Educational Research Association, New Orleans, LA.

Hamilton, R. J. (1985). Adjunct questions and objectives. *Review of Educational Research, 55,* 47–86.

Hartley, J., & Davies, I. K. (1976). Preinstructional strategies: The role of pretests, behavioral objectives, and advance organizers. *Review of Educational Research, 46,* 239–265.

Just, M. A., & Carpenter, P. A. (1976). Eye fixations and cognitive processes. *Cognitive Psychology, 8,* 441–480.

L'Allier, J. J. (1980). *An evaluation study of a computer-based lesson that adjusts reading level by monitoring on task reader characteristics.* Unpublished doctoral dissertation, University of Minnesota at Minneapolis.

McConkie, G. W. (1983, November/December). *Computer-aided reading: A help for illiterate adults.* Paper presented at the meeting of the National Reading Conference, Austin, TX.

Olson, D. R. (1974). Mass media versus schoolmen: The role of means of instruction in the attainment of educational goals. *Interchange, 5,* 11–17.

Olson, D. R. (1976). Towards a theory of instructional means. *Educational Psychologist, 12,* 14–35.

Otto, W. (1980). *Text comprehension research to classroom application: A progress report* (Theoretical Paper No. 87). Madison: University of Wisconsin, Wisconsin Research and Development Center for Individualized Schooling.

Reinking, D. (1985, November). *Using microcomputers to gather on-line processing data.* Paper presented at the meeting of the Georgia Educational Research Association, Atlanta, GA.

Reinking, D. (1986). Six advantages of computer-mediated text for reading and writing instruction. *The Reading Instruction Journal, 29,* 8–16.

Reinking, D., & Schreiner, R. (1985). The effects of computer-mediated text and reader study behavior on measures of reading comprehension. *Reading Research Quarterly, 20,* 536–552.

Rubin, A. (1980a). A theoretical taxonomy of the difference between oral and written language. In R. Sprio, B. C. Bruce, & W. F. Brewer (Eds.), *Theoretical issues in reading comprehension* (pp. 411–438). Hillsdale, NJ: Lawrence Erlbaum.

Rubin, A. (1980b). Making stories, making sense. *Language Arts, 57,* 285–298.

Salomon, G. (1979). *Interaction of media, cognition, and learning.* San Francisco: Jossey-Bass.

Salomon, G., & Clark, R. E. (1977). Reexamining the methodology of research on media and technology in education. *Review of Educational Research, 47,* 99–120.

Samuels, S. J. (1970). Effects of pictures on learning to read, comprehension and attitudes. *Review of Educational Research, 40,* 397–407.

Schallert, D. L. (1980). The role of illustrations in reading comprehension. In R. J. Spiro, B. C. Bruce, & W. F. Brewer (Eds.), *Theoretical issues in reading comprehension.* (pp. 503–524). Hillsdale, NJ: Lawrence Erlbaum.

Tierney, R. J., & Cunningham, J. W. (1984). Research on teaching reading comprehension. In P. D. Pearson (Ed.), *Handbook of reading research* (pp. 609–656). New York: Longman.

Wilkinson, A. C. (1983). Learning to read in real time. In A. C. Wilkinson (Ed.), *Classroom computers and cognitive science* (pp. 183–199). New York: Academic Press.

2
The Construct of Legibility in Electronic Reading Environments

Dan B. Daniel and David Reinking

In the late 19th and early 20th centuries literacy rates in the United States increased rapidly as a result of widespread public education. The publishing industry flourished as more people began to read for work, for learning, and for pleasure. Concurrent with the rise in literacy and the availability of published materials was a concern for the legibility of text. Questions were raised as to whether poor lighting during reading might lead to visual impairment or affect reading performance. Publishers also became interested in improving the quality and appearance of printed materials. Reading researchers responded by conducting numerous experiments investigating the legibility of texts under a variety of conditions. They were interested in determining how physical characteristics of written text affected such factors as visual fatigue, reading speed, and comprehension. This research did not have great impact on printed materials. Conventions for displaying text emerged largely as a result of intuition and technological improvements in printing. As a result, reading researchers turned to other areas of investigation, and interest in legibility waned.

Now, as a result of computer technology, there is renewed interest in legibility, though on a much broader scale. This interest is based on the belief that electronic displays of written text differ significantly from conventional printed materials. There has been concern that text displayed on electronic devices like a computer screen may be less legible than in books and perhaps even hazardous to health. In the late 1970s, a series of studies on computer display devices was conducted by the National Institute of Occupational Safety and Health. The National Research Council (1983) reviewed these studies and concluded that while there was no need for concern about radiation emitted by cathode ray tubes (CRTs), there was justification for concern about visual fatigue. Several studies have found evidence of

24

visual fatigue from CRTs (Gunnarsson & Soderberg, 1983; Jelden, 1981; Mourant, Lakshmanan, & Chantadisai, 1981).

Although an important issue, the effects of electronic display devices extend well beyond visual fatigue. For example, there is evidence that reading is slower on a CRT (Gould & Grischkowsky, 1983; Hoover, 1977; Muter, Latremouille, Treurniet, & Beam, 1982) and that test performance is poorer when items are presented on a CRT (Heppner, Anderson, Farstrup, & Weiderman, 1985). There is also evidence that reading comprehension may be affected by text presented on a CRT (Reinking & Schreiner, 1985). Gambrell, Bradley, and McLaughlin (1985) have found evidence that children have more positive attitudes toward reading text displayed on a computer screen. In fact, readers' beliefs about the difficulty of acquiring information from various media may affect the amount of mental effort they invest in learning (Salomon, 1984; see also Alvermann, chapter 9 of this volume).

In one sense the legibility of electronic texts can be improved by the development of devices that display text with the same clarity as printed materials. However, improved legibility, as considered in this chapter, is also a function of understanding and using productively the differences between printed and electronic texts. Because reading text on a CRT is becoming increasingly common, it is important that such differences be examined. Publishing written materials is also becoming decentralized. With the aid of a microcomputer, a word-processing program, and a printer, almost anyone can engage in "desktop publishing." Thus, just as increased literacy stimulated an interest in examining legibility of printed materials, the increased availability of electronic text leads to questions about what makes electronic text legible. For example, how much do existing notions about legibility of print apply to text displayed on CRTs? Are there new factors associated with legibility that apply only to electronic media? These are the questions addressed in this chapter.

For conventional print, legibility denotes how physical characteristics of written text affect factors such as visual fatigue, reading speed, and comprehension. Tinker (1963) suggested the term as an alternative to "readability," because the latter term is too often linked with readability formulas. In this chapter we propose that although it is a useful construct, legibility should be expanded to include characteristics of electronic text.

Electronic text is defined as reading material that is generated by electronic means (e.g., by a computer) and is displayed on a CRT or similar electronic device (e.g., a liquid crystal display on a flat-screen monitor). Conventional text, on the other hand, is printed on paper or some other surface that is not readily modified. This characteristic (i.e., the degree to which text is easily modified) is the critical difference. Given this difference, we propose a new construct of legibility that encompasses three areas—static legibility, dynamic legibility, and interactive legibility. We will first discuss static legibility, which encompasses factors associated with conventional text; when considering these factors, we will also discuss how they apply to electronic text. We will then introduce two new categories—dynamic and interactive legibility. These categories include characteristics of electronic texts that do not have counterparts in printed texts.

STATIC LEGIBILITY

Legibility of printed text is static in the sense that a printed surface is inert. For example, words on a printed page cannot be easily moved or altered, as they can be on a computer screen with the aid of a word-processing program. Elements of printed texts cannot be flashed like a cursor on a computer screen. Nor is it possible for printed text to respond directly to an individual reader's needs. Thus, *static legibility* refers to display factors usually associated with how easy or difficult it is to read printed texts. Tinker (1963) summarized research in this area and outlined several factors that we include in our definition of static legibility. These are: (1) illumination, (2) color, (3) the printing surface, (4) spacing, (5) typography, and (6) illustrations. In this section we discuss briefly some of the major findings from research on these six factors and consider how the static legibility of printed text might be applied to electronic texts.

Illumination

Much of the previous research on the illumination of printed material in books is not applicable to a discussion of reading from a CRT. Previous studies were concerned with the nature of light reflected from the printed page. However, a CRT is a source of light rather than a reflector of light. Certain conclusions from previous studies, however, suggest variables to consider when reading text displayed on a CRT. For example, Kuntz and Sleight (1973) attempted to establish optimal lighting levels for readers with good and poor visual acuity. A recent review by Dunn, Krimsky, Murray, and Quinn (1985) indicates that there continues to be interest in the effects of illumination on reading performance. There is a need to reevaluate and expand these findings for reading from electronic devices like CRTs.

Another aspect of illumination that has been investigated is brightness contrast. Tinker (1959) found that when illumination was constant, reading speed was gradually reduced as brightness contrast was reduced. When the brightness contrast fell below 60%, greater illumination was required. This finding is of particular relevance to computer displays. Most CRTs have an easily accessible contrast control that allows the user to adjust brightness contrast. Research is needed to establish optimal levels of brightness contrast for CRT displays under varying conditions and whether readers adjust brightness contrast to optimal levels when they are permitted to do so. The type of brightness contrast is also an issue in electronic text. Print is usually displayed with negative contrast (i.e., dark text on a white background), text generated by computers and displayed on CRTs usually has positive brightness contrast (i.e., illuminated text on a dark background). In two studies improved reading performance has been found with negative contrast displays (Bauer & Cavonious, 1980; Radl, 1980).

Color

The effects of color on legibility have also been investigated (Luckiesh, 1923; Luckiesh & Moss, 1938; Preston, Schwankl, & Tinker, 1932; Sumner, 1932). In this early research, two variables were usually manipulated—background color of the page and color of the print. The results of this research indicated that background color was relatively unimportant in affecting visibility, reading speed, and visual fatigue, although in at least one study this was the case only when the print was black (Luckiesh & Moss, 1938). A variety of dependent measures were used in these experiments, including how perceptible the print was at varying distances. In a recent study Bruce and Foster (1982) looked at color in video displays. They examined 42 combinations of colored text with colored backgrounds. They had subjects identify lines of colored characters on seven colored backgrounds and measured the mean recognition time per character. Their findings are summarized in Table 2.1.

The issue of color is especially relevant when considering text generated by a computer. First, text displayed on most computer screens is light on a dark background. The color of the text is often green or amber but may be any of a number of colors, and there has been some speculation as to whether color may be related to fatigue during long periods of reading text displayed on a CRT. Another

Table 2.1 Character and Background Color Combinations on VDTs

Character color	Good background colors	Poor background colors
white	purple, red	yellow
yellow	blue	white
cyan	blue, white	green
green	yellow, white	blue, cyan
purple	white, blue	red
red	white	purple
blue	white	red, purple

Source: Bruce & Foster, 1982

consideration is that multiple colors are becoming more prevalent on computer screens for displaying text, background, and graphics. In general it is much easier and less expensive to manipulate color on a computer screen than on the printed page. Consequently, more options for employing color to highlight text are feasible with the aid of a computer. Technological improvements and reduced cost in hardware continue to expand the possibilities for using color on CRTs. For example, newer color monitors and computers have dramatically improved the resolution of color images on a CRT screen. Nonetheless, many of the computers used in schools have noticeably poor resolution of letters when the monitor is adjusted to highlight colors. Any advantages gained by using color in these instances may be lost by making the text difficult to read.

The Printing Surface

A factor related to illumination is the nature of the surface upon which text is displayed. Early researchers varied factors like the texture, thickness, and light absorbency of paper to manipulate the reflectivity of the surface on which text was displayed. Although the glossiness of the printed surface alone did not seem to negatively affect reading performance (Luckiesh & Moss, 1938; Paterson & Tinker, 1940; Stanton and Burtt, 1935), readers appear to dislike reading text on highly glossy surfaces, and glossiness also interacts with other factors like illumination (Tinker, 1965).

Considering the reflectivity of the surface upon which text is displayed is important when a CRT is used to display text. The typical CRT is covered by glass or plexiglass. The reflectivity of glass coverings on CRTs was quickly recognized as a nuisance by computer users, and manufacturers responded by creating nonglare screens and monitors that permit users to adjust the angle at which they view the screen. Nonetheless, many individuals seem to prefer reading text on a printed page rather than on a CRT, and reflectivity may play a role in explaining this preference. If so, the development of different surfaces for displaying electronic text may influence reading from a CRT.

Spacing

Researchers have also investigated the effects of spacing on legibility. They have varied factors such as page size, width of margins, space between words, and line length. Few of these studies demonstrated clearly that spacing affected legibility in other than obvious ways. For example, Paterson and Tinker (1940) showed that eliminating margins did not significantly affect reading speed, although Tinker (1957) later found that curvature near the spine of a book could distort text and therefore affect legibility. Some recent researchers, however, have examined spacing factors in electronic reading environments. Kolers, Dachnichy, and Ferguson (1981), for example, found that reading speed on a CRT was 17% faster with text printed with 80 as opposed to 40 characters per line.

Varying the space between words has been the focus of more recent research (e.g., Anglin & Miller, 1968; Cromer, 1970; Epstein, 1967; Klare, Nichols, & Shuford, 1957; North & Jenkins, 1951). Unlike earlier legibility research, however, current researchers are more interested in how spacing might directly affect comprehension. In most of these studies words are grouped semantically or syntactically into meaningful chunks separated by additional space. One finding that has been consistent across a number of studies is that chunking text in a fashion that is inconsistent with meaning or phrase structure reduces comprehension (Epstein, 1967; Klare, Nichols, & Shuford, 1957). On the other hand, poor readers' comprehension has been improved by simply adding space at phrase boundaries (Cromer, 1970).

Purposefully varying the space between words to highlight semantic or syntactic word groupings may be more practical when text is displayed by a computer. Geoffrion and Geoffrion (1983), for example, have given an example of how the complex actions required to repair an automobile might be written with the aid of a computer. The computer could group words in a manner that would highlight key actions by increasing the space between the descriptions of actions. Use of spacing in this manner is possible on the printed page but impractical because of the added expense and bulk of such materials. Also, text generated by a computer on a CRT can be adapted to a particular readers' needs. Different readers may benefit from having the same text chunked differently.

Typography

Today typography refers to the total appearance of a printed page and would include the spacing factors discussed above. (See Waller, 1985, who proposes the phrase "text as diagram" in place of typography.) Early researchers used a narrower, literal definition and limited their research to factors like type size and fonts (e.g., Paterson & Tinker, 1929, 1940). Within reasonable boundaries these factors are unlikely to affect legibility (F. Smith, 1978). This is not to say that the boundaries for comfortable reading may not be somewhat different when text is displayed on a CRT. The size of characters on a CRT is determined primarily by the size of the screen. The number and type of fonts used appropriately on a CRT may also vary when compared to printed text. These issues are especially important to beginning reading, because some computer programs for young readers enlarge letters, but also distort them considerably. As improved hardware becomes more widely available, this limitation will probably disappear.

More recently, emphasis has been on typographical cues designed to guide a reader's processing of text (see Glynn, 1978; Glynn, Britton, Tillman, & Muth, 1984). Italics, underlining, and color coding are examples of typographical cues that have been studied. This research is usually based on cognitive theory (e.g., Rothkopf's [1971] notion that typographic cues can function as "perceptual organizers") and addresses how typographical cues affect comprehension. In a review of this research Glynn (1978) concluded that findings were mixed. Any positive effect of typographic cues seems to be limited to the cued information, sometimes at the expense of information not cued. Another conclusion was that typographic cues are probably most effective when they are generated by readers.

To what extent might these conclusions need to be modified in electronic learning environments? First, computers greatly expand the range and practicality of typographic cueing. Many word-processing and similar utility programs allow the user to easily insert and manipulate typographic cues. Although the number and variety of typographic cues in printed texts has increased dramatically over the years

(Duchastel, 1982), the computer enables anyone with a microcomputer to employ typographic cueing. A geometric increase in the amount of typographic cueing in texts may have a general effect on reading protocols. On the other hand, text displayed on a CRT does not permit the reader to examine easily long segments of text at one time and thus may limit the effectiveness of macro-level cues. Such a phenomenon may be consistent with recent studies (e.g., Daiute, 1986) that suggest that limitations in the amount of text displayed at one time on a computer screen may make it more difficult for students to detect certain types of errors while proofreading.

Illustrations

The effects of illustrations that accompany text have been the subject of considerable research and some controversy. Researchers have examined the type, placement, and presence or absence of illustrations and how these factors affect reading performance in a variety of settings. Several reviews of this literature suggest that researchers have not conclusively identified the conditions under which graphic aids are helpful to readers (e.g., Schallert, 1980). Nonetheless, illustrations that accompany text continue to be identified as an important variable in understanding how meaning is derived from text (Jenkins & Pany, 1981).

The use of illustrations in electronic texts further complicates attempts to understand how pictures and text are related. For example, many of the illustrations found in printed texts cannot be reproduced well as computer-generated graphics on a CRT. In addition, most CRTs are too small to permit large or intricate graphic displays, and the amount of text that can be displayed simultaneously on the screen is limited. One way of dealing with this limitation on computer screens is to create the illusion that the screen is a window through which an image larger than the screen can be viewed one part at a time. The user "moves" the window to view different parts of the larger image. On the other hand, a distinct advantage of electronic texts is the fact that illustrations can be animated. Little is known about the effects of animating pictures in conjunction with text. Animation is a characteristic of electronic texts and is included as a factor in dynamic legibility, discussed below.

DYNAMIC LEGIBILITY

Text on a printed page is two-dimensional. The page has height and width, as do elements on the page like letters and words. Factors associated with static legibility have been limited primarily to these two dimensions (i.e., *where* on a plane will elements of a text appear). Electronic reading environments have an added dimension, however. When reading text on a computer screen, one does not flip through a permanent collection of printed pages. Instead, there is only one surface on which to display new information. Displays on this surface can change continuously over time. In other words, a reader of electronic text typically observes printing, not just print. An entire screen of text may appear at once or word by word. Words or letters may be moved to different parts of text displayed on a screen. Displays can be animated to simulate movement. The added dimension, then, is time. For electronic texts, *when* to display text on a computer screen may be as important a decision as *what* to display and *where* to display it. Having the option to control both where and when an image is displayed on a surface permits movement. The capability to use movement on a single surface is a distinguishing feature of electronic text. Thus, *dynamic legibility* refers to a set of factors associated with how text and graphics can be moved relative to other factors and how this capability might affect reading performance.

Factors associated with dynamic legibility are a matter of practical concern just as are factors associated with static legibility. The added dimension of time, however, complicates matters exponentially. The number of reasonable options for manipulating static legibility in conventional texts is almost limitless, yet there are few axioms about how to design legible texts. The problem with dynamic legibility is that not only is there little guidance for using dynamic factors, it is difficult to conceptualize exactly what options are available (see Reinking, chapter 1 of this volume). The flexibility afforded the design of electronic texts also suggests that factors associated with dynamic legibility may have a more direct impact on comprehension than do factors associated only with printed text. What is needed is divergent thinking about the nature of dynamic legibility, creative applications that make use of factors associated with it, and research investigating differences between conventional and electronic reading environments. A starting point for more divergent thinking may be to look at how factors associated with static legibility could be extended into the realm of dynamic legibility. A few examples of issues and possibilities raised by such a comparison are outlined below.

Dynamic Illumination and Color

In an electronic reading environment illumination and color could be used dynamically for aesthetic effect. A poem written for an electronic medium, for example, could be accompanied by changes in luminescence or by shifts in color. This could be done for either the text of the poem or for accompanying graphics.

Dynamic Spacing

Spacing in electronic reading environments can be manipulated relative to time as well as to two-dimensional space. One way of spacing text temporally in computer displays is to purposefully delay the presentation of text (see Wilkinson, 1983, for a discussion of how this option might be used for reading instruction). Sections of text ranging from letters and words to paragraphs can be presented to the reader in segments. A delay could be used to provide information about how the segments are related. For example, a word could be presented followed by a pause and a definition. The pause might be used to highlight how the two elements are related. Or, text that conveys important information can be frozen on the screen to insure that it is not read too quickly. Delays may not always be functional, however. Sometimes a delay may be the result of the computer performing some function or accessing information from a disk. Such delays may have a negative effect on comprehension processes.

Electronic text also permits more flexibility for displaying text in two-dimensional space. For example, line length could be easily adjusted based on the difficulty of the text or the capability of the reader (see Frase, chapter 5 of this volume). Chunking text by strategically inserting additional space between words may also be dynamic on a computer screen. For example, the same text could be chunked differently depending upon whether the reader was a novice or expert.

Dynamic Typography

Conventional typographic cues like underlining and italics can be readily employed to embellish electronic texts. Using word-processing programs, features like font or letter size can be changed by a single keystroke. One of the most promising aspects of dynamic topography, however, is that it may be more powerful than conventional typographic cues in directing a reader's attention to important segments of the text. Segments of electronic text can be slowly underlined, boxed in, flashed, or changed from upper to lower case while the text is displayed on the screen. Research supports the common-sense notion that movement like blinking words directs a reader's attention to that portion of a text (e.g., S. L. Smith & Goodwin, 1971). Since conventional cues tend to have a deleterious effect on information not cued, however, it is reasonable to consider the possibility that dynamic cues may worsen this effect. Also, the ease with which typographic cues can be employed in electronic texts leads to the possibility that they may be overused. When the amount of text cued is greater than the uncued text, the usefulness of typographic cueing is diminished (Glynn, Britton, Tillman, & Muth, 1984).

Dynamic Illustrations

The connection between text and illustrations is more complex for electronic than for printed texts. When a graphic is animated on a computer screen, for example, it can convey information in ways that are impossible given a stationary image. Direction, rotation, occlusion, acceleration, and speed are features of animation that have meaning. In electronic texts these features can be juxtaposed to text in ways that are impossible to duplicate in printed texts and may have value for improving comprehension.

For example, in the real world speakers engaged in a conversation have little difficulty determining who is speaking. Reading the same conversation as dialogue in print, it is more likely that a reader will experience difficulty knowing which character is speaking. The same conversation could be simulated on a computer screen, however. Text representing the words of a character could appear and disappear above a picture of each character in turn; a character leaving the conversation could be shown walking away. Another example would be coordinating a text's description of stages in a process with an animation showing a visual representation of each stage. Text and graphics can be coordinated by alternating the display of segments of text that describe a stage of the process and a visual representation showing the effects of actions described in the text. In printed texts such a coordination is not possible. There is no control over *when* a segment of text is associated with a graphic representation in printed texts, only *where* the text is placed relative to the graphic.

Sound

Books and other conventional reading materials do not enable a reader to hear sound in conjunction with text; thus, it is not included in a consideration of static legibility. Computers, on the other hand, have the capability to coordinate the presentation of a specific segment of text with a specific sound. Sound, therefore, can be considered an aspect of dynamic legibility. Little is known about the affective or cognitive effects of coordinating sound, including speech, with read-ing. Although the use of computer-generated speech is currently being explored for use in reading instruction (see Olson & Wise, chapter 10 of this volume), other applications may be possible. For example, in some computer programs, sound is used to signal an inappropriate action; a reader who attempted to ignore an important segment of text could similarly be alerted to this fact by an auditory signal.

INTERACTIVE LEGIBILITY

Dynamic legibility is primarily a concern for when to display elements of electronic text and how to use movement on a screen to improve reading performance. Dynamic legibility, however, does not encompass another set of differences between conventional printed texts and those presented by a computer. In most cases a computer is designed so people can interact with information that has been pro-grammed into it. Interacting with a computer is a selective process in which the user may request certain information or functions and the computer in turn can be programmed to respond to certain contingen-cies instigated by the user. Although it is common for those in the field of reading to speak of a reader interacting with a text, this is not possible in the same sense that someone can interact with a computer. Readers of printed texts interact with their own knowledge because the text is inert and cannot respond specifically to their individual needs.

Because using a computer can be interactive, reading text gener-ated by a computer and displayed on a computer screen can also be interactive. There are infinite ways that reading text with the aid of a computer can be interactive, and collectively these options define what we call *interactive legibility*. A few examples may illustrate the realm of possibilities in this area.

Consider a reader who is failing to comprehend key ideas in a passage as measured by questions interspersed in the text. When comprehension falls below a certain level, the computer adjusts the text by adding appropriate cueing. In this case the computer has been programmed to monitor reading performance and respond appro-priately. A broad range of performance variables could be incorpo-rated into algorithms that could direct the computer's response to a reader in various situations. In this instance the computer could also be the initiator of corrective action. Alternatively, a reader could request help or additional information from the computer. For example, a reader could direct the computer to simplify or elaborate a segment of the text that is unclear. Or, a reader could identify difficult vocabulary and request that the computer provide a context-specific definition. Individualized assistance provided by the computer may be a useful way of overcoming the fact that the comprehension of good readers reading familiar material may be affected negatively by the presence of unnecessary cues (Hartley & Davies, 1976). Deciding what kinds of interactive options to use and when to use them with what readers are issues of interactive legibility.

Some research has focused on factors associated with interactive legibility as defined here. L'Allier (1980), for example, found that poor high school readers could comprehend as well as good readers when the computer monitored their performance and adjusted text accordingly. Reinking and Schreiner (1985) found that intermediate-grade readers would select computer-based options for help while reading text on a computer screen. Furthermore, comprehension was increased when the computer controlled the presentation of the text (see also Reinking, chapter 1 of this volume). One factor that emerges as important in these studies is the issue of control. Under what circumstances should a reader or the computer be given primary control of the interaction? This question, however, addresses only one aspect of interactive legibility. At present, relevant categories to focus thinking are not clearly defined, yet studies like those cited are a step toward understanding the complexity of interactive legibility.

CONCLUSIONS

In this chapter we compared traditional conceptions of legibility derived from printed materials to how legibility might be considered in electronic reading environments. We expanded the construct of legibility to include static legibility, dynamic legibility, and interactive legibility and defined each of these components to create an expanded construct.

We believe several conclusions are warranted based on our conception of legibility outlined in this chapter. First, legibility is significantly more complex for electronic than for printed texts. Static legibility factors associated with printed texts must be reinterpreted when applied to electronic texts. In addition, new legibility factors associated with electronic texts must be considered, and these, unlike earlier factors, may have more direct impact on reading comprehension. Second, new means for displaying texts electronically may lead to new modes of writing, designing, and reading text. Writing a coherent electronic text using options associated with interactive legibility, for example, implies a different process than writing a printed text. Similarly, reading strategies may be different for a reader attempting to construct meaning from electronic text. Finally, it is apparent that research is needed to investigate the full range of legibility factors outlined in this chapter. There are difficulties in investigating aspects of electronic text, however, not the least of which is the increasing sophistication and complexity of electronic media (e.g., interactive video). Only by having a conceptual framework into which new developments can be incorporated will progress be possible.

REFERENCES

Anglin, J. M., & Miller, G. A. (1968). The role of phrase structure in the recall of meaningful material. *Psychonomic Science, 10*, 343–344.

Bauer, D., & Cavonious, C. R. (1980). Improving the legibility of visual display units through contrast reversal. In E. Grandjean & E. Vigliani (Eds.), *Ergonomic aspects of visual display terminals* (pp. 137–142). London: Taylor and Francis.

Bruce, M., & Foster, J. J. (1982). Visibility of colored characters on colored background in viewdata displays. *Visible Language, 16*, 382–390.

Cromer, W. (1970). The difference model: A new explanation for some reading difficulties. *Journal of Educational Psychology, 61*, 471–483.

Daiute, C. (1986). Instrument and idea: Some effects of computers on the writing process. *Proceedings of NECC 1986*, International Council on Computers in Education, 21–27.

Duchastel, P. C. (1982). Textual display techniques. In D. H. Jonassen (Ed.), *The technology of text* (pp. 167–191). Englewood Cliffs, NJ: Educational Technology Publications.

Dunn, R., Krimsky, J. S., Murray, J. B., & Quinn, P. J. (1985). Light up their lives: A review of research on the effect of lighting on children's achievement and behavior. *The Reading Teacher, 38*, 863–869.

Epstein, W. (1967). Some conditions of the influence of syntactical structure on learning. *Journal of Verbal Learning and Verbal Behavior, 6*, 415–419.

Gambrell, L. B., Bradley, V., & McLaughlin, E. (1985, October). *Young children's comprehension and recall of computer screen displayed text.* Paper presented at the meeting of the College Reading Association, Pittsburgh, PA.

Geoffrion, L. D., & Geoffrion, O. P. (1983). *Computers and reading instruction.* Reading, MA: Addison-Wesley.

Glynn, S. M. (1978, November). Capturing readers' attention by means of typographical cuing strategies. *Educational Technology*, pp. 7–12.

Glynn, S. M., Britton, B. K., Tillman, M. H., & Muth, K. D. (1984, April). *Typographical cues in text: Management of the reader's attention.* Paper presented at the meeting of the American Educational Research Association. New Orleans, LA.

Gould, J. D., & Grischkowsky, N. (1983). Doing the same work with paper and cathode ray tube displays (CRT). *Human Factors, 24,* 329–338.

Gunnarsson, E., & Soderberg, I. (1983). Eye strain resulting from VDT work at the Swedish Telecommunications Administration. *Applied Ergonomics, 14,* 61–69.

Hartley, J., & Davies, I. K. (1976). Preinstructional strategies: The role of pretests, behavioral objectives, and advance organizers. *Review of Educational Research, 46,* 239–265.

Heppner, F. H., Anderson, J. G. T., Farstrup, A. E., & Weiderman, N. H. (1985). Reading performance on a standardized test is better from print than from computer display. *Journal of Reading, 28,* 321–325.

Hoover, T. (1977). *Empirical study of reading and comprehension as a function of CRT display.* (ERIC Document Reproduction Service No. ED 161 002)

Jelden, D. (1981). The microcomputer as a multiuser interactive instructional system. *AEDS Journal, 14,* 208–217.

Jenkins, J. R., & Pany, D. (1981). Instructional variables in reading comprehension. In J. T. Guthrie (Ed.), *Comprehension and teaching: Research reviews* (pp. 163–202). Newark, DE: International Reading Association.

Klare, G. R., Nichols, W. H., & Shuford, E. H. (1957). The relationship of typographic arrangement to the learning of technical material. *Journal of Applied Psychology, 41,* 41–45.

Kolers, P. A., Dachnichy, R. L., & Ferguson, D. C. (1981). Eye-movement measurement of readability of CRT displays. *Human Factors, 23,* 517–527.

Kuntz, J. E., & Sleight, R. B. (1973). Effect of target brightness on "normal" and "subnormal" visual acuity. *Journal of Applied Psychology, 33,* 83–91.

L'Allier, J. J. (1980). *An evaluation study of a computer-based lesson that adjusts reading level by monitoring on task reader characteristics.* Unpublished doctoral dissertation, University of Minnesota at Minneapolis.

Luckiesh, M. (1923). *Electrical advertising.* New York: Van Nostrand.

Luckiesh, M., & Moss, F. K. (1938). Visibility and readability of print on white and tinted papers. *Sight-Saving Review, 8,* 123–134.

Mourant, R., Lakshmanan, R., & Chantadisai, R. (1981). Visual fatigue and cathode ray tube display terminals. *Human Factors, 23,* 529–540.

Muter, P., Latremouille, S., Treurniet, W., & Beam, P. (1982). Extended reading of continuous text on television screens. *Human Factors, 24,* 501–508.

National Research Council. (1983). *Video displays, work and vision.* Washington, DC: National Academy Press.

North, A. J., & Jenkins, C. B. (1951). Reading speed and comprehension as a function of typography. *Journal of Applied Psychology, 35,* 225–228.

Paterson, D. G., & Tinker, M. A. (1929). Studies of typographical factors influencing speed of reading. *Journal of Applied Psychology, 13*, 120–130.

Paterson, D. G., & Tinker, M. A. (1940). *How to make type readable.* New York: Harper and Row.

Preston, K., Schwankl, H. P., & Tinker, M. A. (1932). The effect of variations in color of print and background on legibility. *Journal of General Psychology, 6*, 459–461.

Radl, G. (1980). Experimental investigations for optimal presentation-mode and colours of symbols on the CRT-screen. In E. Grandjean & E. Vigliani (Eds.), *Ergonomic aspects of visual display terminals* (pp. 271–276). London: Taylor & Francis.

Reinking, D., & Schreiner, R. (1985). The effects of computer-mediated text on measures of reading comprehension and reading behavior. *Reading Research Quarterly, 20*, 536–552.

Rothkopf, E. Z. (1971). Experiments on mathemagenic behavior and the technology of written instruction. In E. Z. Rothkopf & P. E. Johnson. (Eds.), *Verbal learning research and the technology of written instruction* (pp. 284–306). New York: Teachers College Press.

Salomon, G. (1984). Television is "easy" and print is "tough": The differential investment of mental effort in learning as a function of perceptions and attributions. *Journal of Educational Psychology, 76*, 647–658.

Schallert, D. L. (1980). The role of illustrations in reading comprehension. In R. J. Spiro, B. C. Bruce, & W. F. Brewer (Eds.), *Theoretical issues in reading comprehension* (pp. 503–524). Hillsdale, NJ: Lawrence Erlbaum.

Smith, F. (1978). *Understanding reading.* New York: Holt, Rinehart, and Winston.

Smith, S. L., & Goodwin, N. C. (1971). Blink coding for information display. *Human Factors, 13*, 283–290.

Stanton, F. N., & Burtt, H. E. (1935). The influence of surface and tint of paper on the speed of reading. *Journal of Applied Psychology, 19*, 683–693.

Sumner, F. C. (1932). Influence of color on legibility of copy. *Journal of Applied Psychology, 16*, 201–204.

Tinker, M. (1957). Effect of curved text upon readability of print. *Journal of Applied Psychology, 41*, 218–221.

Tinker, M. (1959). Print for children's textbooks. *Education, 80*, 37–40.

Tinker, M. (1963). *The legibility of print.* Ames: Iowa State University Press.

Tinker, M. (1965). *Basis for effective reading.* Ames: Iowa State University Press.

Waller, R. (1985). Text as diagram: Using typography to improve access and understanding. In D. H. Jonassen (Ed.), *The technology of text* (Vol. 2, pp. 137–167). Englewood Cliffs, NJ: Educational Technology Publications.

Wilkinson, A. C. (1983). Learning to read in real time. In A. C. Wilkinson (Ed.), *Classroom computers and cognitive science* (pp. 183–199). New York: Academic Press.

3

Implications of Artificial Intelligence Research for Human-Computer Interaction in Reading Instruction

Ernest Balajthy

Teacher-trainers in the field of microcomputers-in-education are aware of resistance among teachers to learning about computer applications (Griswold, 1985; Stimmel, Connor, McCaskill, & Durrett, 1981). While some teachers have latched onto the microcomputer boom with great enthusiasm, a significant number have not. Their skepticism about the importance of computers to education has been occasionally described as a latent "computer phobia," but a closer analysis suggests a general feeling of disappointment with computer applications in the classroom. Indeed, there is a rising tide of criticism against many computer applications (e.g., Sloan, 1985).

Additional evidence for the disenchantment about computers-in-education rests in how computers are being used in classrooms. Primary applications in the teaching of reading and language arts appear to be in two major areas: (1) use of computers as tools for information processing, such as word processing (Schwartz, 1985), and (2) use of computers as motivational drill devices (Balajthy, 1984). Fewer teachers appear to be using computers for direct teaching purposes (i.e., use of tutorial software). In a 1985 listing, 9 of the 10 best-sellers in educational software were programs relating to the language arts, and none of these were tutorials. Eight of the nine involved "computer tool" applications (e.g., word processing, data base management, and special printing programs), and the remaining program was a video drill and practice game (*Classroom Computer Learning*, 1985).

The basis for this rejection of tutorial software—the use of computers to provide direct instruction and modeling in skills—may be due to the computer's inability to interact effectively with students (Balajthy, 1985; Scandura, 1981). So-called interactive software typically requires only low-level interactions. The flexibility of responding like a human teacher, a capability important to meeting the needs of individual students, is sorely lacking in educational software. This lack is felt keenly by teachers in the language arts, where holistic language models (Goodman, 1967; Graves, 1983; Moffett & Wagner, 1983; Smith, 1978) of teaching have become increasingly dominant in the past 20 years.

This chapter begins with a survey and critique of recent attempts to provide human-like interaction between students and computers. The problems involved in developing adequate interactive programs are then discussed, and some existing programs that approach this ideal are described. The final part of the chapter deals with research on the development of artificial intelligence natural language systems.

LIMITATIONS OF "EXACT MATCH" CURRICULUM DESIGNS

The basis of constructing most existing tutorial programs is the capability of the computer to look for an "exact match" between a user's input and material in the program code. The design of instruction based on such exact matches can be carried out in a variety of ways. The common multiple-choice paradigm in which the user is presented a question followed by a series of options and the instructions to "Type A, B, C, or D" is one example. The programming code includes instructions that identify the correct choice and specify what should be done if the correct choice is selected (e.g., to print "Good Work!" on the monitor screen). The code would also contain instructions as to procedures to carry out if the incorrect choice is identified (e.g., state "Try Again" and give the user another chance if it is the first try, or provide the correct answer if it is the second). A third set of instructions specifies what action to take if an inappropriate response is made (e.g., if a number is pressed instead of a letter).

A related "exact match" paradigm involves input of a word instead of a single character. For example, a program aimed at improving spelling or vocabulary may ask the student to type in a word. The computer scans the input to ascertain whether it matches the correct response coded by the programmer. At heart, this paradigm is little different from the single-character paradigm. Common video game formats are based on computer recognition of exact matches, though the graphics involved make such programming more complex than simple text recognition programs. In a vocabulary game such as Word Attack! (Davidson, 1983), for instance, the computer presents a definition at the bottom of the screen, with several words at the top of the screen. The student fires a projectile at the vocabulary word that correctly fits the definition. If the projectile "hits" the correct target word, the computer concludes that a correct word identification has been made by the student.

The exact-match paradigm lends itself to two types of computer instruction: drill and practice exercises, and behaviorally oriented programmed instruction. Much of the existing empirical research on computer-based reading instruction has been of the former type (e.g., Atkinson & Hansen, 1966; Swinton, Amarel, & Morgan, 1978) and most manuals for computer-assisted instructional design deal specifically with these modes of instruction (e.g., Chan & Korostoff, 1984; Landa, 1984). PILOT and other authoring programs are designed to facilitate construction of computer-assisted instructional lessons. The format employed by these programs involves presentation of small bits of information in strictly sequenced, linear frame-by-frame fashion and requires the user to periodically input single-letter or one- or two-word answers to questions. Once considered the educational format of the future (Skinner, 1968), nonelectronic forms of programmed instruction never fulfilled the promises made by educational technologists of the 1950s and 1960s and are in low repute today among educators. While computer-assisted programmed instruction continues to be advocated by some (e.g., Pogrow, 1983) and is frequently used in business and the military, few within the field of reading support its widespread use.

The importance of drill and practice to the development of language skills continues to be recognized today by many in the field of reading (LaBerge & Samuels, 1974; Osborn, 1984; Siegel & Davis, chapter 7 of this volume). Computers can provide some particularly effective methods for delivering such practice exercises, especially because of their motivational qualities and their ability to provide immediate feedback for low-level exercises (Balajthy, 1984; Grabe, 1985). Most teachers, however, look askance on the replacement of drill and practice workbooks with drill and practice computer programs. The increased cost and classroom management problems involved with use of computers overcome the instructional advantages offered by computerized drills. In addition, whole-language advocates who suggest that increased instructional time be spent in actual reading (e.g., Smith, 1978) and in actual writing (e.g., Graves, 1983) rather than in isolated subskill drills continue to exercise considerable influence in the fields of reading and language arts.

OPEN-ENDED CURRICULUM DESIGNS

In an effort to avoid limitations imposed by the exact-match paradigm of computer curriculum design and to allow for more divergent responses, a few attempts have been made to develop computer-based reading activities that allow for open-ended inputs. These programs pose problems or questions and allow students to type in their responses to the computer, but the programs are not capable of analyzing these responses in human terms. By carefully structuring the directions to the students, however, the programs attempt to lead the students through a meaningful appraisal of their inputs.

While some teachers are dissatisfied with the assumption of student competence and the inability of the computer to assess the success or failure of such instruction, the purpose of such programs must be recognized as being process-oriented rather than product-oriented. That is, the aim of these programs is not to arrive at the correct answer—a product. Instead, the purpose is to model effective *processing* involved in the development of a product.

The Puzzler (Gollan, 1985) is an example of open-ended reading instructional software. This program is designed to improve readers' ability to make predictions, confirm hypotheses, and integrate information during reading. In accord with psycholinguistic theory (Goodman, 1967), the program requires readers to use prior knowledge to predict words, sentences, and concepts. The predictions are confirmed or disconfirmed by further reading.

To accomplish this goal, The Puzzler presents parts of a story on separate screen pages. After reading each screen, readers are asked an inference question and are allowed to type their predictions into the computer, which records them for future reference. Instructions suggest to students that a variety of responses are acceptable: "There are many good answers to every puzzle. You can have fun talking about your answers with your friends."

As the story proceeds, each screen page adds information and allows the readers to narrow down their responses by eliminating predictions made invalid by the new information and by adding new predictions. By the end of the story, only a few predictions remain plausible, but the program does not provide a final answer. The students are left to discuss their final predictions with one another and with the teacher. While both students and teachers may find the lack of a final answer somewhat frustrating, the message that predicting is not an exact process is conveyed clearly. Different readers take away different interpretations from the texts they read.

The key advantage of such programs is that they structure the readers' thinking processes to encourage greater inferencing and predicting. Improvement of these higher level skills is crucial to comprehension improvement (Thorndike, 1973–1974). The Puzzler is representative of computer programs that encourage more divergent responses. The key disadvantage is that the program does not provide students with feedback concerning the quality of their responses. The program serves primarily as an impetus for small-group or teacher-led class discussion.

The inability of computers to carry out human-like dialogues is an important limitation when considering reading and writing as holistic language processes. Without such an ability, instructional applications of computers will be severely limited.

THE PROBLEM OF "INTELLIGENT" COMPUTER-HUMAN INTERACTION

Place an individual in a room with a keyboard and monitor. Inform the individual that he or she may communicate using the keyboard and receive communications printed on the monitor. The "person" at the other end, however, may be either another human or a computer. If, after a conversation, the individual is not able to determine with whom he or she had been communicating with a better than 50% accuracy, the computer is "intelligent."

This simplified version of a classic test is called the "Turing Test" after Alan Turing, one of the leading early computer developers, who suggested it (1950). The challenge in meeting the goals of this test is enormous. Ability to communicate with language is among the most complex of all human processes. In order to carry out such a deception successfully, a computer must be able to read and write like a mature reader and writer—for input must be "read" and output must be "written."

As a result, researchers in the field of artificial intelligence (AI) and researchers interested in cognitive processes involved in language communication have a good deal to say to one another. How is background information stored in the mind for easy and effective access? How is this information activated and used as a basis for drawing conclusions and making inferences about material being read? How does the mind make decisions about the levels of importance of the ideas being read? How is new, incoming information integrated with the background information already in the mind? All these questions are central to an understanding of how the human mind operates during reading. They are just as central to the objective of programming an "intelligent" computer.

Consider the following sentence: "As Mary Ann sat back against the tree staring at the clouds, she heard a slither in the grass near her foot and a rattling sound" (Balajthy, 1985, p. 28). How does a human being "read" this sentence? It is certainly true that a variety of interactive cueing systems (Rumelhart, 1977) aid in letter and word recognition and sentence-level syntactic and semantic analysis. But the reading task does not succeed if limited to those levels.

A mature reader draws upon his or her background schemata to "fill in the blanks" assumed by the sentence's author (Anderson, Reynolds, Schallert, & Goetz 1977; Pearson, Hansen, & Gordon, 1979). What are Mary Ann's feelings as she sits back against the tree? Is she relaxed or tense? Is she at peace with the world or is she bitter and depressed? What kind of day is it? Are the clouds the grey rain clouds of an overcast day or a warning of a threatening snow storm? A mature reader would read "Mary Ann sat back against the tree staring at the clouds" and immediately develop some expectations of the situation. Mary Ann might be, for instance, resting peacefully on a warm day, watching a few white clouds floating past in a brilliant blue sky.

The mature reader would further elaborate this scene by instantiating slots in the activated schema (theorists speak in terms of "assigning default values" during instantiation of the schema—e.g., Anderson & Pearson, 1984) as the action occurs to make predictions as to the immediate future situation. Does the slither and rattling sound come from a snake? Will Mary Ann freeze in fear or jump up and run? What happens if there is a snake and it bites her? These possibilities immediately come to mind in a mature reader. Each demands a wealth of background knowledge about people and snakes.

To create a dialogue between the computer and the computer user, computers must be programmed to understand—to comprehend—at a level commensurate with human interactions. They must be programmed to recognize facts, to reorganize information into coherent patterns, to make inferences, to think critically, and to appreciate literary techniques. In essence, they must be taught to simulate the same cognitive processes that occur in human beings during reading. As Huey pointed out years ago (1908), to understand reading is to understand the human mind *in toto*.

A BRIEF HISTORY OF NATURAL LANGUAGE ARTIFICIAL INTELLIGENCE RESEARCH AND DEVELOPMENT

Machine Translation

The earliest attempts to use the computer as an intelligent resource in dealing with natural language involved machine translation, the effort to develop computer programs to automatically translate from one language to another. Machine translation projects originated in the 1950s. Soon afterwards, however, linguists began to recognize the serious limitations of such efforts as the enormous complexity of the task became apparent.

Early researchers assumed that translation was more or less a direct process of dictionary look-up, in which each word from the original sentence was substituted for a word in the target language. Any necessary sentence reordering took place at the end of the process. These early efforts were heavily criticized as being based on a simplistic view of language, and efforts at machine translation died out in the late 1960s and early 1970s. Language is much more than mere word-by-word replacement: One humorous and often-told story has it that an effort to translate the English sentence, "The spirit is willing but the flesh is weak," resulted in the Russian, "The vodka is strong but the meat is rotten." There have been some new attempts to develop machine translation programs in recent years, largely due to an increasing demand for translated materials and a willingness to accept the limitations of such efforts (Slocum, 1985).

Applications Emphases

As interest in direct translation waned, researchers in natural language turned their attention from general efforts dealing with the totality of language to specific problem-solving situations, often with real-world applications. Waltz (1982) has called these "engineering approaches" to highlight the emphasis on practical and specific application. Developers were not interested in modeling the actual processes of human language. They instead focused on achieving successful outcomes—whether or not the performance paralleled human language processes—that had not been achieved in machine translation efforts. As a result of the emphasis on application, developments have filtered down into contemporary microcomputer programs.

Key-Word Systems.   One approach taken to meet application needs was the development of programs that identify key words in user input and perform specified operations accordingly. The well-known programs in the ELIZA family (Weizenbaum, 1976), for instance, simulate a nondirective psychotherapist in conversation with a user-patient. The "doctor" asks leading questions to draw out responses from the "patient." As the patient enters his or her response, it is scanned to identify key words within the program code. A reference to "mother" or "father" in the input might lead to the computer posing the question, "How do you feel about your parents?" or the request, "Tell me more about your mother." If no key word is found, a nonspecific response might be generated, such as, "That is interesting. Tell me more."

Early adventure games were also based on simple key-word programming. An adventure game is a role-playing simulation in which the computer places the user as hero in an adventure setting. The hero may be battling alien starships, exploring mysterious caves, or solving mysteries. The input "West" or "Go West" would be recognized by the program as a request to move the user from one location to another in an imaginary environment. The input "Attack" would be recognized as a command to action.

Text Parsers.   More recent adventure games have incorporated programming that moves beyond the key-word method to allow understanding of inputs of greater complexity. This is possible by incorporating a subprogram called a "text parser" that analyzes sentence components. Early parsers could only handle a maximum input of two words. Parsers in leading microcomputer adventure games of the mid-1980s are capable of dealing with compound sentences and can recognize many parts of speech, including direct and indirect objects. Infocom, for example, a publisher of many of the more complex adventure games, has designed a parser that can deal with up to 1,200 words per game.

The success of such programming efforts is due in large part to the specifically targeted goals of programmers. There is no attempt to deal with natural language with all the flexibility of its organization within the human mind. The only objective is to function appropriately within the tightly confined parameters of the adventure game. In an adventure confrontational situation in which, for example, a hero is beset by a danger, there are very few possible responses: Wait, flee, or attack. The limitations of the adventure game worldview allow success using the very limited text parsers that are themselves only a small improvement on the key-word method. Real-life language and thinking are far too complex to be handled in this manner, though some programs that have appeared, such as Story Machine (Quinn, 1982), apply a similar technology to primer-level story construction with a vocabulary size limited to less than 50 words.

Frase (chapter 5 of this volume) describes work carried out by AT&T in the development of the Writer's Workbench programs that provide analytic feedback to writers. Features of the AT&T system are based on both key-word analysis (as, for example with the spelling checker and identification of poor usage and split infinitives) and text parsing (as with assignment of grammatical parts of speech to words in the text). Writer's Workbench is designed to deal with an almost unlimited variety of topics and writing styles. The analysis and feedback are resultingly rather mechanical in nature and are not in dialogue format.

Data Base Queries.   Another application in which the limited range of possible responses facilitates use of an engineering (as opposed to a cognitive—see below) approach involves use of natural language "front ends" with data bases. A front-end program serves as an intermediary between a major utility program (such as a data base management or word-processing program) and the computer user, making the utility program easier to use. Early research on these front ends, which can translate natural language questions into a structured data base language, was carried out by Green, Wolf, Chomsky, and Laughery (1963) in Baseball, a program designed to obtain information in a sports data base. Today, a variety of front end programs are available that allow natural language querying, either by direct natural language questions or through arranging queries based on choices from a menu of question parts.

Suppose, for example, that a clerk in a business office wanted to use a data base management program to search a data file to find out which Ohio corporations had sales over $5,000,000 in 1987. The clerk would ordinarily need to understand the command system well enough to develop a command that might be exactly like the following: LIST ALL COMPANIES, STATE, SALES87, FOR STATE = 'OH'. AND. SALES > 5000000. Facility in using such a complex command system requires extensive training and frequent practice. With a natural language front-end program, the clerk would be able to input the question phrased in ordinary prose: WHICH COMPANIES IN OHIO HAD SALES OVER $5,000,000 IN 1987? The front end would analyze the natural language input and automatically translate it into the appropriate data base command structure.

Contemporary natural English front ends suffer from several problems. They bog down if an unknown word or a misspelled word is input. For the trained frequent user, they are slower and less precise than the formal command structure. In the long run, for instance, a frequent user of a data base program would find it easier to learn the complex command system rather than the natural language front end. The front ends are of most use to infrequent users and to "naive" users who do not have specialized training.

Cognitive Developments

What is "true" artificial intelligence? Certainly the term is a vague one and will become even vaguer. Buchanan and Shortliffe (1984) have complained that the term *expert system* "is rapidly becoming mongrelized to include any system that is applied, has some vague connection with AI systems and has pretentions of success. Such is the fate of terms that attain (if only briefly) a positive halo" (p. xii). The entire field of *artificial intelligence* may rest under the same halo.

Schank (1979) has suggested that artificial intelligence be defined in terms of stages of research sophistication. Early programs were designed to do something that only a person could do, that is, to exhibit some form of intelligent behavior, as in the applications approaches described earlier. In contemporary stages of research, according to Schank, significant AI programs ought to reveal something about the form, the use, or the nature of knowledge in the domain area. He concludes that, "The ultimate AI program that we are all aiming for is one that specifies the form in which knowledge is to be input to the program, as well as the form of the rules that use that knowledge, and produces a program that effectively models the domain" (p. 220). Artificial intelligence is the study of knowledge in real-world applications, and programs that do not further this study may well lack the prerequisites for designation as AI.

Under this view, perhaps few or none of the existing contemporary natural language reading and writing instructional microcomputer programs are "true" artificial intelligence natural language products. It may well be better to envision them as early—perhaps too early for serious consideration, in some cases—percolations of artificial intelligence research to the limitations of small memory size.

With the early 1970s and the dawn of the cognitive revolution in psychology came an effort to model artificial intelligence natural language programming on the human mind. A variety of researchers, often associated with Stanford, Yale, or MIT projects in artificial intelligence, began to look at ways to build programs that functioned according to information-processing models of cognitive activity.

Of key importance to this effort was the realization by cognitive psychologists that the role of background knowledge was crucial to any form of language understanding and that insight into the organization of that knowledge within human memory must become a primary target for theory and research (Carroll & Freedle, 1972; Lindsay & Norman, 1972). Minsky (1975), for example, proposed that background memory is organized according to interconnecting units, called "frames," that contain information about stereotypical events and objects.

Schank and Abelson (1977) enlarged upon Minsky's concepts, especially in terms of how frame-based knowledge might be applied in given instances. Schank and his colleagues have dealt primarily with the complex world of human actions, suggesting that such actions can be grouped for better understanding into a fairly small number of categories, called "primitives." In an effort to explain the inferential power of the memory system during reading, they postulated the existence of "scripts" (stereotypical action sequences), "goals" (classes of intentions), and "plans" (methods of achieving the goals). More recently (1982), Schank has suggested a dynamic representation of human (and computer) memory in which scenes from stories are organized by Memory Organization Packets (MOPs) according to the low-level goals involved in the stories. Two MOPs, for example, might provide background information necessary to understand a story about a business meeting in a restaurant, drawing on information about business meetings and the serving of food.

One method of comprehending a story is to access generalized knowledge (i.e., "scripts") we have about past experiences—what usually happens in a given situation. Yale's SAM and PAM programs (Wilensky, 1981) can use programmed versions of such scripts to "understand" stories about a limited range of events, such as a trip to a restaurant. They are capable of making limited inferences about missing knowledge and about characters' goals to answer questions about the stories.

The interest in building computer programs based on cognitive processes of reading has resulted in renewed interest in those processes (Dehn, 1984). What, for example, is common sense, and how does it operate in aiding comprehension and refining our understanding of our world? Rose (1984), in his informal history of natural language

research, vividly illustrates the complexity of common-sense processing (McCarthy, 1982) by highlighting an attempt to develop a program
that determines what to do if caught outside in the rain. If research in
this area continues as in the past several years, increased sophistication
will be needed in both understanding of these cognitive processes and
capability of creating computer programs that can model the processes.

CONCLUSION

Research and development in natural language computer systems
has been startingly impressive in the late 1970s and early 1980s. There
is a sense of expectancy among many, encouraged by such writers as
Rose (1984) and by popular media, for the imminent appearance of
computer systems capable of sophisticated dialogues in natural language. One such system might, for example, carry on a discussion with
a student about a reading selection, asking and answering questions
about the topic and drawing conclusions as to the student's learning
and comprehension strategies. Another system might be designed to
teach a specific reading skill, simultaneously constructing a diagnosis
of students' performances on the basis of instructional conversations.
Still another system might carry on a consultative dialogue with
teachers about possible remedial methods for specific skill problems.

Dreyfus and Dreyfus have warned that these expectancies are
based on a "first-step fallacy" (1985, p. 41) about artificial intelligence.
Preliminary research efforts have certainly paid off with promising
results. But these first efforts have been carried out in tightly constrained domains. Attempts to deal with wider domains and more
sophisticated applications have met with much less success. While
intensive research is continuing, at present there is little justification for
concluding that artificial intelligence research in natural language can
continue to have such positive results indefinitely (Weizenbaum,
1976). The problems to be faced in future developments are much
more complex than the problems overcome thus far, for they require a
deeper understanding of comprehension and cognition than is available at present.

The most promising results to date in instructional applications of
artificial intelligence have had to do with very specific skill areas that
involve adherence to strict operational rules. Simple arithmetic, for
example, operates according to sets of exactly specifiable rules. Specialists within the fields of reading and language arts, who deal with

the whole range of language and of thought, will be hard-pressed to find similar specificity and simplicity in their own knowledge domains.

REFERENCES

Anderson, R. C., & Pearson, P. D. (1984). A schema-theoretic view of basic processes in reading. In P. D. Pearson (Ed.), *Handbook of reading research* (pp. 255–292). New York: Longman.

Anderson, R. C., Reynolds, R. E., Schallert, D. L., & Goetz, E. T. (1977). Frameworks for comprehending discourse. *American Educational Research Journal, 14,* 376–382.

Atkinson, R. C., & Hansen, D. N. (1966). Computer-assisted instruction in initial reading: The Stanford project. *Reading Research Quarterly, 2,* 5–25.

Balajthy, E. (1984). Reinforcement and drill by microcomputer. *The Reading Teacher, 37,* 490–495.

Balajthy, E. (1985). Artificial intelligence and the teaching of reading and writing by computers. *Journal of Reading, 29,* 23–33.

Buchanan, B. G., & Shortliffe, E. H. (1984). *Rule-based expert systems.* Reading, MA: Addison-Wesley.

Carroll, J. B., & Freedle, R. O. (Eds.). (1972). *Language comprehension and the acquisition of knowledge.* Washington, DC: Winston.

Chan, J. M. T., & Korostoff, M. (1984). *Teachers' guide to designing classroom software.* Beverly Hills, CA: Sage Publications.

Classroom Computer Learning. (1985). Best-selling software. *Classroom Computer Learning, 6,* 23.

Davidson, J. G. (1983). *Word attack!* [Computer program]. Rancho Palos Verdes, CA: Davidson & Associates.

Dehn, N. (1984). An AI perspective on reading comprehension. In J. Flood (Ed.), *Understanding reading comprehension* (pp. 82–100). Newark, DE: International Reading Association.

Dreyfus, H. L., & Dreyfus, S. E. (1985). Putting computers in their proper place: Analysis versus intuition in the classroom. In D. Sloan (Ed.), *The computer in education: A critical perspective* (pp. 40–63). New York: Teachers College Press.

Gollan, J. (1985). *The Puzzler* [Computer program]. Pleasantville, NY: Sunburst Communications.

Goodman, K. (1967). Reading: A psycholinguistic guessing game. *Journal of the Reading Specialist, 4,* 126–135.

Grabe, M. (1985). Drill and practice's bad rap. *Electronic Learning, 5,* 22–23.

Graves, D. (1983). *Writing: Teachers and children at work.* New York: Heinemann.

Green, B. F., Wolf, A. K., Chomsky, C., & Laughery, K. (1963). Baseball: An automatic question answerer. In E. A. Feigenbaum & J. Feldman (Eds.), *Computers and thought* (pp. 207–216). New York: McGraw-Hill.

Griswold, P. A. (1985). Differences between education and business majors in their attitudes about computers. *AEDS Journal, 18*, 131–138.

Huey, E. B. (1908). *The psychology and pedagogy of reading*. New York: Macmillan.

LaBerge, D., & Samuels, S. J. (1974). Toward a theory of automatic information processing in reading. *Cognitive Psychology, 6*, 293–323.

Landa, R. K. (1984). *Creating courseware*. New York: Harper and Row.

Lindsay, P. H., & Norman, D. A. (1972). *Human information processing*. New York: Academic Press.

McCarthy, J. (1982). Programs with common sense. In M. L. Minsky (Ed.), *Semantic information processing* (pp. 211–232). Cambridge, MA: MIT Press.

Minsky, M. L. (1975). A framework for representing knowledge. In P. Winston (Ed.), *The psychology of computer vision* (pp. 97–120). New York: McGraw-Hill.

Moffett, J., & Wagner, B. J. (1983). *A student-centered language arts and reading curriculum, K–13* (3rd ed.). Boston: Houghton Mifflin.

Osborn, J. (1984). The purposes, uses, and contents of workbooks and some guidelines for publishers. In R. C. Anderson, J. Osborn, & R. J. Tierney (Eds.), *Learning to read in American schools* (pp. 45–112). Hillsdale, NJ: Lawrence Erlbaum.

Pearson, P. D., Hansen, J., & Gordon, C. (1979). The effect of background knowledge on young children's comprehension of explicit and implicit information. *Journal of Reading Behavior, 11*, 201–210.

Pogrow, S. (1983). *Education in the computer age: Issues of policy, practice, and reform*. Beverly Hills, CA: Sage Publications.

Quinn, C. (1982). *Story machine* [Computer program]. Cambridge, MA: Spinnaker Software.

Rose, F. (1984). *Into the heart of the mind*. New York: Harper and Row.

Rumelhart, D. E. (1977). *Introduction to human information processing*. New York: John Wiley.

Scandura, J. M. (1981). Microcomputer systems for authoring, diagnosis, and instruction in rule-based subject matter. *Educational Technology, 21*, 13–19.

Schank, R. C. (1979). Philosophical perspectives in artificial intelligence. In M. D. Ringle (Ed.), *Philosophical perspectives in artificial intelligence* (pp. 156–175). Atlantic Highlands, NJ: Humanities Press.

Schank, R. C. (1982). *Dynamic memory: A theory of reminding and learning in computers and people*. Cambridge: Cambridge University Press.

Schank, R. C., & Abelson, R. (1977). *Scripts, plans, goals and understanding*. Hillsdale, NJ: Lawrence Erlbaum.

Schwartz, H. J. (1985). *Interactive writing*. New York: Holt, Rinehart and Winston.

Skinner, B. F. (1968). *The technology of teaching.* New York: Appleton-Century-Crofts.

Sloan, D. (Ed.). (1985). *The computer in education: A critical perspective.* New York: Teachers College Press.

Slocum, J. (1985). "Machine translation." *Computers and the Humanities, 19,* 109–116.

Smith, F. (1978). *Understanding reading* (2nd ed.). New York: Holt, Rinehart and Winston.

Stimmel, T., Connor, J., McCaskill, E., & Durrett, H. J. (1981). Teacher resistance to computer assisted instruction. *Behavior Research Methods and Instrumentation, 13,* 128–130.

Swinton, S. S., Amarel, M., & Morgan, J. A. (1978). The PLATO elementary demonstration educational outcome evaluation: Final report, summary and conclusions. Urbana, IL: Computer-Based Education Laboratory, University of Illinois. (ERIC Document Reproduction Service No. ED 186 020)

Thorndike, R. L. (1973–1974). Reading as reasoning. *Reading Research Quarterly, 9,* 135–174.

Turing, A. M. (1950). Computing machinery and intelligence. *Mind, 59,* 433–460.

Waltz, D. L. (1982). The state of the art in natural language understanding. In W. G. Lehnert & M. H. Ringle (Eds.), *Strategies for natural language processing* (pp. 3–32). Hillsdale, NJ: Lawrence Erlbaum.

Weizenbaum, J. (1976). *Computer power and human reason.* San Francisco: W. H. Freeman.

Wilensky, R. (1981). PAM. In R. Schank & C. Riesbeck (Eds.), *Inside computer understanding* (pp. 158–185). Hillsdale, NJ: Lawrence Erlbaum.

Part II
RESEARCH ISSUES

As Kamil points out in this section's first chapter, the computer has had an impact on reading research at a number of levels. The computer has led to new models of the reading process, allowed researchers to design experiments and analyze data in a more sophisticated manner, stimulated research into more effective ways to deliver instruction, and created new ways for researchers to disseminate information. His chapter provides a concise overview of research activity and issues in each of these areas. He observes that the computer will continue to change the definition of existing concepts like literacy as well as create new variables for study. In reviewing existing areas of research and speculating about developing areas of interest his chapter establishes a broad agenda for research activity involving the computer.

The chapters by Frase and by McConkie and Zola complement Kamil's overview in that they provide concrete examples of how the computer expands existing lines of research as well as opens up new areas for study. Frase describes how the UNIX operating system developed at Bell Laboratories can be employed to analyze texts in ways that previously were not practical or feasible. As he states, "Few humans have the time, tenacity, or ability to conduct such a tedious, but informative, analysis of all the words in a text." He proceeds to describe several studies that illustrate how "intelligent environments for language analysis" can be used in research. Recent research on comprehension has focused primarily on the reader, but the ability to analyze texts in the fashion described in this chapter may lead to a renewed interest in text-based factors that influence comprehension. Also, using the computer-based analyses described by Frase, researchers could more carefully control the nature of texts used in their experiments.

In the last chapter in this section, McConkie and Zola describe their research, both basic and applied, in the field of reading. In their basic research they have used the computer as a tool to study eye movements during reading. These studies, made possible only through computer technology, have provided valuable data that have implications for theories and models of reading. In addition, the authors point out that eye movement data gathered by a computer may be useful any time a researcher is interested in knowing what text the reader is attending to at a particular moment. Although the sophisticated equipment used to gather reliable eye movement data is not yet widely available, diagnosticians and researchers in the future may have easy access to such information. Finally, the authors describe an application of the computer that allows poor readers to read passages above their instructional level. "Computer-Aided Reading" enables the reader to request the pronunciation of any unfamiliar word in text displayed on a computer screen. The authors suggest that poor readers may benefit more from this type of interaction with the computer than from formal reading instruction.

4
Computers and Reading Research

Michael L. Kamil

In the four decades since the invention of electronic computers, few areas of reading research have been unaffected by either computer technology or by styles of thought associated with computers. Computers and the more recently derivative field of artificial intelligence have given reading researchers opportunities to develop new models of the reading process, to perform and analyze more complex research studies, to deliver instruction more effectively, and even to deal with the publication and dissemination of information in new and different ways. In this chapter, the effects of computers on each of these areas will be surveyed with the intent of showing what has been done as well as what the most probable directions for the future will be.

This review will concentrate on the application of computers to a wide range of reading research problems. There are, however, numerous antecedents to the use of computers in reading research and instruction, and computers have replaced or augmented many of the functions of earlier technologies. For those who are interested, reviews of the effects of these alternate forms of technology are available for reading machines, eye movement trackers, and tachistoscopic devices (Harris & Sipay, 1985), for a variety of other devices (Moe & Johnson, 1980; Johnson & Moe, 1980), and for television (Mason & Mize, 1978).

COMPUTERS AND READING RESEARCH METHODS

Data Collection and Analysis

The first effect computers have had on research in reading is in data collection. Data about reading processes can be obtained with instrumentation ranging from simple paper and pencil to a complex,

computer-controlled apparatus. However, some of the more sophisticated data could not be obtained without appropriate computer technology for data collection. One early application of technology, the
study of eye movements begun by Javal, Dodge and other early
researchers (see Huey, 1908), continues to the present in the work of
such researchers as Fisher, McConkie, Rayner, Just, and Carpenter.
Rayner (1978) reviewed some of this work, and updated reviews have
appeared since (Rayner & Carroll, 1984; Just & Carpenter, 1984).

Other examples of areas where computer control is crucial are the
collection of reaction time data, physiological data, EEG data, and
hemispheric response data, and the use of complicated patterns of text
manipulation done on-line (as in studies where the text is changed as
the reader focuses on it). In some of these examples data can only be
gathered with the use of a computer; in others the computer provides a
means to collect data more precisely or efficiently.

In addition to enabling researchers to collect, through sophisticated instrumentation, new kinds of data about the reading process,
computers also make automated data collection possible. Large
numbers of subjects can be studied in the same experimental setting.
Multiple observations can be made on each of those subjects, with
automatic recording and processing of the data. Further, the computer
can tailor stimulus patterns and presentations from random displays to
those dependent on the prior responses of the participants.

To address concerns about ecological validity (Bronfenbrenner,
1976), researchers can also use computers to collect sufficient data to
describe the experimental environment in a more nearly complete
manner. Only with a computerized data collection system is this even
remotely possible. In subsequent studies, the computer-collected data
could be used to recreate the same conditions under which the first
observations had taken place—or to measure the environment in sufficient detail to indicate how the two situations differed.

Another effect that computers have had on research is in the
analysis of the data once it is collected. It is difficult to imagine
performing multiple regressions or multifactor analyses of variance by
hand, and the statistical analyses that can be computed manually
nearly always require prohibitive amounts of time for calculation.
Only with the aid of a computer is it reasonable to carry out sophisticated analyses on the large amounts of data that can be collected
under automated control. Note, however, that researchers often confuse sophisticated data analyses with the quality of a study. Increasing
the quantity of data collected and analyzed is no guarantee of quality:

Computers only provide a mechanism for the collection and analysis of data; humans must still evaluate the statistical results and make decisions. An old computer slogan applies here: GIGO—Garbage In; Garbage Out.

At one time the analysis of data by computer required a significant amount of effort and technical knowledge of computer hardware. The development of high-speed computers and sophisticated software has changed that. Almost every contemporary reading researcher has used SPSS (Statistical Package for the Social Sciences), or an equivalent statistical package, to analyze some sort of data on a computer. New developments are making that task even easier. A new program, SCSS (Statistical Conversations for the Social Sciences) requires only that the user be able to answer questions regarding the design, variables, number of observations, and so forth. There is no need to do technical formatting of responses, generate card images, or the like.

Microcomputers have become sufficiently sophisticated that most of the commonly used mainframe analysis packages have been adapted for them. In addition there are numerous other statistical packages that make mainframe programming and computing skills less critical.

Reading Research on Computer Hardware

As computers have come into wider use, the characteristics of computer displays have become objects of reading research. One line of this research has tried to determine the optimal sizes for computer displays (see Daniel & Reinking, chapter 2 of this volume).

Microcomputer displays have ranged in size from a few lines to a full page or more in length. Width has ranged from about 40 characters to more than 130. A "normal" display is usually 24 or 25 lines of 80 characters each. Because smaller displays are cheaper, it would be of interest to determine the minimum size of display at which reading is not degraded.

The technique used to study this problem derives from the work of Forster (1970) and is called RSVP (rapid serial visual presentation). Words are presented in the same position on a CRT in sequence. At moderate rates of speed (e.g., 360 words per minute), reading is "surprisingly natural." Comprehension begins to be affected as rates reach 12 words a second (720 words per minute). By the time rates reach 16–28 words per second, subjects no longer have the feeling that they can distinguish all the words or comprehend the material presented (Potter, 1984, p. 91). Mitchell (1984) and Potter (1984) provide more detailed reviews of this material.

A second line of research has compared reading at computer terminals with reading from printed text. For "normal" computer displays, there is almost always a difference between hardcopy and displays (Gould & Grischkowky, 1984; Haas & Hayes, 1985a, 1985b). For display copy, comprehension is poorer when time to read is held constant. If comprehension is a criterion, reading from computer displays takes longer than from hard copy. These effects can largely be mitigated by improvements in the display quality. If computers are ever to be used as primary text presentation devices, this issue will have to be addressed and settled.

Computers and Models of Reading

The final category of effects of computers on reading research is in the use of computers to model the reading process. It is clear that models such as those of Gough (1972), LaBerge and Samuels (1974) or Rumelhart (1977) would not have had their present forms were it not for the use of computer programming and/or simulation techniques. The work of Kintsch and van Dijk (1978) shows how computer simulations have effects on the development of models of text processing. This work has extended notions of readability by using the computer to simulate how well readers can extract and recreate information from a text. In a different vein, Just and Carpenter (1980) have used computer-collected eye movement data to develop a model of the reading process.

A substantial amount of reading research has been oriented toward or derived from "schema theory." Schema theory has been largely shaped by computer modeling and simulation. The work of Schank and Abelson (1977) illustrates much of what can be and has been done with computer simulations of comprehension. The next set of computer influences may be artificial intelligence (see Balajthy, chapter 3 of this volume). Wilson and Bates (1981), for example, give an account of how artificial intelligence might be a factor in language instruction.

Future developments in applications of computers to reading research will be limited only by the imagination of the researchers. Even now, the availability of microcomputers to almost all researchers has an impact on the quantity and quality of reading research. More sophisticated hardware will produce an even broader range of possibilities. There will likely be further noticeable effects in modeling and simulations as more reading researchers gain access to computers; even now, many microcomputers have the capability to run some of the more sophisticated languages used for simulations, like LISP or PROLOG.

The growth of networks that link microcomputers to each other or to central information banks is another development that is likely to benefit reading research. Two principal advantages can be foreseen at the moment, but others may well appear as these systems expand. First, by facilitating communication among researchers, computer networks may lead to more cooperative efforts. Second, information retrieval services available through the computer will increasingly provide easy and instant access to datasets, journals, and other materials for both submission and distribution. Already, for example, computer tapes are available from the National Assessment of Educational Progress so that researchers can perform their own analyses on the coded test data. Another example is use of the Educational Research Forum on CompuServe by a special interest group of the American Educational Research Association. Messages about educational research and interests can be exchanged in computer conferences. Data files can be downloaded for use by others. These are only a few examples of capabilities that will become more common in the future.

COMPUTERS AND READING INSTRUCTION

Teaching reading using computers has been a subject of research since the middle 1960s (Atkinson & Hansen, 1966). However, in order to understand what the issues are in computer-assisted instructional research, a discussion of the general issues in reading research is necessary. These issues include the limitations of computers with regard to reading instruction, alternatives to computers, the definition of computer literacy, and the effects of computer technology on the production of materials.

Some Recent Developments

Sticht and his co-workers (Sticht, Beck, Hauke, Kleiman, & James, 1974) have demonstrated that improvement in reading comprehension can occur as a result of auding (oral comprehension) training. Carver (1977–78) has also shown the connection between reading and listening. While speech compression, recognition, and synthesis devices exist and seem to have some potential for reading applications, little use has been made of them (note, however, that this may be changing; see Olson & Wise, chapter 10 of this volume). Computer reading programs like Writing To Read (Martin, 1986; Educational Testing Service, 1984) incorporate speech as part of the reading instruction. There are even word-processing programs that will allow students the option of having their writing "spoken" to them by the computer (e.g., Talking Screen Textwriter, Computing Adventures, Ltd.). These developments go a long way toward overcoming the objections to early attempts to teach reading by computer (Spache, 1967a).

Another computer-like device that is now available is the Kurzweil reading machine (Cushman, 1980). This machine, which can translate printed text into sound or data files with a high degree of accuracy, is text independent—that is, it can be used without special preparation of the materials to be read. However, the cost has limited the use of these machines to those who require them because of a handicap. Though highly accurate, the Kurzweil reading machine can "misread" when presented with odd-sized type or unusual fonts. Other devices are available for microcomputers that can scan printed text and produce computer-readable text files. These devices are relatively inexpensive and their cost continues to decline.

Materials preparation has been greatly affected by computers. Commercial publishers are beginning to make full use of the capabilities afforded by computerized typesetting and printing, and many now accept manuscripts on magnetic media (diskettes or tapes). At a local level the use of word processing, in particular, has greatly extended the range of materials available to individual instructors for classroom purposes. Desktop publishing—the ability to write and print professional-looking materials with microcomputers and laser printers—has become a reality.

At the same time, instructional management systems have probably become more firmly entrenched in reading instruction due to computer technology. The basal reading series used in schools today frequently require teachers to record students' progress toward mastery of hundreds of reading skills, and the amount of time needed for such monitoring has been a major disadvantage of instructional management systems. Computers, however, have been used in conjunction with these programs to score tests, record students' progress, and prescribe remedial activities. The computer thus makes instructional management systems more attractive to teachers and administrators despite reservations on the part of some authorities that teaching reading as a hierarchy of subskills is inappropriate (see Miller & Burnett, chapter 11 of this volume).

Finally, the areas of computer instruction and computer literacy need to be considered in regard to the preparation and reading of written materials. Under this heading come both instruction and word processing. Word processing is currently a major use of computers for business and represents a potentially large occupational area. It will probably be a major influence in the future of higher education as it becomes the dominant mode for writing. At many universities, students are given access to word-processing systems on the university computer. Theses and term papers are routinely prepared on these systems, which are also used by faculty for preparation of course materials, publications, and other professional papers. The use of plotters can make the production of graphs, charts, and other figures almost a trivial exercise. Many of the more sophisticated plotters can produce figures that are "camera-ready" and acceptable for publication. In addition, electronic mail and data systems connect many institutions with each other through EDUNET or BITNET.

Computers and Literacy

Perhaps the most visible effect of the computer on reading instruction has been its effect on the definition of literacy. It was once the case that being able to sign one's name was a sign of literacy. A combination of technology and military and other large-scale manpower needs has redefined literacy (Venezky, 1978). Though literacy only recently came to mean the ability to read and comprehend new material (Resnick & Resnick, 1977), today, the term is often understood to include the ability to interact with computers—computer literacy. However, even the definition of computer literacy is changing. While ambitious programs to develop computer literacy once involved knowledge of programming and the like (see Johnson, Anderson, Hansen & Klassen, 1980), further technological developments have made some of this training unnecessary. For example, computer literacy for early computers required knowing how to wire program boards by hand. Later machines could be used only if one knew how to keypunch cards. Today, microcomputers rarely have the option of using cards for input. Present-day, state-of-the-art programs for writing CAI/tutorial materials require almost no programming knowledge. Users can interact with the computer in (almost) conversational fashion.

As an analogy, we do not expect people to repair a washer or dryer although they can easily operate them. Beginning drivers are not expected to know auto mechanics. Television viewers would be hard-pressed to explain how their sets worked. Computer literacy may become simply knowing how to use computers, not necessarily how to program them in detail.

What has become vitally important is information. Computers handle information better than other devices, but it is important not to lose sight of the fact that books are highly efficient random-access devices—that is, any information can be accessed without dealing with other information. Tape requires sequential operations in which every preceding piece of information must be covered (or ignored). Only computer-controlled videodiscs (i.e., CD ROM systems) come close to approximating the efficiency of books as random-access devices. Computers can become the first technological advances that even come close to being substitutes for books as storage devices for information. We have little research on this topic, but it will become vital to find out whether the differences in the ways that books and computers store information will have significant educational impacts on learning. For example, the alternative formats for displaying and interacting with written texts that are made possible by the computer may require that students be taught new strategies for finding information.

Early Reading and CAI Projects

The first major efforts to use computers in teaching reading were those of the Brentwood Project, later called the Stanford Project under the direction of Atkinson, Suppes, and their colleagues. A report on the benefits of CAI for reading created some negative reaction (see Atkinson & Hansen, 1966, comments by Spache, 1967a, 1967b, and reaction by Atkinson, 1968). A typical lesson was divided into six parts (Atkinson & Hansen, 1966): letter discrimination, initial vocabulary acquisition, word decoding tasks, syntactic and intonation practice with phrases and sentences, syntactic and semantic practice with phrase and sentence material, and information processing tasks. It was not the general categories that evoked reaction, but the fact that the computer did little more than allow for drill and practice on relatively isolated skills (Spache, 1967b).

It should be noted that the original project used large computers, with remote teletype displays and audio presentations through headsets. Audio communication was unidirectional. This project was the basis for at least one current effort to teach reading with computers. Computer Curriculum Corporation provides commercial services for schools who want entire reading (and other) curricula delivered by computer. While the present Computer Curriculum Corporation materials and hardware are very different from those used originally, they can be traced back to early work on the Stanford Project.

There have been several other large-scale attempts to develop CAI for reading and other curriculum areas. Most notable among these has been the PLATO (Programmed Logic for Automatic Teaching Operation) project originally developed at the University of Illinois and now largely based at the University of Delaware and Control Data Corporation (see Obertino, 1974, for a review of the PLATO system). PLATO offered several advantages over other computer systems: a special terminal, with superior graphics; touch panels for simplified responding; special easy-to-use languages for programming instructional materials; and random access audio output. PLATO has been used to teach beginning reading, college-level English, and GED reading comprehension, among many other subjects.

Another major system is the TICCIT system (Time-shared Interactive Computer-Controlled Information Television) developed by Hazeltine and Mitre Corporation using Data General computers. Much work has been done with TICCIT at Brigham Young University. The unique advantages of TICCIT are a special keyboard to make input easier and a display that incorporates television video tapes, normally or frame by frame. Other large-computer applications in reading are described by Mason, Blanchard, and Daniel (1983).

Advantages of CAI

There are, theoretically, several major advantages to CAI. Instruction can be individualized with regard to rate and content. A totally unique curriculum (in terms of actual content) can be developed for each student, given the large number of different alternatives a computer program can select based on student performance. Strategies for enhancing attention and motivation can be built into CAI fairly easily. The "addiction" to video games is often utilized in instructional environments for such purposes. Computer programs are also objective; they are unaffected by factors not directly relevant to learning. Since computer programs make instructional decisions solely on the basis of academic performance, they are unaffected by the social and interpersonal factors that sometimes mistakenly capture the attention of teachers in the classroom (Duffy, 1981). Finally, some tasks can't be done by humans—clear examples are most readily found in mathematics. An iterative solution to a complex mathematics problem can be found in a few seconds or minutes with a computer; it might involve a lifetime of work for a mathematician. Similarly, in reading the computer can provide information at the reader's fingertips that would be far less accessible without a computer.

Problems with CAI

Despite the advantages of CAI, there has been less than stellar progress toward realizing them. The major obstacle has traditionally been the expense. Large computer systems for CAI were beyond the fiscal reach of most school systems. Even time-sharing on large systems did not reduce the cost sufficiently. It has only been in the last few years that microcomputers have been inexpensive enough for most schools to be able to afford them.

Additionally, large computer systems have a major fault: They often go "down." When a large computer is not working properly, all of the terminals connected to it on a time-sharing basis are affected. Again microcomputers have effectively eliminated this problem. Each machine stands alone, if one goes "down" it does not affect the others.

Mason (1980) lists the following additional problems: the cost of software, the difficulty of reading at a CRT (cathode ray tube), the computer's inability to listen to someone read in order to help improve his/her fluency, and the fact that the computer is limited to the responses that are programmed. Many of these problems have been addressed and at least partly resolved; others will await new technological developments.

Cost is by no means the sole instructional problem entailed in software selection. Since software may be more complex and less flexible than other materials, a series of different questions arise. Who is to do the authoring? Who should decide where computer materials fit in the curriculum? How should software be evaluated? Who should do the evaluation? Should computer software be correctable at local sites? All of these questions and more need to be addressed. A part of the reason that CAI did not become more popular in the 1960s was the lack of what might be called "humanistic" software. It will take a concerted and cooperative effort on the part of reading professionals, computer programmers, and publishers to make high-quality materials available for use with microcomputers. Moreover, the materials will have to make use of the special capabilities of computers to be widely accepted by reading professionals.

Research on Reading and CAI

Most of the studies that have investigated reading and CAI have involved mainframe or minicomputer systems. These studies are not always exactly relevant to the present state of affairs in which there are far larger numbers of microcomputers in use than were available when most of the studies were conducted. In light of such a strong caveat, what do the research results have to suggest about CAI and reading?

In their 1972 survey of the literature on drill and practice in CAI, Vinsonhaler and Bass found an advantage of .1 to .4 school years for CAI drill and practice groups in language arts. Edwards, Norton, Taylor, Weiss, and Dusseldorp (1975) did a similar survey, but did not restrict their search to drill and practice. Of the six studies cited in reading or English, none showed negative results. Only one showed the effects of traditional instruction and CAI to be equal; five showed advantages for CAI.

Jamison, Suppes, and Wells (1974) compared the effects of many alternative instructional media. In many of the studies they surveyed involving programmed instruction and CAI, no significant differences were found. Overall, however, it did appear that there could be some savings in time. Most important, small amounts of CAI, when used as supplements, led to improvements in achievement, particularly for slower students. The survey also indicated that the overwhelming majority of efforts in developing educational technology were directed toward improving quality with little regard to cost.

Kulik, Kulik, and Cohen (1980) have done a meta-analysis that shows the benefits of CAI at the college level. There are consistent, though small, benefits in achievement and affect as the result of CAI. The authors also report a substantial savings in time when CAI is used.

Niemiec, Samson, Weinstein, and Walberg (in press) have done a meta-analysis of 48 studies of CAI. In general, the findings were that, overall, students who were in CAI treatment groups had performances that were .45 standard deviation units better than the controls. Other effect sizes of interest were: vocabulary, .40; comprehension, .11; total reading, .24; language arts, .48; and spelling, .38. Microcomputers fared better than mainframes, with an effect size of 1.26 (although this is based on only two studies). One other important finding emerged from this analysis: Computer-managed instruction was not substantially better than conventional instruction—its effect size was only .03.

In 1981, Gleason summarized the effects of CAI as follows:

1. CAI can be used successfully to assist learners in attaining specified instructional objectives.
2. There is substantial savings (20%–40%) in time required for learning over traditional instruction.
3. Retention is at least as good as if not superior to retention following conventional instruction.

4. Students react positively to good CAI programs; they reject poor ones.

The Niemiec et al. (in press) analysis seems to suggest that teaching reading by computer can result in some achievement improvements, such as a student's performance rising from the 50th percentile to about the 65th when CAI is used. However, managing instruction is not a particularly beneficial use of computers, since the effect size is essentially nil—that is, there seems to be no advantage over (at least) conventional management. Finally, there is a hint in these data that microcomputers may be more effective than mainframes for delivery of CAI. This finding may simply be attributable to the fact that the materials and assessment devices are more carefully matched in local environments where microcomputers are used, or it may be due to some real technological advantage of microcomputers. In either case, the "hint" is based on only two studies. Obviously, broadening the research base of microcomputer studies should be a priority.

CAI AND METACOGNITION

Another aspect of computers and reading relates to research on metacognitive activity. In much CAI software, students are called on to make decisions like how many problems or questions they wish to have in a lesson, how difficult the items should be, and even when to terminate the lesson. Garhart and Hannafin (in press) have shown that there is very little relation between self-assessed understanding of lesson content and subsequent performance on tests. Students who do control their own instructional decisions tend to terminate instruction prematurely.

A growing number of studies point out the potential disadvantages of providing too many options for CAI students (Carrier, 1984; Tennyson, 1980). Reinking (1986) suggested that restricting options in certain CAI situations may be beneficial for learners. This view calls into question the value of a capability often cited as an advantage of the computer—its ability to present students with a much larger number of options than conventional instruction can provide. Since so much CAI software entails making independent "metacognitive" decisions, these are crucial issues that need to be explored in much greater detail.

COMPUTERS AND READING AND WRITING RESEARCH

One of the most intriguing areas of application has been in the use of computers for writing. Since some current thought favors the holistic teaching of reading and writing, these applications are important concerns for reading research (see Miller & Burnett, chapter 11 of this volume).

Rubin has described both the story maker technique of writing instruction (1980) and adaptations of that technique for computers (1983). In this technique, students use the computer to string together different parts of stories that they (or others) have written to create almost unlimited variations. While there is improvement in story structure comprehension and story-writing ability after story grammar instruction, research is still needed to determine whether exposure to computer programs like these will have similar effects.

Perhaps the most common use of computers today is in word processing. Because reading and writing share some, but not all, skills (Shanahan, 1984; Shanahan & Lomax, 1986), studies of the effects of composition and word processing are relevant to reading research. What are some of these findings?

Most importantly, writing, in and of itself, does not seem to lead to "better" or "different" writing styles. Bridwell and her colleagues (Bridwell, Johnson, & Brehe, in press; Bridwell, Sirc, & Brooks, in press) have demonstrated that writing styles on computers are primarily a function of the writing a person has already learned.

Daiute (in press) has shown that there is no substantial difference between revising during word processing and revising during conventional writing unless students are taken through a "prompting" program that "encourages" thinking about revisions on a paragraph-by-paragraph basis. In fact, in some conditions, there was even a bit more revising when students used a pen than when they used a word processor. These conclusions are reinforced by preliminary findings with college-level students (Shapiro, MacGregor, Berman, & Niemiec, 1986). They demonstrated that without a carefully designed writing curriculum, there may be little improvement in writing. By inference, given the relatively specific overlap in reading and writing skills (Shanahan, 1984), there may be little or no concurrent improvement in reading without a very specific curriculum. However, there are more unanswered than answered questions in this area. The progress of CAI in reading and writing will ultimately depend on answering these questions.

THE FUTURE OF COMPUTERS AND READING

No review of this sort is complete without some speculation about what the future will hold for the use of computers in reading research. The premise of futurists such as Toffler (1970) is that technology is developing at an exponential rate. If that is true, the task of prediction is close to futile. However, a few guesses are still in order.

Future Directions for Research on CAI

Gleason (1981) points out that there are few researchers who are asking questions of the form: Is CAI better than method X? While there are only a few researchers doing comparative methods research in CAI, there are researchers and practitioners working on the following types of problems and questions:

1. What are the most effective CAI strategies? What is best in terms of feedback? Are different paradigms better for different curricular areas?
2. How do individual learning styles interact with CAI? How much cognitive complexity can students handle?
3. What are the effects of individual learner characteristics (e.g., memory span, perception, IQ, motor skills, sensory preferences, and literacy levels) in CAI situations?
4. What hardware configurations are most effective, efficient, or necessary? How important are audio outputs, touch panels, video capabilities, and light pens?
5. How does affect relate to CAI? What are the roles of motivation, persistence, delayed gratification, and locus of control?
6. What are the most effective strategies for program development? How should programmers and practitioners relate to each other?
7. What are the most effective strategies for integrating CAI with other instructional activities?

The answers to these questions, combined with present knowledge, will shape the future role of computers in reading instruction. Presently, we have few answers; future research needs to focus on these and related questions.

Educational Concerns

In the future, there will be a new definition of literacy. Being an educated person will involve knowing how to interact with computers. It will probably become impossible to complete school without being able to deal with computers at some level. Most students will learn how to interact with a computer as a basic skill.

An extensive array of hardware will be available. Computers will eventually have excellent synthesized speech output and will also have speech recognition capabilities. The machines in the near future will have highly improved graphics, extensive memory capacity, and easy access to video tape/disk input and output. Costs will probably not decrease substantially but capabilities almost certainly will be greater.

Computers will be used to teach a wide variety of skills, from creative writing to art and music. Computer software will move away from drill and practice formats toward more innovative applications. The choices for learning will not be location-specific: A student will not have to be face-to-face with an "expert" to learn. Thus, for all practical purposes, the choices of subject matter will become unlimited.

Students will be able to make use of computers for word processing, learning to write, preparing of materials for class projects, and interacting with information banks of all sorts. A new form of "literacy" may appear. Even now, computerized video disks are being used to replace some training manuals, even in the area of medical diagnosis. Some tasks are more easily demonstrated than described—for example, it is probably easier to show someone how to tie a bowline knot than it is to explain how to tie it. Thus, the reading requirements for certain tasks would certainly be minimized.

There will be extensive networking of microcomputers among schools, in a manner similar to that used by the Minnesota Educational Computer Consortium. Libraries, as we know them, may become outmoded. The contents of only a few CD ROM disks could contain the entire written works of any library. Lambert and Ropiequet (1986) presage such changes in their compilation of articles dealing with the emergent CD ROM technology. The notion of Dynabooks could become a reality—text could be expanded at any point to pursue topics, elaborate concepts, or remediate reading behaviors. This capability requires no new technology. All that is needed is the appropriate developmental work.

To be prepared for the changes in reading research and instruction, we must adjust not only our thinking about the reading process, but the manner in which we investigate it and teach it. We will have to account for a much wider range of reading variables and behaviors in a vastly broader range of environments in the years to come. In addition to studying the processes of reading, we will have to be concerned with the social implications of literacy as access to information. Thoughtful research concerning computers and reading will play an important role in shaping these changes.

REFERENCES

Atkinson, R. (1968). A reply to Professor Spache's article, "A reaction to 'Computer-assisted instruction in initial reading: The Stanford Project.'" *Reading Research Quarterly, 3*, 418–420.

Atkinson, R., & Hansen, D. (1966). Computer-assisted instruction in initial reading: The Stanford project. *Reading Research Quarterly, 2*, 5–25.

Bridwell, L., Johnson, P., & Brehe, S. (in press). Composing and computers: Case studies of experienced writers. In A. Matsuhashi (Ed.), *Writing in real time: Modeling production processes*. New York: Longman.

Bridwell, L., Sirc, G., & Brooks, R. (in press). Revising and computing: Case studies of student writers. In S. Freedman (Ed.), *The acquisition of written language: Revision and responses*. Norwood, NJ: Ablex.

Bronfenbrenner, U. (1976). The experimental ecology of education. *Educational Researcher, 5*(9), 5–15.

Carrier, C. (1984). Do learners make good choices? *Instructional Innovator, 29*, 15–17.

Carver, R. (1977–78). Toward a theory of reading comprehension and rauding. *Reading Research Quarterly, 13*, 8–63.

Cushman, R. (1980). The Kurzweil reading machine. *Wilson Library Bulletin, 22*, 311–315.

Daiute, C. (in press). Physical and cognitive factors in revising: Insights from studies with computers.

Duffy, G. (1981). Teacher effectiveness research: Implications for the reading profession. In M. Kamil (Ed.), *Directions in reading: Research and instruction* (pp. 113–136). Washington, DC: The National Reading Conference.

Educational Testing Service. (1984). *The ETS evaluation of Writing to Read* (Unpublished technical report). Princeton, NJ: Educational Testing Service.

Edwards, J., Norton, S., Taylor, S., Weiss, M., & Dusseldorp, R. (1975). How effective is CAI? A review of the research. *Educational Leadership, 33*, 147–153.

Forster, K. I. (1970). Visual perception of rapidly presented word sequences of varying complexity. *Perception and Psychophysics, 8*, 215–221.

Garhart, C., & Hannafin, M. (in press). The accuracy of cognitive monitoring during computer-based instruction.

Gleason, G. (1981). Microcomputers in education: The state of the art. *Educational Technology, 21*, 7–18.

Gough, P. (1972). One second of reading. In J. F. Kavanagh & I. G. Mattingly (Eds.), *Language by ear and eye* (pp. 331–358). Cambridge, MA: MIT Press.

Gould, J., & Grischkowky, N. (1984). Doing the same work with hardcopy and with CRT terminals. *Human Factors, 26*, 323–337.

Haas, C., & Hayes, J. (1985a). *Effects of text display variables on reading tasks: Computer screen vs. hard copy* (CDC Technical Report No. 3). Pittsburgh, PA: Carnegie-Mellon University, Communications Design Center.

Haas, C., & Hayes, J. (1985b). *Reading on the computer: A comparison of standard and advanced computer display and hard copy* (CDC Technical Report No. 7). Pittsburgh, PA: Carnegie-Mellon University, Communications Design Center.

Harris, A., & Sipay, E. (1985). *How to increase reading ability* (8th ed.). New York: Longman.

Huey, E. (1908). *The psychology and pedagogy of reading.* New York: Macmillan.

Jamison, D., Suppes, P., & Wells, S. (1974). The effectiveness of alternative instructional media: A survey. *Review of Educational Research, 44*, 1–67.

Johnson, D., Anderson, R., Hansen, T., & Klassen, D. (1980). Computer literacy—What is it? *Mathematics Teacher, 73*, 91–96.

Johnson, D., & Moe, A. (1980). Current approaches, part two. In P. Lamb & D. Arnold (Eds.), *Teaching reading* (2nd ed., pp. 205–236). Belmont, CA: Wadsworth.

Just, M., & Carpenter, P. (1980). A theory of reading: From eye fixations to comprehension. *Psychological Review, 87*, 329–354.

Just, M., & Carpenter, P. (1984). Using eye fixations to study reading comprehension. In D. Kieras & M. Just (Eds.), *New methods in reading comprehension research* (pp. 151–182). Hillsdale, NJ: Lawrence Erlbaum.

Kintsch, W., & van Dijk, T. (1978). Toward a model of text comprehension and production. *Psychological Review, 85*, 363–394.

Kulik, J., Kulik, C., & Cohen, P. (1980). Effectiveness of computer-based college teaching: A meta-analysis of findings. *Review of Educational Research, 50*, 525–544.

LaBerge, D., & Samuels, J. (1974). Toward a theory of automatic information processing in reading. *Cognitive Psychology, 6*, 293–323.

Lambert, S., & Ropiequet, S. (Eds.). (1986). *CD ROM: The new papyrus.* Redmond, WA: Microsoft Press.

Martin, J. (1986). Learning to read by first learning to write. *The Reading Instruction Journal, 29*, 35–42.

Mason, G. (1980). Computerized reading instruction: A review. *Educational Technology, 20*. 18–22.

Mason, G., Blanchard, J., & Daniel, D. (1983). *Computer applications in reading* (3rd ed.). Newark, DE: International Reading Association.

Mason, G., & Mize, J. (1978). Teaching reading with television: A review. *Educational Technology, 18,* 5–12.

Mitchell, D. (1984). An evaluation of subject-paced reading tasks and other methods for investigating immediate processes in reading. In D. Kieras & M. Just (Eds.), *New methods in reading comprehension research* (pp. 69–89). Hillsdale, NJ: Lawrence Erlbaum.

Moe, A., & Johnson, D. (1980). Current approaches, part one. In P. Lamb & D. Arnold (Eds.), *Teaching reading* (2nd ed., pp. 171–204). Belmont, CA: Wadsworth.

Niemiec, R., Samson, G., Weinstein, T., & Walberg, H. (in press). The effects of computer based instruction in elementary schools: A quantitative synthesis.

Obertino, P. (1974). The PLATO reading project: An overview. *Educational Technology, 14,* 8–13.

Potter, M. (1984). Rapid serial visual presentation (RSVP): A method for studying language processing. In D. Kieras & M. Just (Eds.), *New methods in reading comprehension research* (pp. 91–118). Hillsdale, NJ: Lawrence Erlbaum.

Rayner, K. (1978). Eye movements in reading and information processing. *Psychological Bulletin, 85,* 618–660.

Rayner, K., & Carroll, P. (1984). Eye movements and reading comprehension. In D. Kieras & M. Just (Eds.), *New methods in reading comprehension research* (pp. 129–150). Hillsdale, NJ: Lawrence Erlbaum.

Reinking, D. (1986). Six advantages of computer-mediated text. *The Reading Instruction Journal, 29,* 8–16.

Resnick, D., & Resnick, L. (1977). The nature of literacy: An historical exploration. *Harvard Educational Review, 47,* 370–385.

Rubin, A. (1980). Making stories, making sense. *Language Arts, 57,* 285–298.

Rubin, A. (1983). The computer confronts language arts: Cans and shoulds for education. In A. C. Wilkinson (Ed.), *Classroom computers and cognitive science* (pp. 201–217). New York: Academic Press.

Rumelhart, D. (1977). Toward an interactive model of reading. In S. Dornic (Ed.), *Attention and performance VI* (pp. 573–603). Hillsdale, NJ: Lawrence Erlbaum.

Schank, R., & Abelson, R. (1977). *Plans, scripts, and understanding.* Hillsdale, NJ: Lawrence Erlbaum.

Shanahan, T. (1984). Nature of the reading-writing relation: An explanatory multivariate analysis. *Journal of Educational Psychology, 76,* 466–477.

Shanahan, T., & Lomax, R. (1986). An analysis and comparison of theoretical models of the reading-writing relationship. *Journal of Educational Psychology, 78,* 116–123.

Shapiro, J., MacGregor, S., Berman, S., & Niemiec, R. (1986, April). *Evaluation of computer assisted instruction for higher education students in a developmental writing program.* Paper presented at the annual meeting of the American Educational Research Association, San Francisco.

Spache, G. (1967a). A reaction to "Computer-assisted instruction in initial reading: The Stanford Project." *Reading Research Quarterly, 3,* 101–109.

Spache, G. (1967b). Reading technology. In G. Schick & M. May (Eds.), *Junior college and adult reading programs—Expanding fields* (16th yearbook of the National Reading Conference, pp. 178–184). Milwaukee, WI: The National Reading Conference.

Sticht, T., Beck, L., Hauke, R., Kleiman, G., & James, J. (1974). *Auding and reading: A developmental model.* Alexandria, VA: Human Resources Research Organization.

Tennyson, R. (1980). Instructional control strategies and content structure as design variables in concept acquisition using computer-based instruction. *Journal of Educational Psychology, 72,* 525–532.

Toffler, A. (1970). *Future shock.* New York: Random House.

Venezky, R. (1978). Fantasy and realism in literacy assessment. In R. Beach & P. D. Pearson (Eds.), *Perspectives on literacy* (pp. 42–52). Minneapolis, MN: College of Education, University of Minnesota.

Vinsonhaler, J., & Bass, R. (1972). A summary of ten major studies on CAI drill and practice. *Educational Technology, 12,* 29–32.

Wilson, K., & Bates, M. (1981). Artificial intelligence in computer-based language instruction. *The Volta Review, 83,* 336–349.

5

Computer Analysis of Written Materials

Lawrence T. Frase

COMPUTING ENVIRONMENTS FOR TEXT ANALYSIS

Computers give us an opportunity to analyze the written word in new and more efficient ways and to study and apply the principles of cognitive science and text design. Today, models of decision processes used by experts have been incorporated into programs that make design recommendations—for example, recommendations for the most suitable column width to use for a particular text (Frase, Macdonald, & Keenan, 1985). Knowledge-based expert systems (Duda & Shortliffe, 1983), developed by researchers in artificial intelligence, allow us to build into computers the expertise derived from various disciplines.

Just as cognitive science and text design reflect theoretical and practical aspects of documentation, computer science and software engineering reflect theoretical and practical aspects of a common domain (computation). The existence of these two components, theoretical and applied, shows that it isn't enough to have tools and an understanding of how to use them. We also need an environment in which to develop and extend software tools to the solution of everyday problems. When it comes to computers, a systems development environment is a critical condition for converting knowledge into new applications.

Intelligent Environments for Language Analysis

Today we have the capacity to develop intelligent environments for language analysis. What is an "intelligent environment"? Intelligence has two components—a base of knowledge and a set of procedures for transforming, using, and sharing that knowledge. An intelligent environment, then, is one that has information resources and ways to change that information and send it to others. The more knowledge and procedures a system has the more intelligent it is. This conception does not distinguish between machines, people, and social systems; each is a resource that contributes to outputs from the system. Any assessment of a computer environment must include all these cooperating elements. The "intelligence" of an environment depends on how well people and machines work together.

Recent developments in computer systems have given us the resources to support an evolving environment for intelligent text processing that will continue to grow and invent new applications. A major step in this evolution includes the widespread use of several shared operating systems. One purpose of this chapter is to show how such shared environments can aid research on written materials.

UNIX Operating System

Bell Laboratories has had a well-developed computer applications environment for many years. The UNIX[1] operating system has been a major resource for text processing and other applications within AT&T and in schools, universities, and businesses, here and in other countries (see Bourne, 1978; Pike & Kernighan, 1984; Ritchie & Thompson, 1978). The UNIX system includes a hierarchical file arrangement; file, device, and inter-process input and output; various programming languages; and many applications systems. The system has many software development tools, as well as network capabilities. Furthermore, the UNIX system is widely used in education, government, and industry, so developments can be disseminated rapidly from one institution to another. System philosophy emphasizes portability of tools across environments. The system already has many text processing tools, including the UNIX Writer's Workbench[2] Software, discussed below.

The shell language of the UNIX operating system is simple to use because commands execute complex functions that are hidden from the user. For instance, typing the command SPELL, followed by the name of a file containing a text, delivers a list of misspelled words in the text. Another command, WC, followed by the name of a file containing text, counts characters, words, and lines in the file. Commands have options, signaled by a minus sign, that allow them to be modified in certain ways. For instance, the command WC –L, followed by the file name, counts just the lines in the file. In the UNIX system, one can string commands together using the pipe (symbolized by "|")

facility. Using the pipe, the output of one command is fed to another command. Hence, the string of two commands SPELL *filename* | WC -L delivers a count of the misspelled words in a file, which could be stored in a file with other statistics on text problems.

Another example is the Writer's Workbench command SYL, which determines the number of syllables in words. For instance, the command SYL -3 *filename* lists the unique words in a file that have three or more syllables. A slightly modified version of this program (contributed by N. H. Macdonald, and further modified by me) lists repeated occurrences of the same word, not just the unique words, so that the new command SYL.NEW -3 *filename* | WC -L, delivers a count of the words of three or more syllables in a text file. That simple sequence of commands has become part of a program I wrote to calculate the Gunning Fog Index (Gunning, 1963), which uses the number of words greater than 2 syllables as a variable. In that program, the number of words greater than 2 syllables is calculated and stored in a variable called "w," using the command W = `SYL.NEW -3 *filename* | WC -L`.

In summary, each command, no matter how complex its inner workings, becomes a resource for others to use in their own programs. I have given a few examples of simple commands, how they combine, and how they are shared between people and programs. This shared tool environment, aside from the specific features of the UNIX operating system, is a major resource for research and application of language analysis. The flexibility to choose from a wide range of tools is an important asset for the scientific investigation of language.

ANALYSIS OF WRITTEN MATERIALS

This section describes various examples of the uses of computer text analysis based on the Writer's Workbench programs and other UNIX system commands. The first four subsections describe how the computer was used to help understand a problem of text layout, the nature of text evaluation programs, the outcomes of their use for writing instruction, and how the programs were used to help evaluate a new test of writing ability. The final two subsections describe new programs designed to study additional text properties: measures of metric and syntactic features, and a measure of content similarity.

Text Design

One way we have used UNIX system tools is to explore the physical design of text. Physical design includes all elements of page layout that might affect how well people read and comprehend a text; for example, the amount of text on a page, the size of margins, whether text is aligned at the margins, and length of text lines. Below I consider line length, in particular, and how it affects how efficiently a text can be read.

Humans decide how to design a text by imagining the effects that the design might have on readers. Computers, too, can make design decisions about the format of text. To do this, the computer needs two models: first, a cognitive model of the information processing demands of different linguistic features; second, a model of text features that can be changed. Using these models, computer-based projections of the demands that a document will make on a reader, when a text is designed in different ways, can be developed. This approach is illustrated below with a computer program that determines the best line length for individual texts based on the occurrence of meaningful units of information, or "chunks," on lines.

The Problem

Expert designers are aware that the arrangement of words on a page is important for comprehension and artistic effect; hence, there is concern for the cognitive consequences of typographic formats. We know that people process complex information by segmenting and grouping related items together. For example, discriminations occur in segmenting episodes in a film (Carroll & Bever, 1976) or in the processing of symbolic materials. In reading aloud, readers pause at the boundaries of words that form meaningful units of information. Poetry often reinforces cognitive boundaries typographically by starting a new line when a new unit of thought begins. Ordinary text, on the other hand, obscures meaningful units by running them together, perhaps several on a line, or by separating words that belong in the same unit.

Studies show that if each line of a text contains only one meaningful segment (or "chunk"), memory, reading speed, and problem solving are improved over standard texts (Frase & Schwartz, 1979). Ordinarily, text is formatted in a uniform line length. Line length affects the probability of a reader's obtaining exactly one chunk on a line; a very short line length prevents complete chunks from fitting on one line, and a very long line length might contain several chunks. Unless all the chunks in a text are of equal length (an unlikely occurrence), no line length will result in the ideal case of one chunk on each line. (See Keenan, 1984, for qualifications to the assumption that one chunk on a line is ideal.) We might expect that some line lengths will yield a higher percentage of single chunks on a line than others. Furthermore, the best line length should differ according to text difficulty. For instance, as words and sentences become longer, more space is needed to express an idea.

The Study

The aim of this study (reported in detail in Frase, Macdonald, & Keenan, 1985) was to explore computer recommendations for text line length, and to determine whether those recommendations correspond to human judgment and findings from research.

Sixty 150-word text passages, of easy, medium, and difficult readability levels, were the objects of study. As measured by the Kincaid readability formula (Kincaid, Fishburne, Rogers, & Chissom, 1975), the easy passages were at the fourth-grade reading level, the medium passages at the tenth-grade reading level, and the difficult passages were at the eighteenth grade. Each passage was segmented into meaningful chunks of information by a human. Segmentation was also done by computer (see Hartley, 1981, for an example of output). The computer segmentation algorithm (implemented by Nina Macdonald) was based on an analysis I did of the boundaries used by humans in segmenting text into meaningful chunks. There was high agreement among human judges on chunk boundaries, and also high agreement between human and computer segmentations of the text (90% of the boundaries were the same).

We used a simple model to analyze the occurrence of meaningful chunks on lines under different text designs. In ordinary text, chunks are arranged haphazardly. Various outcomes are possible within each line; for instance, some lines contain several chunks, others contain only parts of a chunk. We classified lines into four categories: (a) no complete chunks (called "particles"), (b) exactly one chunk, (c) one chunk, plus chunk particles, and (d) two or more chunks, with or without chunk particles (called "overloads"). This model considered one chunk on a line the optimal condition for efficient reading. We assumed that multiple chunks (overloads) require the reader to break lines into meaningful segments, and chunk parts (particles) require the reader to assemble components, broken by the typographic design, into meaningful groups. Both of these, chunk overloads and chunk particles, we considered undesirable design outcomes.

Computer design analysis proceeded in three stages: (a) segment and mark chunk boundaries, (b) format the text, and (c) categorize lines into the four categories described above and count them. After segmentation into chunks, each passage was formatted by the computer into line lengths ranging from 5 to 75 characters. Five or ten characters on a line approximates a "vertical" typography, which uses only one word on each line. A line length of 25 corresponds to the line length used in two-column formats such as those found in *McCall's* magazine, and a line length of about 66 characters is often used for business letters. The UNIX system AWK command was used to classify each line of formatted text (with the chunks marked) into one of the four categories of the cognitive model. The percentage of lines in each category for each text was then calculated. The computer analyzed each of the 60 passages at each of 15 line length formats (900 analyses).

Outcomes

As expected, at low line lengths almost all the lines were chunk particles. This percentage decreased rapidly as line length increased. Chunk overloads seldom occurred at short line lengths, but increased rapidly with line length. There were few instances of a single chunk on a line at any line length.

Chunk particles and overloads are undesirable outcomes. If we assume that both are equally undesirable, then these undesirable outcomes can be minimized by formatting text at the line length where the sum of particles and overloads is the least. The best line length for the easy passages, with this analysis, was 44 characters. Since lines were forced to have the same length, as is commonly done in text production, at all line lengths there was a high percentage of undesirable outcomes. The best design, at 44 characters per line, resulted in about 75% undesirable outcomes. The data suggest that, for texts of all readability levels, line lengths between 40 and 60 characters minimize undesirable outcomes. This figure agrees well with human preference data (Tinker, 1963).

Our analysis shows, however, that this general rule applies only roughly to any one text, because the chunk characteristics of texts vary with readability and other features. The mean best line lengths for passages in different readability groups were significantly different: 44, 50, and 56 characters for the easy, medium, and difficult groups, respectively. However, there was much variability within readability groups, and texts varied in whether improvements would result from reformatting. For some texts an equal number of unfavorable outcomes resulted regardless of line length. Hence, our results illustrate why the design of a text must be determined by the linguistic characteristics of that text, not by group norms.

This study shows how computers can be used to analyze a text into cognitive units, and to assess whether these units are displayed effectively to the reader. Few humans have the time, tenacity, or ability to conduct such tedious, but informative, analyses involving all the words in a text. The computer recommended line lengths of 40–60 characters, which agrees well with the research literature, but it also showed that recommendations must vary with the characteristics of individual passages. An additional study, by Stacey Keenan (1984), shows that variability in line length is also an important factor in reading efficiency.

Text Evaluation

Programs that give detailed information about the language of text can be built quickly within a computing environment that contains tools developed by others. While working on problems of text design, it became clear that resources of the UNIX system could be used to provide extensive evaluation of reading materials. The Writer's Workbench system evolved as new programs were created to provide more and more information to writers of technical documents.

Rationale and Programs

Three important principles guided the Writer's Workbench software development. First, the programs should incorporate the knowledge of experts. The literature of rhetoric and psychology provide widely accepted text assessments and standards that people use in evaluating writing. Second, the programs should provide many assessments, thereby encouraging a multidimensional analysis of text, not a superficial one. Finally, users should have control over the programs. An author should be able to adjust the standards the programs use to make judgments, the form in which a text is submitted to the programs as input, and the form of output from the programs. For instance, it should be possible to change the standards used to evaluate text readability, include or exclude lists from analyses, and make the amount of editorial advice that one gets brief or long, as one desires.

Today's Writer's Workbench programs are a greatly expanded version of the earlier programs, which are described elsewhere at length (Cherry, 1980, 1982; Frase, 1983; Frase, Macdonald, Gingrich, Keenan, & Collymore, 1981; Macdonald, 1983; Macdonald, Frase, Gingrich, & Keenan, 1982). The PARTS and STYLE programs (Cherry, 1980, 1982) are the basis for several assessments. PARTS assigns a grammatical part of speech to each word in a text and STYLE converts this information into summaries of text variables. For instance, STYLE reports 73 text measures, including counts of words and sentences, and raw numbers and percentages of grammatical parts of speech. PROSE, another program, evaluates and discusses an author's writing style. Copyediting can be done interactively using the PROOFVI program. After running PROOFVI on a file, the author can see the text with errors, such as faulty diction and misspellings, highlighted. The program will suggest changes and for some errors, such as spelling, will automatically make corrections if desired. Table 5.1 lists the current Writer's Workbench programs and shows their structure. After typing a command (shown on the left) and the name of a file containing the text, the author gets the information shown on the right of the table.

User Response

Aside from testing the validity and reliability of the programs, we have tracked user response to the programs since they first became available within AT&T Bell Laboratories. A survey of users (Frase, Macdonald, Gingrich, Keenan, & Collymore, 1981) showed that a statistically significant number of users think that the documentation and program output are clear, that the programs don't miss much, and that the programs are likely to find things the writer would miss. In addition, authors believe that the programs improve their writing skills. Gingrich (1983) reported trials of the programs in two AT&T company locations. Her results showed that technical writers are more likely to detect editorial problems using the programs, and they have the same positive response to the programs as do staff at AT&T Bell Laboratories.

Writing Instruction

Rationale and Programs

Computer analysis of written materials has great instructional potential. In 1980, the English Department at Colorado State University (CSU) began a project to use editing programs to help composition students revise and edit their papers (Kiefer & Smith, 1983; Smith & Kiefer, 1982). A research agreement between AT&T Bell Laboratories and CSU resulted in studies to explore the use of the Writer's Workbench software in college composition. The Writer's Workbench system needed to be altered for specific classroom needs. A pilot study, for example, showed that writers with limited time at a terminal

Table 5.1 Writer's Workbench Programs

ON LINE HELP WITH WRITER'S WORKBENCH PROGRAMS	
wwbaid..............................	describes programs and explains how to use them
wwbhelp word.....................	gives information about programs and functions
wwbinfo..............................	prints this table
ON LINE HELP WITH GRAMMAR, SPELLING, PUNCTUATION, AND USAGE	
prosestnd...........................	prints prose standards used to evaluate documents
continris............................	explains clear ways to present contingencies
punctris.............................	explains punctuation rules
spelltell word.....................	finds the correct spelling of a word
splitris..............................	explains split infinitives
tmarkris............................	explains correct use of trade/service marks
worduse word.....................	explains correct usage of words and phrases
PROGRAMS FOR COPYEDITING	
acro file.............................	finds acronyms
consist file.........................	runs three consistency checking programs
tmark file.......................	finds inaccurate trade marks
conscap file.....................	checks for inconsistent capitalization
conspell file....................	checks inconsistent British/U.S. spellings
proofvi file.........................	proofreads text and corrects errors interactively (runs *diction*, *double*, *punct*, and *spellwwb*)
sexist file...........................	finds sexist phrases and suggests changes
switchr file........................	finds words used as both a noun and a verb
wwb file.............................	runs *proofr* and *prose* (style analysis program)
proofr file........................	runs five proofreading programs
spellwwb file..............	checks spelling
punct file....................	checks punctuation
double file...................	finds consecutive occurrences of the same word
diction file.................	finds awkward phrases, suggests changes
gram file....................	finds split infinitives and wrong articles
PROGRAMS FOR STYLE ANALYSIS	
findbe file...........................	prints file, highlights forms of verb "to be"
match style-file(s)...............	collates style statistics from different texts
morestyle file.....................	runs four additional stylistic analyses
abst file.........................	evaluates text abstractness
diversity file....................	measures vocabulary diversity (type/token ratio)
neg file............................	finds negative words
topic file.........................	lists frequent words to give an idea of the topic
org file...............................	prints short version of text to show organization
parts file............................	assigns grammatical parts of speech to words
reroff file............................	puts *mm* / *nroff* macros back in formatted text
syl file................................	counts syllables of each different word in file
wwb file.............................	runs *proofr* and *prose*
prose file.........................	gives detailed commentary about text style
style file......................	calculates and summarizes style statistics
PROGRAMS TO ANALYZE PROCEDURAL DOCUMENTS	
continge file........................	analyzes contingencies in procedural text
murky file...........................	finds difficult sentences in procedural text
PROGRAMS TO CUSTOMIZE DICTIONARIES AND STANDARDS	
dictadd..............................	adds phrases to user's personal dictionaries
personal dictionaries:	*ddict* - dictionary of awkward phrases
	sexdict - dictionary of sexist terms
	spelldict - dictionary of correct spellings
	tmarkdict - dictionary of trade/service marks
spelladd.............................	adds words to *spelldict* dictionary
mkstand............................	calculates standards for prose from user documents

Note: Indented commands are automatically run by the command that immediately precedes them. Indented commands can be run singly as well.

needed paper copy so they could mull over the computer comments. Furthermore, students did not need the entire set of Writer's Workbench programs, several of which were designed for specialized vocabularies used in AT&T Bell Laboratories.

CSU altered and added program dictionaries, selected and organized programs and program parts, and made it possible for students to run all relevant programs by giving one simple command. (The architecture of the UNIX operating system and the Writer's Workbench software were designed to facilitate such changes.) To help students apply program advice to their papers and to replace the Writer's Workbench system's on-line informational programs, a user manual was prepared and distributed to all students in computer-assisted composition classes (Smith & Kiefer, 1983). Thus, a major contribution of the staff at CSU was to tailor the system for composition instruction.

User Response

CSU's implementation of the Writer's Workbench system runs as a writing lab outside the classroom; hence, teachers can, if they choose, teach their classes just as they have in the past, or they can integrate laboratory and classroom work. Kiefer and Smith found that students heed the computer suggestions more if they have specific guidance from an instructor or a well-informed peer editor.

Performance of students who used the programs was compared to that of students taught in the noncomputer classes (see Kiefer & Smith, 1983, and Frase, Kiefer, Smith, & Fox, 1985, for detailed reports). An attitude survey showed that 85% of the students easily learned to use the computer and that over 75% found the course more enjoyable because of it. Instructors in the experiments agreed that the programs sensitize students to language more quickly than do standard grading procedures. Data show that students who use the computer go through additional revisions of their papers compared to students who do not use the computer. Although the quality of student writing showed no global difference in holistic scores between the writing of experimental and control subjects, students who used the programs did significantly better on editing tests, especially items that required them to revise written material.

To summarize, use of the Writer's Workbench system had positive effects on attitude and editorial performance. Two things apparently helped students; the use of a word processor and the use of the Writer's Workbench software. Using a word processor, students were easily able to revise and format their papers; using the text analysis software improved their revision skills. Use of the programs at CSU has grown. Today, over 4,000 students at CSU use the programs each year; the programs are also used in other schools in the United States and elsewhere.[3]

Evaluation of Writing Abilities

The Problem

Stylistic measures may be sensitive enough to reveal differences in student writing abilities, provided one selects the right variables to analyze. Language offers a range of ways to say things; hence, authors must make stylistic choices. Flexibility in choice should reflect skill in writing. Potentially important stylistic variables include sentence length and complexity and ornateness of language. Average sentence length has been used to compare the writing styles of individuals and groups of writers and to chart historical trends in style. Cluett (1976) looked at samples of English literature by 50 different authors from the past 400 years, finding a decline from an average of 50 words per sentence in the 17th century to less than 25 words per sentence in the 20th century, while Rankin (1979) found differences between contemporary rural and urban American authors, with urban authors writing longer sentences with more subordination than rural authors.

Frequency counts of grammatical parts of speech have also been used to characterize different writing styles (see Cluett, 1976; Coke, 1981). A high verb-adjective ratio, or VAR (Busemann, 1925; Boder, 1940), indicates a sparse, active style, whereas a low VAR indicates a more ornate style.

The Study

Recently, Lucy Pollard-Gott proposed a new test of students' sensitivity to stylistic variation. The test is analogous to the cloze procedure (Taylor, 1953), but instead of single words full sentences serve as the cloze units. She collected data, and together we used the UNIX Writer's Workbench programs, and others I wrote, to determine the sensitivity of this test (this work is reported at length in Pollard-Gott & Frase, 1985).[4]

College students read two short stories representing two very different writing styles, one plain and one ornate. The first story was in a plain style characteristic of much modern fiction—short sentences (more than half simple), and an active style (reflected by a high VAR).

This story had 80 sentences. The second story had an ornate style—long and complex sentences with many subordinate clauses and a low VAR. This story had 40 sentences. Both stories were written by well-known authors. In each story every fourth sentence was deleted and replaced by a blank. Students were asked to read the story (the remaining 75% of the sentences) and then go back and write sentences of their own to replace those missing from the text. The computer was used to obtain a style profile for the cloze sentences produced by each student, and this style was compared with the style of the original stories. The style information was designed to answer two questions. Do students adapt their writing styles to different text contexts? Does amount of advanced writing instruction influence performance on the test?

Part 1.   One part of the study tested students' spontaneous sensitivity to variation in story style. No mention of style was made in the instructions; students were simply asked to complete the story. Forty-four subjects were paid to participate. Of the 44, 18 had taken one or more creative writing courses at the college level (Group CW, for "creative writing"). The remaining 26 participants had not taken advanced writing courses in college (Group NCW, for "no creative writing"). Writing samples from the subjects received high quality ratings from expert raters.

Each participant came for two sessions on separate days. In the first session, subjects read one of the two cloze stories, and then went back over it to write one full sentence of their own for each numbered blank. In the second session, subjects read the other story and completed the blanks.

Part 2.   In Part 1 of the study, no mention of style was made in the instructions to the story completion test. The style requirements were therefore left implicit for both Group CW and Group NCW. This part of the study added another group (Group NCWE, for "no creative writing, explicit instuctions") in which less experienced writers were given explicit directions to imitate story style when writing their completions. There were 20 college students in this group. Subjects were told to put themselves in the author's place and to write in the same way. No specific stylistic advice was given.

Results

Average sentence length was one striking difference between the original stories used for the completion task. Groups CW and NCW differed in their tendencies to adjust to these styles. Group CW wrote significantly longer sentences to complete the ornate story than to complete the plain story, $t(17) = 6.36$, $p < .001$. This was true as well for Group NCW, $t(25) = 5.60$, $p < .001$, but the difference in average cloze sentence length of the two stories was greater for Group CW. The mean difference of 6.56 words per sentence for group CW was larger than the mean difference of 3.37 words per sentence for group NCW, $t(42) = 2.67$, $p < .02$. The ratio of the average length of cloze sentences for the two stories (a measure of writing flexibility) differed for Groups CW and NCW, as well ($p < .01$).

In Part 2 of this study, students without advanced writing courses were given explicit instructions (Group NCWE) to imitate the style of each cloze story in the story completion task. The emphasis on style for these subjects raised the flexibility of their writing equal to Group CW. The mean length of completions for the ornate story significantly exceeded that for the plain story, $t(19) = 8.90$, $p < .001$. Furthermore, the difference, 6.08 words per sentence, was comparable to that for the creative writers (Group CW), and different from the results for Group NCW. The mean difference in average cloze sentence length between Groups NCW and NCWE was significant ($p < .01$), as was the difference in style ratios ($p < .01$).

The ratio of the number of verbs to the number of adjectives in a text reflects the lexical choices a writer makes. VARs were computed by a program I wrote that used the results from the parts of speech analysis of the Writer's Workbench system, which assigns each word a part of speech. The category "verb" includes all main verbs except forms of "to be" and auxiliaries. "Adjectives" are single words. The VAR picked up large differences in style between the two experimental stories. The active style of the plain story was reflected in the high VAR, 1.50. The ornate story had a low ratio, .77.

The VARs of cloze sentences for Group CW reflected story differences. The mean ratio for the plain story significantly exceeded that for the ornate story, $t(17) = 2.97$, $p < .01$. In contrast, sentences of Group NCW did not reflect this lexical choice. For Group NCW, the VARs for completions of the two experimental stories were similar. Furthermore, the difference in VAR between the plain and ornate completions was significant for Group NCWE, $t(19) = 2.59$, $p < .02$. Apparently, attention to a particular dimension of text is an important component of writing flexibility.

To summarize, Pollard-Gott's story completion task has useful features that make it attractive for research on writing performance. It is a compromise between essay tests, which call for full-length compositions, and objective tests, which call for linguistic judgments but no original writing. This research shows that carefully selected stylistic measures are sensitive to differences in educational background among good writers. Beyond that, however, the study is an example of how computer text analysis can facilitate the detailed analysis and scoring needed for such research.

Additional Measures of Writing Style

The Problem

The Writer's Workbench system provides mostly static measures of linguistic variation. For instance, it reports the average word and sentence length and the percentage of simple as opposed to complex sentences. But a certain average word or sentence length could arise from texts with entirely different sequential properties—one text might use all its short words in the introduction while another text might distribute the long and short words equally throughout its discourse. The rhythm of text, its flow of cadences, affects how interesting a passage is to read and possibly how well it is remembered (Lanham, 1983). Measures of these sequential properties would provide a more sophisticated view of text properties and they might help in development of future programs. My purpose here is to show how combinations of UNIX text-processing tools can help analyze important features of language.

Studies

Metrical Analysis.   English language rhythms are based on three major meters: accentual, syllabic, and free verse. (Turco, 1968, provides diagrams of all major verse forms in Anglo-American prosody.) Composition teachers (Lanham, 1983) advise novice writers to pay attention to the flow of their words and to avoid strings of words of equal syllable length, while linguistic discussions reinforce the assertion that syllabic structure can be a significant prose characteristic (Turner, 1977). Syllabic meter is thus a candidate for analyzing the rhythm of text. Furthermore, the Writer's Workbench system has a program to count syllables in words, so we can build a sequential measure using this syllabic output.

As an example, I wrote a program (SYLREP) that determines the number of syllables in each word and lists the syllable counts for each consecutive pair of words in the text, using existing UNIX system commands; the program then calculates the proportion of pairs that show a repeated syllabic pattern. For instance, the sentence "I am here today" contains four words of 1, 1, 1, and 2 syllables, consecutively. Consecutive pairs are then 1-1, 1-1, and 1-2. There are thus two repeated patterns out of three total pairs. This produces a SYLREP output of .6666.

Except for poetic effect, repetitious syllabic patterns are generally considered an undesirable characteristic of text. Saintsbury goes so far as to say, "the essence of prose and verse rhythm lies in variety and divergence" (cited in Lanham, 1974, p. 103). One might expect, then, that poor writing would show more syllabic repetition than good writing. Forty-seven samples of writing from introductory students at Colorado State University were used to test this hypothesis.[5] Students read a one-page, single-spaced article on a controversial topic. They had one hour to read the article and to write an essay about it. The passages were then scored by English Department staff, who assigned them high, medium, or low quality ratings. There were 11 high-quality passages, 15 medium passages, and 21 low passages.

The mean proportion of repetitions for the high, medium, and low groups was .42, .46, and .51, respectively. A t-test on the differences between each pair of the means shows that they all differed significantly ($p < .05$) from each other. Therefore, in line with the prediction, syllabic redundancy increased as the quality of text decreased. Another measure of redundancy, the type-token ratio (proportion of unique words in a text) calculated on content words (again, a static measure), did not show differences among texts of different quality.

To summarize, the present study showed two things: (1) The SYLREP program detected differences in syllabic meter among texts of differing quality, and (2) low-quality texts exhibited the least rhythmic variation.

Syntactic Analysis.   Programs that measure grammatical patterns might be used to assess the syntactic constraints in writing. Just as the pairs of syllable counts reflect metrical rhythm, pairs of grammatical parts of speech that occur consecutively in text reveal rhythms at a higher, syntactic level of analysis. Different languages have different syntactic rules, which show up in the way grammatical parts of speech are chained together (Greenberg, 1963; Pullum, 1977). Unlike redundancies in meter, which are best avoided in ordinary writing, redundancies in syntax reflect constraints that speakers of a language share. Speakers of other languages do not share those constraints. That's one reason why foreigners seem to speak oddly. The oddness, to some extent, depends on how distant the structure of one's native language is from that of the language one is trying to speak. If this is true, there should be differences in the regularity of grammatical patterns in English compositions of people from different language backgrounds.

The GRAMREP program, which I based on Writer's Workbench programs, changes each word in a text into its part of speech, lists all consecutive pairs of the parts of speech as they occur in text, then calculates the proportion of repetitions by dividing the number of pairs showing a repetition by the total number of pairs. For instance, the sentence "I see the great big cat" is transformed into "pron verb art adj adj noun," and the resulting consecutive pairs are pron-verb, verb-art, art-adj, adj-adj, and adj-noun. One of the pairs (adj-adj) is repeated, and there are five total pairs, which gives a syntactic redundancy of .20 (1/5). A high score on this measure, indicating redundant use of grammatical parts of speech, in one sense shows flexibility in language, since additional items from one word class can be called up with ease.

Sixty passages of English writing were obtained, twenty each written by students whose native language was either Arabic, Chinese, or Spanish.[6] The passages were administered to all students under the same conditions, including the requirement that they write about the same topic. The 60 passages, selected from a larger sample, were above the 60th percentile on quality ratings; hence, the passages reflect adequate writing ability. These passages were run through the GRAMREP program. The question was whether the measure would detect differences among the different linguistic groups.

The mean proportion of repetitions was .056, .058, and .069 for the Arabic, Chinese, and Spanish speakers, respectively. The Spanish speakers differed from the Arabic $t(38) = 2.22$, $p < .05$.

For a further perspective on these data, the GRAMREP program was run on texts written by English-speaking students at Colorado State University (used in the previous study). The mean repetition score for native English speakers was .070, .067, and .072 for high-, medium-, and low-quality passages, respectively. These English-speaking groups did not differ among themselves; furthermore, the English- and Spanish-speaking groups were similar and uniformly higher than the Arabic and Chinese speakers in grammatical redundancy.

To summarize, the GRAMREP program detected differences in the patterns of syntax used by different language groups. The similarity of Spanish- and English-speaking groups, which showed higher repetition of grammatical patterns than Arabic and Chinese groups, makes sense when we consider the linguistic similarities among the groups, although the detailed causes for this are not clear.

Summary

Metrical and syntactic studies show that useful linguistic measures can be easily constructed from available UNIX system tools. The present studies did not pursue theoretical and experimental questions at length; the purpose has been rather to provide examples of how an intelligent environment might facilitate research on written materials.

Text Content

The Problem

Programs are available for creating concordances or tables of contents for files or directories (Burton, 1981), but good overall measures of text similarity are still needed. The TOPIC program of the Writer's Workbench provides a list of frequently occurring words and phrases in a text, but this leaves the reader to make judgments about how closely two texts might overlap in content. It does not provide a metric for comparison.

Using FGREP, COMM, and other commands in the UNIX operating system, I developed a measure of content similarity (called SIMILARITY). The FGREP command can find words in a file that are or are not on a list of words supplied to it. Thus, by supplying a list of function words, it is possible to gather only content words from files. The COMM command can print words that are common to two files. The SIMILARITY program, based on the FGREP and COMM commands, provides a metric for content similarity based on word frequency distributions in texts. It gets rid of function words, determines the number of remaining content words that are common to two passages, and divides the number of common words by the square root of the product of the number of words in the two passages. This gives a rough index of the percentage overlap in content between two passages. Such indices have been used to measure the associative overlap among samples of words in psychological research (Deese, 1962, 1965). Other indices could be used to measure content similarity (see Stalker, 1978); there is a wide literature on content analysis for library research. However, overlap seemed most appropriate for the present studies.

The Study

The similarity measure was tested on a variety of passages. For example, I conducted the following experiment on systematically constructed passages provided by Earl Woodruff, from the Ontario Institute for Studies in Education in Toronto, Canada (Woodruff, Bereiter, & Scardamalia, 1981–1982).[7] Thirty-six eighth-grade students each wrote three passages—one about junk food, one about whether parents should be present at students' parties, and one about the content of school courses; henceforth, I refer to these simply as topics 1, 2, and 3. The passages ranged from 43 to 380 words long, with an average length of 160 words. When these 108 passages (36 writers $\times$ 3 topics = 108) were run through the SIMILARITY program, 5,778 passage similarities were obtained.

Passages on the same topic had average similarities twice as high as those of passages on different topics. Generally, an index above .2 reflected similar content. Statistical comparison between the similarities of passages on the same topic (mean = .24) and on different topics (mean = .11) showed a highly significant effect, $t(5776) = 75.6$, $p <$ .0001. This is equivalent to a point biserial correlation of .71, which is reasonably high. It means that, in classifying passages into those that were written about the same topic, about 84% of our judgments would be correct.

In an independent study, Esther Coke (personal communication) asked subjects to rewrite passages to create different impressions of authors. The rewritten passages thus contained the same content as the originals, but the tone differed. Coke compared the similarity indices of 447 pairs of rewritten passages of similar content with 5,319 pairs of rewritten passages of different content. Her results showed a discontinuity in the indices of content-related and content-unrelated passages: The indices for unrelated passages fell below .2, while the related passages extended from .4 to .8. These findings confirm the results obtained with the 108 passages written by children.

Summary

Development of the similarity index is another example of how computer resources can grow into new tools to measure features of written text. Studies show that the measure is sensitive to content difference among texts. Such a measure might be used to determine how well students focus when told to write about a particular topic. The similarity index could also be used as part of a formal topic recognition system, in which stored files of content words, characterizing domains of interest, were the basis for assigning texts to certain categories. In this way, the standards for content assignment would be based on norms (for whatever purpose) and the similarity index would merely be a vehicle for making comparisons.

CONCLUSION

The developments and studies reported here were intended to suggest possibilities for the application of computers to instruction and the analysis of written materials. Some of the studies explored new possibilities for the Writer's Workbench system, including programs that measure the rhythm, syntax, and semantics of text.

Data reported on new measures of text were encouraging. The studies here suggest that some simple programs could provide additional, higher level linguistic information that we do not currently get. But more important is the concept of a shared intelligent text processing environment. We have the capacity, and obligation, to provide such an environment for all those teaching and studying reading and writing.

NOTES

1. Trademark of Bell Telephone Laboratories.
2. Trademark of AT&T.
3. The Writer's Workbench Collegiate Edition, available from AT&T, is a complete writing lab based on the CSU implementation of the programs. It includes 24 terminals, a printer, an AT&T 3B2 processor, software for administering the writing lab, and the Writer's Workbench system. The system is currently used in high schools and colleges throughout the country.
4. Lucy Pollard-Gott designed this study and collected the data.
5. I thank Kate Kiefer and Charles Smith, of the English Department at CSU, for providing these passages. Patricia Gingrich, of AT&T Bell Laboratories, planned some of the data collection.
6. The passages were kindly provided by Sybil Carlson, of the Educational Testing Service, as part of a cooperative research project. Her encouragement is greatly appreciated.
7. I thank Earl Woodruff for his kindness in sharing these passages.

REFERENCES

Boder, D. P. (1940). The adjective-verb quotient: A contribution to the psychology of language. *Psychological Record, 3*, 309–343.

Bourne, S. R. (1978). UNIX time-sharing system: The UNIX shell. *Bell System Technical Journal, 57*, 1971–1989.

Burton, D. M. (1981). Automated concordances and word indexes: The process, the programs, and the products. *Computers and the Humanities, 15*, 139–154.

Busemann, A. (1925). *Die Sprache der Jugend als Ausbruck der Entwicklungs-rhythmik.* Jena: Fischer.

Carroll, J. M., & Bever, T. G. (1976). Segmentation in cinema perception. *Science, 191,* 1053–1055.

Cherry, L. L. (1980). *PARTS—A system for assigning word classes to English text* (Computing Science Technical Report No. 81). Murray Hill, NJ: Bell Laboratories.

Cherry, L. L. (1982). Writing tools. *IEEE Transactions on Communication, COM-30*(1), 100–105.

Cluett, R. (1976). *Prose style and critical reading.* New York: Teachers College Press.

Coke, E. U. (1981, April). *Computer analysis of style based on grammatical usage.* Paper presented at the Annual Meeting of the American Educational Research Association, Los Angeles.

Deese, J. (1962). On the structure of associative memory. *Psychological Review, 69,* 161–175.

Deese, J. (1965). *Structure of associations in language and thought.* Baltimore: Johns Hopkins.

Duda, R. O., & Shortliffe, E. H. (1983). Expert systems research. *Science, 220,* 261–268.

Frase, L. T. (1983). The UNIX Writer's Workbench Software: Philosophy. *Bell System Technical Journal, 62*(6, part 3), 1883–1890.

Frase, L. T., Kiefer, K. E., Smith, C. R., & Fox, M. L. (1985). Theory and practice in computer aided composition. In S. W. Freedman (Ed.), *The acquisition of written language: Revision and response* (pp. 195–210). Norwood, NJ: Ablex.

Frase, L. T., Macdonald, N. H., Gingrich, P. S., Keenan, S. A., & Collymore, J. L. (1981). Computer aids for text assessment and writing instruction. *Performance & Instruction Journal, 20,* 21–24.

Frase, L. T., Macdonald, N. H., & Keenan, S. A. (1985). Intuitions, algorithms, and a science of text design. In T. Duffy & R. Waller (Eds.), *Designing usable texts* (pp. 97–112). New York: Academic Press.

Frase, L. T., & Schwartz, B. J. (1979). Typographical cues that facilitate comprehension. *Journal of Educational Psychology, 71,* 197–206.

Gingrich, P. S. (1983). The UNIX Writer's Workbench Software: Results of a field study. *Bell System Technical Journal, 62*(6, Part 3), 1909–1921.

Greenberg, J. (1963). Some universals of grammar with particular reference to the order of meaningful elements. In J. Greenberg (Ed.), *Universals of language* (pp. 58–90). Cambridge: MIT Press.

Gunning, R. (1963). *More effective writing in business and industry.* Boston: Cahners.

Hartley, J. (1981). Eighty ways of improving instructional text. *IEEE Transactions of Professional Communication, PC-24,* 17–27.

Keenan, S. A. (1984). Effects of chunking and line length on reading efficiency. *Visible Language, 18*(1), 61–80.

Kiefer, K. E., & Smith, C. R. (1983). Textual analysis with computers: Tests of

Bell Laboratories' computer software. *Research in the Teaching of English, 17*, 201–214.

Kincaid, J. P., Fishburne, R. P., Rogers, R. L., & Chissom, B. S. (1975). *Derivation of new readability formulas (Automated Readability Index, Fog Count, and Flesch Reading Ease Formula) for Navy enlisted personnel* (Research Branch Report 8-75). Chief of Naval Technical Training, Naval Air Station, Memphis, Millington, TN.

Lanham, R. A. (1974). *Style: An anti-textbook*. New Haven: Yale University Press.

Lanham, R. A. (1983). *Analyzing prose*. Los Angeles: Scribner's.

Macdonald, N. H. (1983). The UNIX Writer's Workbench Software: Rationale and design. *Bell System Technical Journal, 62*(6, Part 3), 1891–1908.

Macdonald, N. H., Frase, L. T., Gingrich, P. S., & Keenan, S. A. (1982). The Writer's Workbench: Computer aids for text analysis. *IEEE Transactions on Communication, COM-30*(1), 105–110.

Pike, R., & Kernighan, B. W. (1984). Program design in the UNIX environment. *AT&T Bell Laboratories Technical Journal, 63*, 1595–1605.

Pollard-Gott, L., & Frase, L. T. (1985). Flexibility in writing style: A new discourse-level cloze test. *Written Communication, 2*, 107–127.

Pullum, G. K. (1977). Word order universals and grammatical relations. In P. Cole & J. M. Sadock (Eds.), *Syntax and semantics* (vol. 8, pp. 249–277). New York: Academic Press.

Rankin, D. L. (1979). Syntactic elements of style in urban and rural American prose. *Language and Style, 12*, 91–115.

Ritchie, D. M., & Thompson, K. (1978). The UNIX time sharing system. *Bell System Technical Journal, 57*, 1905–1929.

Smith, C. R., & Kiefer, K. E. (1983). Using the Writer's Workbench programs at Colorado State University. In S. K. Burton & D. D. Short (Eds.), *Sixth International Conference on Computers and the Humanities* (pp. 672–684). Rockville, MD: Computer Science Press.

Stalker, G. H. (1978). Some notions of "similarity" among lines of text. *Computers and the Humanities, 11*, 199–209.

Taylor, W. L. (1953). "Cloze procedure": A new tool for measuring readability. *Journalism Quarterly, 30*, 415–433.

Tinker, M. A. (1963). *Legibility of print*. Ames: Iowa State University.

Turco, L. (1968). *The book of forms*. New York: Dutton.

Turner, G. W. (1977). *Stylistics*. Great Britain: Penguin.

Woodruff, E., Bereiter, C., & Scardamalia, M. (1981–82). On the road to computer-assisted compositions. *Journal of Educational Technologies Systems, 10*(2), 133–148.

6

Two Examples of Computer-Based Research on Reading: Eye Movement Monitoring and Computer-Aided Reading

George W. McConkie and David Zola

Before the advent of computer technology it was possible for reading researchers to think of experiments that would be wonderful to do, but were impossible to carry out because of the speed or complex contingencies required in data collection or stimulus manipulations. One could enjoy futuristic speculation about fascinating but completely impossible studies that could be conducted only in some impossible world. There was a sort of smugness that came in knowing that one's aspirations outstripped the realm of possibility.

But then came computers, and all this began to change. As one's understanding of computer technology grows, so does one's humility. In this new reality, we are limited not so much by what is possible, but more by our own lack of creativity and vision in recognizing and exploiting the possibilities we have available. Certainly this has always been the case, but it becomes more apparent in the electronic age. The possibilities for innovative new approaches to reading research, using current technology, far outstrip our vision of the many ways in which reading can be investigated.

For those of us studying reading, then, the challenge is to expand our research creativity to match the limits of what is possible in this new age. This book represents the accumulated efforts of a number of researchers who are trying to accomplish this task. In the present

The research reported in this chapter has been supported by NIMH grant MH32884 to the first author and by NIE contract NIE-C-400-76-0116 to the Center for the Study of Reading. Laboratory personnel who contributed to the studies described here include Gary S. Wolverton, Carlisle Trimble, Harry E. Blanchard, and Tavakoli Behrooz.

chapter, we will briefly summarize examples of our work in two areas: first, using the computer to monitor readers' eye movements in order to study perceptual processes, and second, using the computer to create a new reading environment that allows poor readers to read material that would normally be beyond their ability.

MONITORING READERS' EYE MOVEMENTS

There is a variety of commercially available equipment today which senses the rotational position of the eyes, and which provides output that a computer can sample at a high rate. We currently use an SRI Dual Purkinje Image Eyetracker (Cornsweet & Crane, 1973), and sample eye position 1,000 times per second, with each sample indicating where the eye is being directed at that millisecond (msec) in time in both horizontal and vertical dimensions. This yields 4,000 bytes of data for every second of reading, resulting in very large data files. For example, for one study we had third-grade children read an entire novelette over a series of several sessions as their eyes were being monitored, resulting in data files of more than one million bytes per chapter for each child. These data are then reduced to files indicating the letter position on which the eyes were centered during each fixation and how many thousandths of a second they remained at that location. This information is being used to explore properties of children's eye movements and to investigate questions about the mental processes taking place during reading. Of course, neither the rapid sampling rates nor the ability to handle such large data sets would be possible without computer technology.

Eye movement recording can actually play three different roles in reading research. First, eye movement records are themselves a source of valuable data. Where the eyes are centered, for what period of time, and in what sequence reflects certain aspects of the mental processes taking place. Thus, fixation probabilities and times, and lengths and directions of eye movements, can be used to test hypotheses about the nature of the mental processes occurring during reading. Second, eye movement records can be the basis for analyzing other data collected simultaneously. For example, information about eye position can be used to select brain wave or skin conductivity data taken as a person was fixating different parts of the display. The eye movement data indicate when the relevant parts of the text were being fixated, thus indicating what segments of the simultaneously collected physiological data should be analyzed. Third, eye movement data can be used as

the basis for making eye-movement contingent stimulus manipulations. For example, it would be possible to sound a tone 50 msec after
the first fixation on a particular part of the display, and to measure the
time the subject takes to press a key in response to the tone, as an
indication of the processing load at that point in time during an ongoing reading task.

Our research has involved all three of these uses. We have established a laboratory in which we record the eye movements of people
as they read text displayed on a cathode-ray tube (CRT) under computer control. With this system, it is possible to make changes in the
text display, contingent upon characteristics of the subjects' eye movements. The eye movement data can then be analyzed to determine
whether the experimental manipulations disturb the reading process,
and if they do, to further study the nature of that response. To illustrate some of the uses of this system we will briefly describe three
recent studies that employ its characteristics in rather different ways.

Spatial Transformations of the Text During Reading

About four times a second during reading, the eyes are moved to a
new location. These eye movements, which are called *saccades*, typically require about 20 to 40 msec. The pauses between saccades are
called *fixations*, and their average duration is about 225 msec. The
question that one series of our studies addressed is whether saccades
are programmed to take the eyes to specific locations, or whether the
eyes are simply being sent further down the line of text, with the
location of each fixation being of little significance, as long as it is in
approximately the right region. In order to investigate this issue, an
experiment was carried out to examine the effects of causing certain
fixations to be misplaced in the text. This misplacement was produced
by simply moving text to the right or left a certain distance on the CRT
during selected eye movements. Since we are able to refresh a single
line of text every 3 msec, and the shortest saccades require nearly 20
msec, it was possible for the computer to identify when the eyes had
begun to move and then to move the line of text while the eyes were
still moving. Thus, the text was in a slightly different location during
one fixation than it was during the last.

In one study, the text was shifted to the left or right by two
character positions during selected saccades. As a result, when the eyes
stopped for the next fixation, they were centered at a position in the
text which was exactly two character positions away from where they
normally would have been centered. If the eyes would normally have

been centered on the letter *r* of the word *word,* and the text were shifted to the right, the eyes would instead be centered on the letter *w.* This happened twice during the reading of certain lines. There was no movement of the text during the reading of other lines, which served as the control condition.

The readers reported no awareness that the text was being moved, but an analysis of their eye movement data indicated that there was a great increase in the likelihood that the following saccade would be a short eye movement in the direction in which the text had been shifted. Thus, in many instances, the next eye movement took the eyes back closer to the location to which they were originally being sent. From this finding we concluded that eye movements are being initiated to take the eyes to specific text locations, and not simply to advance the eyes some reasonable distance along the line. The exact nature of this control is still being investigated.

Studies of this type require that the computer be programmed to sample eye position every msec and to determine with each sample whether a saccadic movement has been initiated. This is done by comparing the current eye position with that obtained 4 msec earlier. If the difference is above a certain threshold, then a saccade has begun. A test must then be made to determine whether this is a saccade on which a display change is desired. The decision might be made by counting (i.e., shift the text during the 3rd and 6th forward saccades on a line) or by location (i.e., shift the text during the saccade that follows the first fixation to the right of the 20th character position on the line). More complex contingencies are also possible, of course. If it is determined that the saccade in progress is the one on which a change should be made, the computer then causes the displacement of the text on the CRT. With our equipment, the testing and initiation of the display change is accomplished within less than 1 msec and the shifting of the text requires 3 msec. More information about the equipment and programs used is presented elsewhere (McConkie, Zola, Wolverton, & Burns, 1978).

Manipulating Words in the Text During Reading

In a second series of studies the computer was programmed to manipulate the display in ways that caused different words to be present at a given location in the text during different fixations as the text was being read. One of these studies was conducted to investigate the nature of the region within which letters are acquired and used during fixations in reading. This study required that we be able to determine on which fixation the letter at a particular location in the text was actually perceived. In order to accomplish this, the letters at selected positions were changed from fixation to fixation. This was done in the following way. First, pairs of words were identified which differ at a single letter position, like *leaks* and *leans*. For each such word pair, a sentence was created into which either word would fit appropriately, such as *John does not store his tools in the garage any more because it leaks/leans too much*. As a subject read a short paragraph containing this sentence, the critical letter was changed during each eye movement. Thus, the word *leaks* was present during one fixation, *leans* during the next, *leaks* during the next, and so on. After reading each paragraph, the subject was presented with four words, one at a time, and was asked to indicate which words had been seen in the passage. Both target words were included in this list. If readers identify the same word on two successive fixations, this manipulation would be extremely disruptive to reading. However, we found no evidence of disruption, indicating that the words of the length studied (3 to 7 letters in length) are identified on a single fixation. Only in those instances in which subjects regressed back and reread the part of the sentence containing the changing word did they sometimes become aware that a word was different than it had been previously, as indicated by their self-reports and by abnormalities in the eye movement records.

Since we had a record of which word was present during each fixation, and which words the subjects reported having seen, it was possible in most cases to identify the fixation on which the letter at the changing letter position was acquired. An examination of this information indicated that the readers were acquiring the letters in word units, within an area of about 4 letter positions to the left of the fixated letter, and perhaps 8 letter positions to the right of it. Furthermore, if a word was identified during one fixation it was not attended during the next, even when it was within the area where identification was possible. In the extreme case, there were many instances in which the eyes were centered on the last letter of a word but that word (including the letter being directly fixated) was not attended during that fixation. Apparently the word had been read during the prior fixation, so that during the current fixation, even though the eyes were centered directly on it, the letter was not attended.

In general, the data indicated that whether or not a letter was acquired during a particular fixation depended on whether the word containing it was attended during that fixation, rather than simply on where it was located on the retina.

In order to conduct this study, two versions of each line containing a critical word were prepared. For the sentence given in the example above, one version contained the word *leaks* and the other contained the word *leans*. When the computer detected that a saccade was beginning, it checked to see whether the prior fixation had been within a certain region, extending 11 letter positions left of the critical letter to 11 letter positions to the right of it. If so, then the line was changed on the CRT, which resulted in the desired change in the critical word. Thus, while the eyes were within a certain region near the critical word location, the word in that location was different on each fixation than it had been on the last fixation.

More recently, an algorithm has been developed for predicting, part way through a saccade, where the eyes will be centered for the next fixation. This makes it possible to identify the saccade that is taking the eyes to a certain word during reading and to change that or some other word during that saccade.

Interrupting Reading at Certain Points in the Text

It is commonly assumed that skilled readers form predictions or have anticipations of what they will encouter next in the text and that these expectancies facilitate word perception and other aspects of reading. In order to try to investigate these mental activities, one of us (GWM) spent several hours reading a novel as his eyes were being monitored. At preselected locations in the text (but unknown to the reader), during a saccade the text was replaced by X's. Thus, when the eyes came to rest for the next fixation there was no text available to read and reading was interrupted. When this occurred, the subject attempted to grasp any sense of anticipation that was available to consciousness and record these introspections on a note pad, as well as to write down the last words that had just been read. This study was motivated by the hope that, if such anticipations were being made, it might be possible to gain introspective access to them if reading were interrupted in midstream.

The results indicated a remarkable lack of conscious anticipations. The reader seemed to be aware only of the words that had just been read and of their meaning. The data indicated that the last word of which the reader was aware was typically that being fixated during the last fixation on which text was present or the word immediately to the right of it. There was little or no sense of being aware of what the next word or words were going to be. It was possible to make guesses, but they did not seem to come naturally as part of the normal ongoing reading task that was taking place. The reader also showed consider-able doubt as to the accuracy of the guesses. Thus, it appeared either that the role of such expectancies in reading has been overemphasized or that they are being formed at an unconscious level to which there is little conscious access.

To conduct this study, certain text locations were identified where reading would be interrupted. Each of these was specified as a certain character position on a certain text line. When one of the lines contain-ing a target location was displayed for reading, at the beginning of each saccade the location of the prior fixation was checked to see if it was to the right of the specified character position. If so, the text was immediately replaced by a line of X's. This line remained on the CRT until the experimenter pushed a button, following the subject's intro-spective report, which then brought the original line back on the screen and allowed reading to continue.

With this technique it is possible to unexpectedly interrupt the normal flow of reading at any point in the text in order to collect data on specific aspects of the processing taking place or the knowledge that has been acquired.

Future Uses of Eye Movement Technology

The use of eye movement monitoring in reading, and particularly eye-movement contingent display control, has led to major advance-ments in our knowledge about the perceptual processes taking place during reading. A review of this research can be found in McConkie (1983). This research has recently been extended to study language processing during reading (Frazier & Rayner, 1982; Just & Carpenter, 1980). Eye movement studies investigating reading disorders have also been initiated (Olson, Kliegl, & Davidson, 1983; Pavlidis, 1981). A major project now underway in our own laboratory uses eye move-ment techniques to study the perceptual development that takes place as children learn to read.

These eye movement techniques make it possible to obtain spe-cific information about particular aspects of perceptual or language processing from a person who is in the act of reading. It is our hope that as further knowledge is acquired, these techniques will be found useful for diagnostic purposes. Children suspected of having reading problems will be able to read a series of passages as their eye move-ments are being recorded. These passages will be carefully designed to contain specific types of complexities that have diagnostic potential. In addition, during the reading certain types of display manipulations will take place. The computer will immediately analyze the data to see which manipulations did and did not have effects on the reader, and to examine the reader's response to the various complexities present in the text. The computer will then print out for the reading specialist a report that describes specific characteristics of the reader's perceptual and language processing, and how these are similar to and deviate from those of successful readers. Such information may be useful in identifying particular disorders and suggesting lines of remediation that are needed. Ideally, it will be possible to identify deviations in the nature of the processing taking place early enough to allow for correction before a student's reading progress has been seriously retarded.

Eye movement monitoring techniques can be used for many purposes in the reading field. In the examples described here, they were used for studying eye movement control, what is being seen during a fixation, and the nature of higher mental processes taking place during reading. In other studies they are used to time mental processes, examine the use of peripheral vision in reading, and provide evidence about reading strategies under certain circumstances when difficulties are encountered. The eye-movement contingent display control technique, which we developed and are using, makes it possible to manipulate certain spatial characteristics of text, which letters and words are at which positions in the text during a specific fixation, and when during the fixation certain aspects of the stimulus pattern are present. All this is done in response to characteristics of the reader's eye movements through the use of computer technology. It is possible to use the system to interrupt reading at certain points in the text and obtain readers' reports of their conscious experiences, or to initiate the collection of other types of data during the reading of certain critical parts of a passage. We have also speculated about the potential for diagnosis of reading problems using eye movement monitoring techniques.

   Any line of research aimed at studying reading as it is in progress is likely to find eye movement recording techniques either useful or necessary as a means of detecting just where the reader is attending in the text at any moment in time.

COMPUTER-AIDED READING

   In another project, we have developed a computer system to assist people with poor reading skills to read passages that are beyond their normal reading ability level. We refer to this as *computer-aided reading.* We interfaced an IBM-PC computer to an EIS Instavox audio unit and a light pen, and programmed this system to "say" a word when the reader is not able to identify it independently. To do this, all the words in a passage are previously recorded and stored in the audio unit, which has space for recordings of over 2,500 words, each individually accessible by the computer within less than .5 sec. The text is displayed a page at a time on the CRT, and if the reader touches any word with a light pen, the computer immediately accesses and plays the audio recording of that word. From the reader's point of view, when a word is touched the computer "says" that word through earphones.

With this system, readers are no longer constrained by their sight vocabularies. If they cannot identify a particular word, all they must do is touch the word with the light pen and the computer tells them what it is, enabling them to continue their reading without interruption or frustration.

Our initial research with this system has been with adults reading at or below the fourth-grade level. With the computer's help, they are able to read and understand passages written for normal adult audiences, such as short stories, magazine articles, instructional materials, and poetry. The computer-aided reading system drastically changes the nature of the materials that these people can read in their reading instruction, and this has important implications for instruction. No longer is it necessary to be able to independently identify the words in order to read passages of interest. Content reading can begin much earlier. Reading is less frustrating. And the focus of instruction can be on gaining knowledge from text rather than on learning decoding skills. Word identification skills can then be taught in the context of actual reading, presented as techniques for helping people to become independent of computer assistance, rather than as prerequisites for reading. Other instructional implications of computer-aided reading are discussed elsewhere (McConkie, 1984).

Pilot studies show that adults find the computer-aided reading environment to be comfortable and helpful (McConkie, Winograd, & Zola, 1984). Furthermore, spending time reading each day can be even more beneficial to the development of reading ability than an equivalent amount of time spent in reading instruction.

The concept of computer-aided reading actually involves using computer technology in whatever ways possible to assist people in reading passages that they would not be able to read on their own. Thus, future developments of the system will allow a person to find out what a word means, and perhaps to get a paraphrase of a difficult sentence, among other things. We are investigating what types of assistance are actually used by, and helpful to, both adults and children.

Computer-aided reading also provides an interesting environment in which it is possible to investigate a number of issues about reading instruction and learning to read. Most significantly, it opens the door to studying the extent to which reading skill develops through simply reading, and what sorts of additional instruction can hasten the development of reading ability. It also provides an environment in which to study the development of sight vocabulary through reading.

Computer-aided reading can be used to give people access to text that they need or desire to read but are unable to comprehend on their own. For instance, remedial readers can read the same material their classmates are studying, adults can read training manuals that are beyond their reading level, and college students with poor reading skills can read complex college texts. Thus, it may be of considerable social significance to people who have traditionally been deprived of opportunities because of their inability to read.

Computer-aided reading holds great potential both for providing an interesting environment for studying the development of reading skill, and for serving as a means by which people with low reading ability can gain access to information available only in written form.

Eye movement research and computer-aided reading serve as two examples of ways in which computer technology makes new forms of reading research possible. Studies involving eye movement contingent display control can be conducted in no other way than with the use of computers. Data are collected msec by msec, and decisions must be made and implemented within extremely short periods of time. Thus, where speed and complex contingencies are required, computer technology is essential.

Computer-aided reading, on the other hand, uses computer technology to create a responsive, information-rich environment for the reader. Information that might be useful to a reader is stored in a form that can be readily accessed. While our initial implementation of this concept, in which the reader can find out the identity of any word, is extremely interesting and appears to be highly beneficial, this is only the first step in initiating the total computer-aided reading concept.

REFERENCES

Cornsweet, T. N., & Crane, H. D. (1973). Accurate two-dimensional eye tracker using first and fourth Purkinje images. *Journal of the Optical Society of America, 63*, 6–13.

Frazier, L., & Rayner, K. (1982). Making and correcting errors during sentence comprehension: Eye movements in the analysis of structurally ambiguous sentences. *Cognitive Psychology, 14*, 178–210.

Just, M. A., & Carpenter, P. A. (1980). A theory of reading: From eye fixations to comprehension. *Psychological Review, 87*, 329–354.

McConkie, G. W. (1983). Eye movements and perception during reading. In K. Rayner (Ed.), *Eye movements in reading: Perceptual and language processes* (pp. 65–96). New York: Academic Press.

McConkie, G. W. (1984). *Reflections on reading instruction from the perspective of computer aided reading.* Unpublished manuscript.

McConkie, G. W., Winograd, P., & Zola, D. (1984). *Computer aided reading with illiterate adults.* Unpublished manuscript.

McConkie, G. W., Zola, D., Wolverton, G. S., & Burns, D. D. (1978). Eye movement contingent display control in studying reading. *Behavior Research Methods and Instrumentation, 10*, 154–166.

Olson, R. K., Kliegl, R., & Davidson, B. J. (1983). Dyslexic and normal readers' eye movements. *Journal of Experimental Psychology: Human Perception and Performance, 9*, 816–825.

Pavlidis, G. T. (1981). Sequencing, eye movements and the early objective diagnosis of dyslexia. In G. T. Pavlidis & T. R. Miles (Eds.), *Dyslexia research and its applications to education* (pp. 99–163). New York: Wiley.

Part III
INSTRUCTIONAL ISSUES

The chapters in this section discuss applications of the computer to reading instruction and present computer-based research focusing on instructional variables. Taken together, they illustrate that computer technology makes available a diversity of new options for reading instruction. Each chapter also raises important issues for instruction. Some of these issues are new and have been created by widespread availability of computers for instruction. Other issues, although familiar, take on a new dimension when considered in light of computer technology.

For example, Siegel and Davis argue that there is a place for drill and practice programs in teaching reading comprehension. To be of value, however, drill and practice programs must employ the capabilities of the computer to move beyond paired-associate learning. They argue that with the aid of a computer, examples used for drill can help students generalize comprehension skills beyond a particular practice item. To illustrate this viewpoint they describe the format of a computer-based curriculum for helping students practice comprehension skills. Among the important features of the programs described are: a bank of variable items, item-specific corrective feedback, instructional uses of graphics, an algorithm for interspersing the review of missed items, and items that set up minimal contrasts to help students avoid discrimination errors.

Instructional uses of computers in reading are most often discussed in the context of developmental reading as taught in elementary and secondary schools. Vinsonhaler and his colleagues, however, present an interesting application of computer technology to the preparation of reading specialists. They cite the low correlations among professionals who diagnose the same reading cases as an indication that more training is needed in this area. They present the results of several training studies which suggest that using a computer to simulate diagnostic cases can improve inter- and intra-clinician agreement in diagnosing reading problems. Likewise, Alvermann describes an interactive video program designed to help preservice teachers learn how to administer an informal reading inventory. Her chapter also shows how a research study can employ computer technology to investigate learners' thought processes and their responses to text presented under various conditions. She suggests that the continued development of interactive video technology may lead to novel ways to match instructional content, texts, and characteristics of the learner. Both of these chapters also demonstrate how the computer may be only one component, although an integral one, of a larger more encompassing program of instruction.

The chapter by Olson and Wise points to the fact that ongoing improvements in computer technology will have a continuing impact on options for instruction. They describe methods employed to create computer speech and provide insights into how this capability might be used to expand options for reading instruction. Also reported are the results of their investigations of a computer program designed to individualize the learning of phonemic segmentation by disabled readers. Their work is a useful example of how computer technology can be applied to instructional problems in a context of theory and research.

The use of computers for language arts in elementary schools is a relatively new issue. In the final chapter Miller and Burnett point out, however, that the issues surrounding the use of computers cannot be divorced from more fundamental issues concerning how the language arts should be taught. They do so by comparing how two elementary school teachers with different notions about language arts select computer applications and software for use in their respective classes. In one sense their chapter is a commentary on the commercial reading software currently available for use in elementary school classrooms. Their comparison of the two teachers, one subscribing to a subskill orientation, the other committed to a whole-language approach, also allows them to show how each viewpoint leads to different conceptions of computer use and software selection.

7

Redefining a Basic CAI Technique to Teach Reading Comprehension

Martin A. Siegel and Dennis M. Davis

As with any subject, the universe of things students must master in learning to read might roughly be divided into two main parts: factual information and generalizations. Such areas as symbol-sound identification fall into the first category, while comprehension skills most often fall into the latter. Both categories are important, but their relative importance seems to vary from subject to subject. In a subject like elementary math, for example, it is easy to see the importance of teaching a body of factual knowledge—like the basic addition, subtraction, and multiplication facts. Reading, however, seems to be mainly skill learning from the outset.

Unfortunately, many of the computer-based education teaching techniques and lesson formats that have been used with most success in other subject areas have been those that seem best suited to teaching factual knowledge. Drill and practice lessons, for example, seem to be best at teaching paired associates; tutorials seem best for presenting basic knowledge (often followed by a drill and practice segment to test and solidify the content presented in the tutorial).

As a consequence, many educators—both reading teachers and university reading specialists—have neither seen much good computer-based reading instruction nor held out much hope for a successful computer application in this area. To the extent that they retain any interest in the application of computers to the teaching of reading, they often transfer their hopes to the "next generation" of "intelligent" programs capable of analyzing students' learning patterns, diagnosing the kinds of errors a student most often makes, and prescribing on that basis. Unfortunately, despite the exciting promise of this work, these programs remain mostly unrealized potential in the laboratories of artificial intelligence researchers (see Balajthy, chapter 3 of this volume). According to this point of view, then, we face a dilemma: The courseware available now seems unsuited to teaching reading, but well-designed instruction may be years in coming. To some it may seem simpler to abandon altogether the application of computers to the teaching of reading.

While we understand and sympathize with this statement of the problem, we cannot accept the direction in which it leads us to find a solution. It seems to imply that what is wrong with educational computers today is that they are too machinelike, that their utility in education will increase the more successfully they come to imitate human teachers. To accept this explanation for current ills and invest in this remedy for the future might well foreordain the death of computer-based instruction in reading. Just as "page turner" programs available for today's computers have shown us that a computer cannot be as good at being a book as a book can, computers and software of the future, to the extent that they aim at imitating human teachers, ultimately will be unsuccessful in achieving their goal. Human teachers will always be better at being human teachers.

Perhaps, as Siegel and Davis (1986) have suggested, instead of pinning our hopes on a future generation of smarter computers, we might be better off accepting the computer as a mechanical medium for delivering instruction. It is not that computer-assisted instruction (CAI) is bad, but that we have not been sufficiently imaginative in our exploitation of the instructional methods it makes available. After all, we once held out great hope for the CAI techniques now so frequently derided. It is not that we were naive then but sadly more sophisticated now; we actually had good reason to believe in the traditional CAI techniques. Even the simplest computer-based drill possessed several promising instructional features now often overlooked or forgotten:

1. Simple as they are, drills go a long way toward *individualizing instruction*. Each student can choose the drill-based lesson that best serves his or her needs—every student in the classroom can work on a different lesson. Students can work at their own pace. The drill format is conceptually simple enough that students can truly work independently—with no help from the teacher or anyone else—and receive all the motivational benefits of self-direction.
2. In a rudimentary but nevertheless significant way, computer-based drills are often *adaptive instruction*. Whenever a computer-based drill tags missed items and returns them for review, the lesson is adapting to the individual's needs. It becomes in effect a different lesson for each student, redesigning itself according to a student's performance.

3. "Individualized" and "adaptive" instruction are buzz words today in education. A less exciting but equally important feature of computer-based drills is that they are *appropriate to the computer.* Instead of trying to make the computer imitate some other teaching medium, they exploit the computer's own strengths for organizing and presenting information.[1]

Despite these strengths, however, drills have one serious disadvantage: They can only teach paired associates. This limitation does not, of course, make drills useless for instruction. Many things students must learn—from basic math facts in elementary school, to the names and symbols of the chemical elements in high school, to the names and locations of the bones of the body in medical school—have the form of paired associates. Unfortunately, other subjects, like reading, involve the learning of skills, which must be generalized. It is principally for this reason that some have come to view drill and practice programs as too limited in scope to have significant impact on the teaching of reading.

One promising way to address this problem is to create instructional methods that capitalize on the computer's strengths for providing drill but can teach a wider range of knowledge and skills in more interesting, compelling ways than traditional CAI lessons usually do. A chief direction of our research at the Computer-based Education Research Laboratory, therefore, has been to attempt to find how to extend the drill format to teach important generalizable skills of reading comprehension while retaining the strengths of the drill as a computer-delivered instructional format. In the sections that follow we shall present our development efforts (describing some instructional formats in our reading comprehension curriculum for educationally disadvantaged adolescents and adults) and discuss the research in computer-based instructional techniques that they embody.

EXTENDING THE DRILL FORMAT

We begin by asking this basic question: What changes would have to take place in the structure of drills to make them capable of teaching generalizations? Computers deliver paired-associate drills effectively because the collection of items in the drill is a stipulated set for each member of which a single correct response exists. Conversely, teaching generalizations on computers is difficult because the set of exemplars for each generalization is potentially infinite and many correct responses are possible. The key instructional design insights necessary to extend the drill format to teach generalizations, therefore, are (1) to devise a way to store, search, and retrieve a set of items large enough to demonstrate the range of the concept to the slowest learner; and (2) to cast these items in instructional formats that teach the generalization effectively while still accepting only "one correct response." Two major changes in the drill structure are required to accomplish these objectives: variable items and item-specific corrective feedback.

Variable Items.   In the typical "flashcard" drill, missed items are tagged and come up later for review. This method of handling review is appropriate for teaching paired associates but inappropriate for generalizations. In teaching generalizations the goal is not mastery of the drill item but of the rule of which the item is one example. If an extended drill is to teach generalizations, therefore, missed items must be varied slightly when they recur in a review sequence to make each iteration a minimally different example of the generalization rather than a recurrent stimulus that can be memorized without comprehension of the rule it illustrates.

Item-Specific Corrective Feedback.   In a "flashcard" drill teaching paired associates, learning can take place even when feedback is of the "no, try again" variety. Since the goal is memorization, not understanding, it is sufficient for the student merely to know when he has produced the correct response. If an extended drill is to teach generalizations, however, feedback for missed items (examples of the generalization) must not just state what the correct response should have been but must explain how that response was an example of the generalization. To do that, feedback must refer specifically to the content of the individual item—general explanation of the rule is insufficient.

APPLICATION OF THE EXTENDED DRILL TO READING

The example in Figure 7.1, drawn from an extended-drill lesson in the PLATO Curriculum Project (PCP) reading comprehension curriculum (Siegel, DiBello, Bruner, & Felty, 1977–78), serves to illustrate both these lesson features. Though it may not at first look like one, the information presented in the figure constitutes a drill item. It is a stimulus and requires from the student a single correct response. To

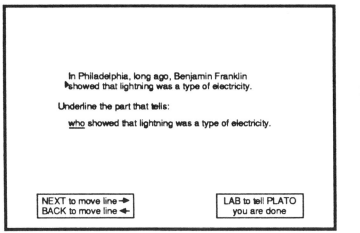

Figure 7.1

produce his response the student presses keys to move a cursor (that takes the form of an underline) through the sentence. With each keypress the cursor underlines the next sentence part. When the student thinks he has underlined the correct part, he presses another key to record his answer.

If the student answers correctly, he is given appropriate feedback and routed on to the next item. Figure 7.2 shows what happens when a student misses the item. Notice that the feedback is specific to the item and illustrates the rule the lesson seeks to teach. Notice, too, that the lesson uses graphics in an economical but powerful way to aid instruction.

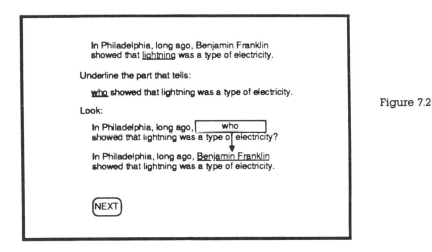

Figure 7.2

A difficulty one faces in designing individualized reading instruction for computers on which students can work independently is that explanations in feedback easily may become more complex than the item itself—which the student already has demonstrated he cannot read! Instructional graphics of the kind shown in Figure 7.2, as opposed to graphics used only to motivate students, help address this problem.

After the feedback shown in Figure 7.2 is delivered, this missed item is returned to the stack. When it comes up for review, however, the *who* element is changed slightly to teach the generalization. The figure cannot show it, but the item is actually programmed with a series of "flipbook" parts that can be substituted for the original form. Then, when this item comes up for review, "Benjamin Franklin" may be replaced by "an American scientist," "a famous political figure," "an inventor," or "an American." These semantically equivalent *who* elements greatly increase the number of items available for practice when the student needs it, while minimizing the amount of information the program has to store, search, and retrieve. In fact, in this reading curriculum more than 200 million different sentences can be generated. And because both the item variants and their feedback are generated by algorithm rather than merely being stored whole, it is also possible to keep the instructional routines in the corrective feedback specific to each individual item variant.

In the context of our opening remarks it is worthwhile to stress that these features—item variants and graphical instructional feedback specific to each item variant—are not imitations of teachers, books, or any other instructional medium. They are *computer* features, as "mechanical" as any other "traditional CAI" technique. They are instructionally powerful and compelling precisely because they are designed to exploit the computer's peculiar strengths as an instructional medium.

In fact, these features are not possible without the computer. Imagine a human teacher using flashcards and attempting to vary individual items minimally before returning them to the stack for review for even one student! The computer is capable of doing it simultaneously for many students on an individual basis. We are not arguing that teachers cannot teach generalizations. We are saying instead that computers derive their educational power from software that exploits their own strengths—not from imitating other instructional media. (The enthusiasm with which word processors are being incorporated into the educational process provides another excellent example of software that exploits the computer's potential rather than imitating other media.)

THE PCP READING COMPREHENSION CURRICULUM

The extended-drill item shown in Figures 7.1 and 7.2 is one of 10 items that comprise the first lesson in the strand of the curriculum that teaches the general skill of finding information in text. Other strands deal with the skills of paraphrasing and answering paraphrase questions about text, synthesis of text (identifying main ideas, themes, etc.), making inferences from text (comprehending information implied but not stated explicitly), vocabulary development, following directions from text, skills for taking reading comprehension tests, and metacomprehension (monitoring and adjusting one's reading behavior so as to increase comprehension).

The nine additional items in the extended drill of which the illustrated item forms a part explore the wider range of the generalization. Some of the ways in which the range is sampled include:[2]

1. Varying the placement of the *who* element within the sentence:
     Roger Bacon used lenses to make a telescope in England sometime in the thirteenth century.
2. Varying the syntax of the *who* element (by making it the direct object, indirect object, or object of a preposition):
     Lightning struck Roberto and spoiled the shine on his high-heeled shoes.
3. Adding additional *who* elements among which the student must discriminate:
     Diannah had a date to meet Cedric in the town square on Saturday.

Each of the 10 items has flipbook parts for the *who* elements similar to those discussed in Figure 7.2, and these increase by many times the number of discrete practice items available to students. Notice, too, that while our focus in the discussion so far has been on *who* questions, each item is carefully constructed to include elements that answer other *wh-* questions: where, when, what, and what kind of. The lesson also teaches these information-finding skills in similar fashion—by changing the direction to, "Underline the part that tells *when* . . . ," etc. Within each item, each of these other *wh-* elements is also provided with a set of flipbook parts for generalization training. Thus, by utilizing the computer's unique capabilities, a group of only a few well-chosen items have a greater potential to teach complex skills.

Later, lessons within the information-finding strand of the curriculum introduce more difficult and complex items, but they also vary instruction along a continuum from highly structured tasks to more independent learning. As the student moves through the strand, the format of lessons changes gradually, shaping the student from the highly structured and well-cued task shown in Figures 7.1 and 7.2 to full autonomy. The formats that constitute the stages in this process are summarized below.

1. "Underline the part that tells . . ." (cued).   This format has been described above and illustrated in Figures 7.1 and 7.2.

2. "Underline the part that tells . . ." (uncued).   This format, illustrated in Figure 7.3, is identical to the cued format above but requires the student to determine where the appropriate phrase begins and ends. In this task, the student must underline the four words that tell "*what* the bearded old man did for a living." By pressing the key marked "NEXT," the student moves the cursor from word to word; by pressing "m" the student marks or underlines the word.

3. Direct question after the sentence.   This format is similar to the previous format, except that the student is asked a direct question and required to underline the words that tell the answer to the question. Figure 7.4 provides an example.

4. Direct question before the sentence.   By placing the question before the sentence, as in Figure 7.5, the student is led to search the passage for the correct answer.

5. "What does the boxed part tell?"   As Figure 7.6 shows, this format is the inverse of the first format. The student first reads a passage. Then a box is drawn around one of the phrases, and the student must select from several alternatives the one corresponding to the meaning of the boxed part.
Notice that the distractors are not random. Each choice refers to a different phrase in the passage. Thus, as Figure 7.7 illustrates, rather than merely saying, "No, try again," to an incorrect response, the feedback can show the phrase that matches the student's choice, graphically demonstrating not just that he or she is wrong, but why. When the student matches the boxed phrase with the correct choice, a bold animated arrow, illustrated in Figure 7.8, connects the choice with the box.
An item of this type presents a potential problem for generalization training. When it comes up for review, the same distractors must appear, so the danger exists that the student will merely memorize the location of the correct choice (as a paired associate) rather than master

The bearded old man who built cabinets
▶for a living went to visit the hard working young
man who grew soybeans and corn for a living.

Underline 2 words that tell:

<u>what</u> the bearded old man <u>did</u> for a living.

| NEXT to move line ➡
 BACK to move line ⬅ | Press "m" to mark a <br> line, ERASE to erase | LAB to tell PLATO <br> you are done |

Figure 7.3

The bikini swimsuit was designed by a Frenchman
▶and first modeled in 1946 The model who wore the
first bikini received 50,000 fan letters.

Underline 2 words that tell the answer.

When was the bikini swimsuit first modeled?

| NEXT to move line ➡
 BACK to move line ⬅ | Press "m" to mark a <br> line, ERASE to erase | LAB to tell PLATO <br> you are done |

Figure 7.4

<u>Why</u> is metal galvanized?

Underline 4 words that tell the answer.

▶The process of applying zinc coating to iron or
steel to protect against corrosion is called
galvanizing.

| NEXT to move line ➡
 BACK to move line ⬅ | Press "m" to mark a <br> line, ERASE to erase | LAB to tell PLATO <br> you are done |

Figure 7.5

119

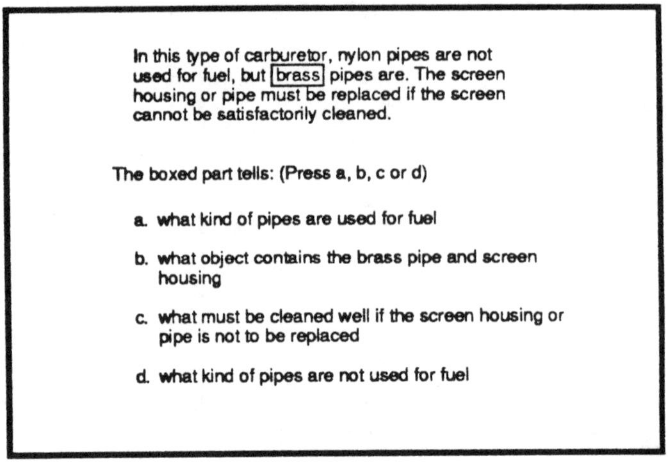

In this type of carburetor, nylon pipes are not used for fuel, but [brass] pipes are. The screen housing or pipe must be replaced if the screen cannot be satisfactorily cleaned.

The boxed part tells: (Press a, b, c or d)

a. what kind of pipes are used for fuel

b. what object contains the brass pipe and screen housing

c. what must be cleaned well if the screen housing or pipe is not to be replaced

d. what kind of pipes are not used for fuel

Figure 7.6

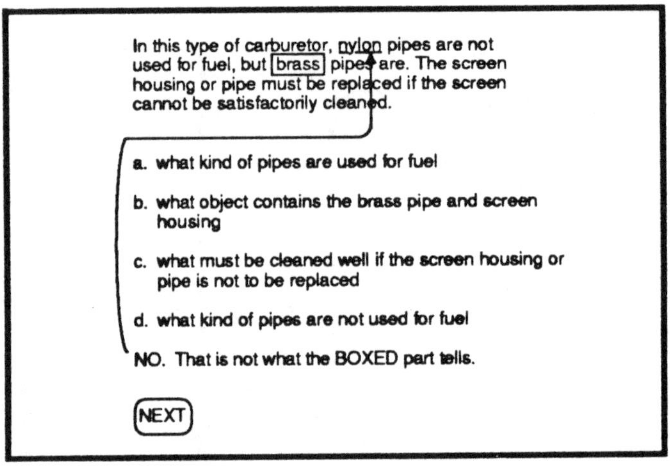

In this type of carburetor, nylon pipes are not used for fuel, but [brass] pipes are. The screen housing or pipe must be replaced if the screen cannot be satisfactorily cleaned.

a. what kind of pipes are used for fuel

b. what object contains the brass pipe and screen housing

c. what must be cleaned well if the screen housing or pipe is not to be replaced

d. what kind of pipes are not used for fuel

NO. That is not what the BOXED part tells.

(NEXT)

Figure 7.7

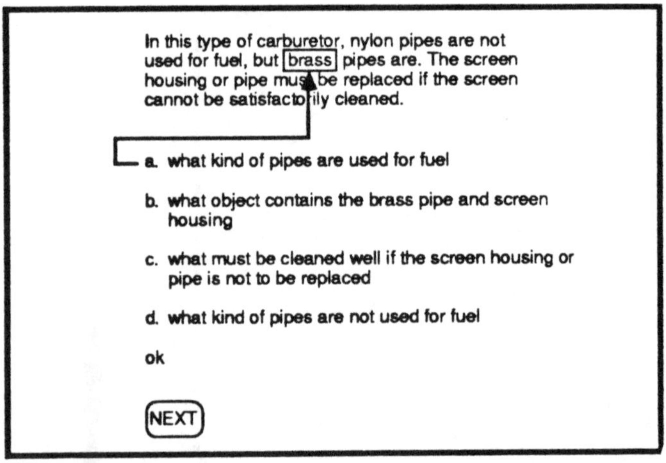

In this type of carburetor, nylon pipes are not used for fuel, but [brass] pipes are. The screen housing or pipe must be replaced if the screen cannot be satisfactorily cleaned.

a. what kind of pipes are used for fuel

b. what object contains the brass pipe and screen housing

c. what must be cleaned well if the screen housing or pipe is not to be replaced

d. what kind of pipes are not used for fuel

ok

(NEXT)

Figure 7.8

the generalization. To avoid this outcome, the order of the choices is randomly varied and semantically equivalent phrases are substituted whenever the item appears again.

6. "Does this sentence tell . . . ?" (cued). In this format, the student first decides whether the passage answers the question and touches one of the boxes illustrated in Figure 7.9. If the correct answer is "yes," the student then must underline the correct segment as in the first format. If the student responds "no" when the correct answer is "yes," the format underlines the phrase that tells the answer.

7. "Does this sentence tell . . . ?" (uncued). This final format is identical to the previous one except that, when it passes to the underlining phase, the student must delineate the beginning and end of the phrase that answers the question—as in the second format.

OTHER INSTRUCTIONAL FEATURES OF EXTENDED DRILLS

In addition to variable items and graphic, item-specific corrective feedback, two other important features can be incorporated into the extended drill format. Both address problems associated with learning through drills, and both rely on the special capabilities of the computer for effective implementation.

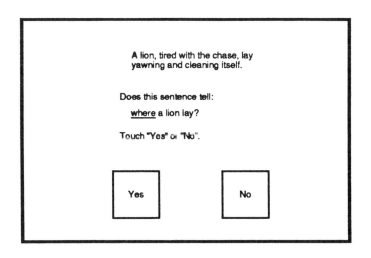

Figure 7.9

Increasing Ratio Review

The first problem to consider is one endemic to all drills—those that teach paired associates as well as those that are extended in the manner we have described to teach generalizations. The problem is that, while drills are often adaptive instruction (because they provide review only of items missed by the individual student), review is not always effective in ensuring long-term memory. Items missed early in the queue and returned to the end are likely to be forgotten by the time they recur. Items missed late are likely to be remembered solely because they were seen only moments ago.

Once again, the computer's unique capabilities provide a possible solution. Suppose that, instead of moving a missed item to the end of the queue, it were inserted into the queue at *several* positions, each with a greater number of intervening items—that is, in an increasing ratio. An individual student's trip through the item queue might then be represented schematically as in Figure 7.10.

In the diagram, the letters *a* through *k* represent items in the drill. Boxes denote items the student has missed. The brackets above the items indicate the review positions for item *a*, which recurs in the queue two items later, then four later, then six later. The brackets below the item queue show what happens when item *c* is missed again during review: The process starts over again each time the item is missed. (Space does not permit the diagram to show that when the student misses items near the end of the queue, the program can be built to resurrect items to which the student has responded correctly, so that the more important goal of building long-term memory for missed items can be achieved.) When several items are missed, the procedure quickly becomes more complicated than any human teacher could reasonably manage. This procedure differs for extended drills used to teach generalizations only in that recurrences of the item in review slots randomly select an alternate flipbook part.

Figure 7.10

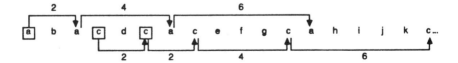

Discrimination Training

To be maximally effective, a drill-based lesson must acknowledge that there are two main classes of errors possible within drills. Siegel and Misselt (1984) describe these types as out-of-list errors and discrimination errors and discuss them fully. In the present context, it suffices to note that the chief difference between them is that discrimination errors involve confusing members of the drill set with one another, while out-of-list errors do not. The distinction is important, because discrimination errors should receive special treatment.

The PCP reading comprehension lessons we have discussed treat discrimination errors in several ways, depending on the format. In the "underline the part that tells . . ." format, for example, the possible discrimination error is to confuse one *wh-* question for another. Figure 7.11 illustrates discrimination training for this error type.

In this figure, the student answered a *who* question with a part that tells *when*. The feedback points out the confusion, and the normal progress of the drill is interrupted to provide additional training on the error in the form of a small drill within the drill:

In Philadelphia, long ago, an American scientist showed that lightning was a type of electricity.

Underline the part that tells:
who showed that lightning was a type of electricity.

In Philadelphia, long ago, Benjamin Franklin
showed that lightning was a type of electricity.

Underline the part that tells:

who showed that lightning was a type of electricity.
No. That answer tells:

when an American scientist showed that lightning
was a type of electricity.

Figure 7.11

Now underline the part that tells:
<u>when</u> an American scientist showed that lightning
was a type of electricity.

This process is then repeated two or more times until the student
demonstrates mastery. On subsequent iterations, the *who* and *when*
elements are randomly flipped in the sentence:

In Philadelphia, in the 18th century, an American scientist showed
that lightning was a type of electricity.

In Philadelphia, in the 1700s, a famous political figure showed that
lightning was a type of electricity.

In addition, the order of the *who* and *when* questions that follow
these sentences is also randomly varied. When the student has demonstrated mastery of the discrimination, the program returns to the
regular queue of items.

The example above teaches what may be called a "ballpark"
discrimination (that is, whether or not a given stimulus is an example
of a generalization). The "Does this sentence tell . . . ?" format employs another form of discrimination training. It teaches a "borderline"
discrimination (that is, just when does a given stimulus become an
example of a generalization). In this format, the student sometimes
will be presented with a sequence of sentences coupled with an invari-
ant task:

A cheetah lay yawning and cleaning itself.
    Does this sentence tell <u>where</u> a cheetah lay?

A cheetah, tired from the chase, lay yawning and cleaning itself.
    Does this sentence tell <u>where</u> a cheetah lay?

A cheetah, tired from the chase, lay yawning and cleaning itself
under a shady tree.
    Does this sentence tell <u>where</u> a cheetah lay?

A cheetah lay under a shady tree while yawning and cleaning
itself.
    Does this sentence tell <u>where</u> a cheetah lay?

Tired from the chase, a cheetah lay yawning and cleaning itself.
    Does this sentence tell <u>where</u> a cheetah lay?

This small drill within the drill holds all elements constant except the discrimination being taught. The goal is to teach the relationship between the *where* question and the sentence. The minimal changes in the sentence focus the student's attention on this relationship.

CONCLUSION

Summative evaluational studies on the information-finding, paraphase, and inferential segments of the PCP reading curriculum have demonstrated educationally as well as statistically significant results among adolescents and learning disadvantaged adults (Alessi, Siegel, Silver, & Barnes, 1982–83; Stevens, 1983), and 10 years of implementation have yielded informal verification of the formal studies. These results are significant in the context of this paper chiefly because they indicate the instructional power of the extended drill format and, by extension, other CAI techniques that might be revitalized in similar ways.

All the techniques we have discussed—variable items, item-specific corrective feedback, instructional use of graphics, increasing ratio review, and discrimination training techniques—extend both the scope of instructional applications for computer-based drills and the effectiveness with which they teach generalizations.

More significantly, they indicate that it may not, after all, be necessary to wait for the "next generation" of "intelligent" programs. They indicate that to begin to make significant progress in fulfilling the potential of computer-based education it may not be necessary for computers to become more like human teachers in their ability to understand and diagnose (see Balajthy, chapter 3 of this volume, for another point of view). In fact, they indicate that we may be able to leave the design of instruction to curriculum designers and continue to use the computer to deliver instruction, but in increasingly effective ways.

In sum, we hope that both the techniques discussed in this paper and their demonstrated effectiveness in the PCP reading curriculum combine to suggest that, in large part, the dearth of excellent courseware that threatens the future of computer-based education is not the fault of the machines and their machinelike instructional methods. Instead, we hope that the discussion helps to focus attention on what we perceive to be the more critical need: more imaginative and insightful ways to exploit the peculiar strengths of the computer not as an imitation human teacher but as a powerful means to individualize and increase the effectiveness of instruction delivered by teachers.

NOTES

1. See Siegel & Davis (1986) for a more detailed examination of the computer's strengths as an instructional medium.

2. Some skills, like tracing the antecedents of pronouns used as *who* elements, are introduced later in the sequence, since they depend on skills taught in the PCP Language Curriculum.

REFERENCES

Alessi, S. M., Siegel, M. A., Silver, D., & Barnes, H. (1982–83). Effectiveness of a computer-based reading comprehension program for adults. *Journal of Educational Technology Systems, 11*(1), 43–57.

Siegel, M. A., & Davis, D. M. (1986). *Understanding computer-based education.* New York: Random House.

Siegel, M. A., DiBello, L. V., Bruner, E. C., & Felty, J. M. (1977–78). *PCP reading comprehension I–IV.* Urbana, IL: University of Illinois, Computer-based Education Research Laboratory.

Siegel, M. A., & Misselt, A. L. (1984). An adaptive feedback and review paradigm for computer-based drills. *Journal of Educational Psychology, 76*(2), 310–317.

Stevens, R. J. (1983). *Strategies for identifying the main idea of expository passages: An experimental study.* Unpublished doctoral dissertation, University of Illinois, Urbana-Champaign.

8

Computers, Simulated Cases, and the Training of Reading Diagnosticians

John F. Vinsonhaler, Annette B. Weinshank, Christian C. Wagner, and Ruth M. Polin

Diagnosis is accorded great importance in remedial reading instruction. In both research and practice, it is widely used as the major basis for remediation (Carter & McGinnis, 1970; Ekwall, 1976; Otto, McManemy, & Smith, 1973; Spache & Spache, 1973). This central role of the diagnostic act led the present authors to perform a series of studies on the diagnostic and remedial decisions made by reading specialists and teachers (Vinsonhaler, Weinshank, Wagner, & Polin, 1983). One important aspect of this work was to determine the reliability or agreement of the diagnostic judgments. Thus, the written diagnoses and remedial plans of reading specialists were analyzed to determine the agreement of clinicians about a set of simulated cases. Agreement could occur either between any two clinicians for the same case or for the same clinician for the same case on two separate occasions. In the initial study of the series, neither measure was significantly different from zero.

The average interclinician correlation (diagnosis of the same case by two clinicians) was −.10 (measured by the Phi coefficient). The average intraclinician correlation (test-retest correlations for the same clinician diagnosing the same case) was .13. These findings were

This work is sponsored in part by the Institute for Research on Teaching, College of Education, Michigan State University. The Institute for Research on Teaching is funded primarily by the Program for Teaching and Instruction of the National Institute of Education, United States Department of Education. The opinions expressed in this publication do not necessarily reflect the position, policy, or endorsement of the National Institute of Education. (Contract No. 400-81-0014) startling, considering that the subjects were trained, experienced, and highly regarded reading specialists.

A series of five additional observational studies was performed to see if these unexpected findings could be replicated and generalized. New samples were drawn from additional populations, including other reading specialists, classroom teachers, and learning disability clinicians. Additionally, new simulated cases and case formats were developed and used. Potential researcher-induced unreliabilities were eliminated. Finally, remedial reliability was studied by comparing the remedial plans of the same and different clinicians for the same cases of reading disability. Individual diagnostic and remedial reliability remained very low. Across all the studies, interclinician reliability averaged .03 (Phi) and intraclinician reliability averaged .21 (Phi).

In our view, the explanation for the low diagnostic agreement found in our studies lies in the inadequacies of the training that reading specialists receive. A comparison of training programs in medicine and reading is instructive. Medical training is based on the supervised diagnosis, treatment, and follow-up of hundreds of simulated and real cases, with feedback from expert clinicians (Shapiro & Lowenstein, 1979; Simpson, 1972). By contrast, training in reading features supervised diagnosis, remediation, and follow-up of only one or two cases.

COMPUTER-BASED DIAGNOSTIC TRAINING STUDIES

This chapter reports the results of two follow-up studies investigating the use of computer-based simulated cases to improve diagnostic reliability. The training and the simulated cases are based upon two interrelated models of reading. The first is a performance model that specifies the characteristics of a proficient reader; the second is a learning model that specifies how one becomes a proficient reader.

The performance model is based on seven critical reading performances frequently discussed in the literature and observed in the combined diagnoses of the clinicians in the observational studies previously cited. Thus, a poor reader is characterized by deficiencies in one or more of the following:

1. Instant word recognition: the ability to recognize a set of words instantly
2. Decoded word recognition: the ability to recognize a set of words using various phonetic strategies
3. Vocabulary: the ability to give word meanings

4. Oral reading: the ability to read text aloud with appropriate phrasing, fluency, and intonation
5. Silent reading comprehension: the ability to answer specific questions on text read silently
6. Listening comprehension: the ability to answer questions on text read aloud by someone else
7. Attention/Motivation: the ability to concentrate on a reading task

The learning model used in these studies specifies causal factors associated with each of the critical reading performances. For example, if the problem of poor instant word recognition is established, the learning model suggests probable causal factors, such as poor visual discrimination, insufficient practice, etc. For a more extended discussion of the models, see Vinsonhaler et al. (1983); Weinshank, Cureton, and Blatt (1980); and Cureton, Stewart, and Patriarca (1980).

The Computer-Based Diagnostic Internship

Three features characterize the diagnostic training used in these studies. First, instruction was given on the performance and learning models that served as the foundation for diagnostic decision-making. Second, decision aids were used to insure systematic data collection and diagnostic categorization. Two major types of decision aids were created: diagnostic/remedial forms designed for use during the diagnostic decision-making act and diagnostic checklists designed to permit the translation of written diagnoses to a common vocabulary. Third, practice in diagnosis was provided by a computer-based internship consisting of a set of eight simulated cases stored on a text-processing mainframe computer (i.e., the Amdahl 470 using Textform) and presented to the reading specialists, either by a researcher or by a microcomputer (i.e., DEC/PDP8 and Apple II Plus and IIe). Most of these cases were those used in the series of observational studies of reading specialists described earlier.

The First Training Study

The purpose of the study was to test the hypothesis that training, based on the decision aids and systematic practice with simulated cases, would improve diagnostic agreement. As in the observational studies, agreement was measured by correlations between the diagnoses of different clinicians for the same case.

Method

Subjects. Subjects were 28 experienced teachers who were master's degree candidates with prior coursework in reading. Training was in the context of a graduate level reading diagnosis course. Thirty hours of instruction were provided across a five-week period.

Materials. The stimulus materials used for training were the computer-based simulated cases of reading difficulty that form the Diagnostic Internship. There were four basic cases, each of which had an equivalent form—that is, a superficially disguised replicate of the original case prepared by changing the student's name, using alternate forms of tests, and so forth (Lee & Weinshank, 1978). Thus there were eight simulated cases in all. A cue inventory listing all the information available for each case was provided. The cue inventory for one of the simulated cases is shown in Figure 8.1.

Figure 8.1 Case Information (Case Inventory) for Case 4, Dan

Physical Information
Vision Test
Audiometric Record

Background Information
School Record
Teacher Form
School Information
Parent Form

Assessment Information
Basic Sight Vocabulary (Dolch)
Sentence Completion
Gates - McKillop Reading
    Diagnostic Tests
        Recognition & Blending
            Common Word Parts
            Auditory Blending
            Phonic Spelling of Words
            Giving Letter Sounds
Auditory Discrimination
    (Wepman)
Durrell List-Read Series
    Intermediate Level
    Vocabulary
    Paragraphs

Assessment Information (Cont.)
Durrell Diagnostic Analysis of
    Reading Difficulty
        Oral Reading
        Silent Reading
        Word Recognition & Word
            Analysis
        Hearing Sounds in Words -
            Primary
        Visual Memory of Words -
            Primary
        Intermediate Spelling - List 1
Achievement Test (Iowa Test of
    Basic Skills)
        Vocabulary
        Reading
Graded Word List (Slosson Oral
    Reading Test)
Reading Achievement (Gates
    MacGinitie)
        Speed/Accuracy
Cognitive Ability (Weschler Intel-
    ligence Scale for Children)
        Verbal
        Performance
        Full Scale

Instruction. Students were required to diagnose one practice case each week under the supervision of an instructor familiar with the performance and learning models. Students interacted with the cases, using the decision aid as a guide, and prepared a written diagnosis. Subsequently, the students transferred their written diagnoses onto two checklists: one based on the performance model (Critical Reading Performance Checklist) and the other based on the learning model (Causal Factors Checklist). The entire group received feedback and had the opportunity to discuss the cases with their instructor.

Testing. The students were randomly assigned to one of the four simulated cases, yielding seven students for each case. The procedures and cases used for the pre- and posttests were manually based (i.e., presented by the researchers) so that artifacts due to computer practice could be eliminated. Otherwise, the testing was identical to the training procedure and to the method used in the original observational studies previously cited.

Analysis and Results

Data analysis focused on the diagnostic agreement of the students with each other on the same case (interclinician agreement). As in the observational studies, two agreement statistics were used (Phi correlation and Porter statistic). In both statistics, zero (0) means no agreement and one (1.0) means perfect agreement. Both the Phi and Porter coefficients are derived from a four-cell agreement table containing the four diagnostic categories, which are: (a) present in both diagnoses (N++); (b) present in Diagnosis i, but absent in Diagnosis j (N+−; (c) absent in Diagnosis i, but present in Diagnosis j (N−+); and (d) absent from both diagnoses (N−−). The Phi coefficient is a Pearson Product-Moment correlation based upon the four-cell table. The Porter coefficient is obtained by dividing the number of categories present in both diagnoses (N++) by the sum of the number of categories present in both or in either diagnosis (the sum of N++, N+−, and N−+). The major difference between the two statistics is that the Porter calculation considers only statements actually made by one or both clinicians, while the Phi calculation also includes statements that could have been made, but were absent, from both diagnoses. Since no significant differences between these statistics were found, only the results for Phi are reported.

The dependent variable was mean interclinician agreement for pre- and posttests as measured by the Phi and Porter coefficients.

Tests of statistical significance for the difference between means were performed using cases as the unit of analysis. First, the mean correlations among the individuals diagnosing the same case were calculated separately for both the pre- and posttests. Second, the difference between the pre- and posttest means was calculated separately for each case. Lastly, the t-test of the difference between means for paired observations was applied to the differences between pre- and posttest means obtained for each case (Edwards, 1954, pp. 278–282). Table 8.1 shows the results for the Phi coefficients. Results for the Porter statistic were comparable. Mean agreement on the pretest for the Critical Reading Performances was much higher than that obtained in the observational studies (Phi = .26 versus .03). Mean agreement on the pretest for the Causal Factors was also higher than in the observational study (Phi = .16 versus .03).

Students' diagnostic agreement also improved from pre- to posttests. For the Critical Reading Performances, agreement increased from .26 to .38 (Phi); however, this difference was not statistically significant ($t = 2.77$, $p > .05$). For the Causal Factors, agreement also increased from the pretest [.16 (Phi)] to the posttest [.38 (Phi)], and this difference was statistically significant ($t = 15.70$, $p < .001$). Thus, the data strongly support the hypotheses that decision aids and computer-based training on simulated cases improve diagnostic agreement.

Table 8.1 First Training Study

Type of checklist	Pretest	Posttest
Critical Reading Performances		
M	.26	.38
SD	.08	.07
Causal Factors		
M	.16	.38
SD	.02	.01

The Second Training Study

The objective of the first training study was to determine the improvement in diagnostic agreement that would result from tightly controlled training. In the study, instruction in the learning model was based on a text developed expressly for training (Weinshank et al., 1980). The decision aids were redesigned so that students were forced to: (1) make a "problem" or "no problem" decision on the status of each critical reading performance; (2) support that decision with case data; and (3) list probable causes underlying performance.

The objective of the second study was to establish whether or not the results of the first study could be replicated with other instructors and generalized to teachers who had no specialized training in reading. These considerations led to a design in which instruction was provided for three separate groups of teachers, each taught by an experienced clinician trained in the use of the performance and learning models for diagnosis.

Another objective was to compare computer-based training with training based on real children, the latter being a much more costly, labor-intensive procedure.

Methods

Subjects.   The subjects, who were paid for their participation, were fifteen experienced classroom teachers with minimal formal training in reading or reading diagnosis.

Instruction.   The subjects were assigned at random to three training groups, each with a different preceptor, i.e., an experienced clinician who diagnosed and proposed remediations according to the performance and learning models and provided feedback on student decision-making for specific cases. All groups were instructed for 30 hours, supplemented by 10 hours of practice. Two groups received computer-based simulated case training. The other group was trained with real children who had reading disabilities. All groups received instructor feedback. Progress was monitored by means of pre-, mid-, and posttests on a simulated case and an additional transfer-of-training test on a case not previously diagnosed. Five simulated cases were used; one subject from each preceptor training group was tested on each case.

The materials used in this study included the same set of simulated cases, four originals and their replicates, used in the first training study. In addition, a fifth simulated case and replicate were developed to provide an example of a reading comprehension problem in an older student. These ten cases comprised our reading internship: five cases for training and five for testing.

Testing.   The testing procedure was identical to that used in the earlier training study except that: (1) there were five simulated cases rather than four; (2) there were four testing sessions (i.e., pre-, mid-, post-, and transfer-of-training tests) rather than just two (i.e., pre- and posttests); and (3) a revised model-based diagnostic decision aid (discussed above) and checklist were developed.

A portion of the decision aid is shown in Figure 8.2. This format, based on the problem-oriented medical record developed by Weed (1976), forces the individual to:

1. Make a decision about the adequacy or inadequacy of each critical reading performance
2. Indicate the case information used in making the decision
3. List likely causal factors underlying performance
4. Suggest remedial strategies

The checklist listed the seven critical reading performances as major categories and required a decision as to the subject's adequacy in each area. Subsets of diagnostic categories under each performance included causal factors related to each of the seven critical reading performances. Under each critical performance an "Other" category was listed to accommodate diagnostic statements that could not be translated into existing categories.

The pretest was administered prior to any training. Identical procedures were followed for the midtest approximately five weeks later and the posttest at the end of the ten-week session. In all these tests students diagnosed the same case, thus enabling a progress profile to be established. A week after the posttest, a transfer test was given in which students diagnosed a different simulated case they had never seen before.

Results

Although the computer case simulation groups showed slightly higher agreements than the real case group, the differences did not approach statistical significance. Hence, results for all groups will be reported together.

Figure 8.2 Sample Page from the Diagnostic Decision Aid

Case Name: Dan (Grade 4)

Does the student have a problem with INSTANT WORD RECOGNITION?

(Circle One)   Yes   No

On what basis was this decision made?
  SORT Score: 2.1
  Durrell Word Analysis and Word Recognition = low first grade

If no, then continue with the next critical Reading Performance on page 3.

If yes, describe the important factors that have contributed to this problem.
For each factor, suggest remedial procedures for its improvement.
Continue on the next page, if required.

1. Describe one factor contributing to the problem with Instant Word
   Recognition.

   Dan has poor visual memory of words.

   Suggest remedial procedures for alleviating this factor.

   He needs to look at the whole word, not just the beginning letters.

2. Describe another factor contributing to the problem with Instant Word
   Recognition.

   Dan does not do enough reading outside of class.

   Suggest remedial procedures for alleviating this factor.

   Parents need to devise a plan to encourage Dan to read more, possibly
   using a reward system for the amount of reading he does.

Figure 8.3 and Table 8.2 summarize the findings for agreement
among students across training groups on a given case. For the un-
trained students, initial mean diagnostic agreement (Phi = .39) was
much higher than that obtained by the experienced specialists in the
observational studies (Phi = .03). These data provide further support
that the decision aids have a positive effect on diagnostic agreement.
As in the first study, training improved agreement from pretest (mean
Phi = .39) to posttest (mean Phi = .66). In the second study, the
difference is statistically significant ($t = 2.78$, $p < .05$). There was little
change in agreement on the transfer test (mean posttest Phi = .66,

Figure 8.3 Mean Phi Coeffecients among Students for Critical Reading Performance and Causal Factors

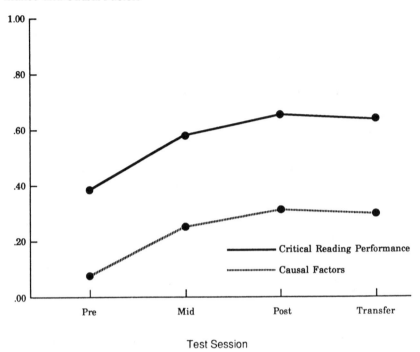

Test Session

Table 8.2 Second Training Study

Type of checklist	Pretest	Posttest	Transfer test
Critical Reading Performances			
M	.39	.66	.64
Causal Factors			
M	.08	.31	.30

mean transfer test Phi $= .64$). The difference is not statistically significant ($t = .19$, $p > .05$). Thus the improvement in agreement was
transferred to simulated cases not directly used in the training.

Figure 8.3 and Table 8.2 also summarize the findings for causal
factors. In general, agreement on causal factors is much lower than
that for critical reading performance. The improved agreement obtained by the use of the decision aid alone can be seen by comparing
the interclinician agreement in the observational studies (mean Phi $=$
.03) with the pretest agreement of the students on causal factors (mean
Phi $= .08$). This small difference suggests that the decision aid alone
was *not* effective in improving diagnostic agreement for causal factors. The effects of training on causal factors can be seen by comparing pretest agreement (mean Phi $= .08$) with the posttest agreement
(mean Phi $= .31$). This difference is statistically significant ($t = 5.88$, p
$< .01$). There was little change in agreement from posttest (Phi $= .31$)
to transfer test (Phi $= .30$). The difference was not statistically significant ($t = - .42$, $p > .05$). Apparently, training is effective in improving
agreement and the effect can be transferred to simulated cases not
specifically used in the training.

DISCUSSION

The findings of these training studies can be explained by an
existing theory of clinical decision making (DeGowin & DeGowin,
1976) that implies three sources of diagnostic agreement: (1) agreement on a systematic procedure for case data collection; (2) agreement
on the set of diagnostic categories to be used for all cases; and (3)
agreement on rules of inference associating the diagnostic categories
with observable case data. The role of a theoretical model in diagnostic decision making is to provide a rational method for selecting cues,
choosing the diagnostic categories, and specifying the rules of inference.

In our studies, the independent variables were: (1) use of the
decision aid, (2) training on the models, and (3) practice with feed
back on computer-based simulated cases. The effect of the variables
can be interpreted in terms of their probable reduction of interclinician variation on the three theoretical sources of agreement: data
collection procedures, diagnostic categories, and rules of inference.

In retrospect, we interpret the effects of the independent variables as follows. First, the effect of the use of the decision aid was to
constrain all decision makers to collect data relevant to seven common

diagnostic categories and to make forced judgments of "problem" or "no problem" for these seven categories. This effect was probably responsible for the sharp increases in individual agreement from the observational studies (in which no decision aid was present) to the pretests of the training studies (where decision aids were used).

Second, we believe the effect of training and computer-simulated practice with the performance model was to develop consensus on rules of inference associating test results (and other data) with diagnostic judgments of "problem" or "no problem" for each of the critical reading performances. The effect was probably responsible for the significant increases in individual agreement from pre- to posttest.

Finally, the probable effect of training and practice on simulated cases with the learning model was to develop consensus on the rules of inference associating causal factors with problems in the critical reading performances. This effect may have been responsible for significantly increased agreement on the causal factors from pre- to posttest.

CONCLUSIONS

Research on clinical trials in medicine has shown conclusively that the evaluation of treatment effects depends upon reliable diagnostic categorizations and the systematic monitoring of outcomes. Low diagnostic reliability dilutes the impact of differentially effective treatments and leads to incorrect estimates of clinical validity (Collen et al., 1964; DeDombal, Leaper, Horrocks, Staniland, & McCann, 1974). Thus, diagnostic agreement and reliability is fundamental to the evaluation of treatments and must be improved in the field of reading.

We would propose the following method for implementing training to improve diagnostic reliability. First, one should choose any model for the reading process that lends itself to selecting diagnostic categories and rules of inference. The skills-oriented models chosen here are but one example. Second, one should derive decision aids and instructional materials that teach the diagnostic categories and rules of inference. Third, one should provide a microcomputer-based internship which provides practice on simulated cases. Such an internship can be provided at a fraction of the cost of typical clinical training and appears to be at least as effective as more traditional methods of instruction. Finally, one should combine all these resources and integrate them into existing courses in reading diagnosis or in-service clinical practice.

In summary, earlier studies by the present researchers uncovered severe problems with diagnostic reliability in reading. The present studies have documented a potential solution to the reliability problem based on changes in the training of reading specialists. The computer was an integral part of this training. In the future, training of reading clinicians may benefit from the capability of the computer to effectively and efficiently simulate the diagnosis of reading problems.

REFERENCES

Carter, H. L., & McGinnis, D. J. (1970). *Diagnosis and treatment of the disabled reader*. Toronto: Macmillan Company.

Collen, M., Rubin, L., Neyman, J., Dantzig, G., Baer, R., & Siegelaub, A. (1964, May). Automated multiphasic screening and diagnosis. *American Journal of Public Health, 54*, 5.

Cureton, D., Stewart, G., & Patriarca, L. (1980). *Diagnosis and remediation in reading*. Unpublished manuscript, Michigan State University, Institute for Research on Teaching, East Lansing.

DeDombal, F. T., Leaper, D., Horrocks, J., Staniland, J., & McCann, A. (1974). Human and computer-aided diagnosis of abdominal pain: Further report with emphasis on performance on clinicians. *British Medical Journal, 1*, 376–380.

DeGowin, E. L., & DeGowin, R. L. (1976). *Bedside diagnostic examination* (3rd ed.). New York: Macmillan.

Edwards, A. L. (1954). *Statistical methods for the behavioral sciences*. New York: Rinehart & Company.

Ekwall, E. (1976). *Diagnosis and remediation of the disabled reader*. Boston: Allyn & Bacon.

Lee, A., & Weinshank, A. (1978). *Case production and analysis: CLIPIR pilot observational study of reading diagnosticians* (Research Series No. 14). East Lansing, MI: Institute for Research on Teaching, Michigan State University.

Otto, W., McManemy, R. A., & Smith, R. J. (1973). *Corrective and remedial teaching* (2nd ed.). Boston: Houghton Mifflin.

Shapiro, E., & Lowenstein, L. (Eds.). (1979). *Becoming a physician: Development of values and attitudes in medicine*. Cambridge, MA: Ballinger.

Simpson, M. (1972). *Medical education: A critical approach*. London: Butterworth.

Spache, G. D., & Spache, E. B. (1973). *Reading in the elementary school* (3rd ed.). Boston: Allyn & Bacon.

Vinsonhaler, J. F., Weinshank, A. B., Wagner, C. C., & Polin, R. M. (1983). Diagnosing children with educational problems: Characteristics of reading and learning disabilities specialists and classroom teachers. *Reading Research Quarterly, 18,* 134–164.

Weed, L. (1976). A new paradigm for medical education. In E. F. Purcell (Ed.), *Recent trends in medical education* (pp. 55–93). New York: Macy Foundation.

Weinshank, A. B., Cureton, D., & Blatt, G. (1980). *A model of reading and learning to read.* Unpublished course material, Michigan State University, Institute for Research on Teaching, East Lansing.

9
Using Computer-Simulated Instruction to Study Preservice Teachers' Thought Processes

Donna Alvermann

Until recently it was assumed that instruction was the dominant variable related to student achievement. The advent of computer-simulated instruction and a growing acceptance of students' self-reports as valid research data, however, have led to studies that examine how students' cognitive and affective thought processes mediate the effects of instruction. The mediational paradigm holds that instruction influences student thinking, and student thinking, in turn, influences what is learned (Doyle, 1977; Wittrock, 1986).

In this chapter preservice teacher education students' thinking (e.g., their perceptions of instruction, their attentional and affective processes, their background knowledge) is explored through their participation in an interactive video simulation of a diagnostic reading technique. The technique involved students in administering, scoring, and interpreting an informal reading inventory (IRI), a term used to describe a series of graded word lists and paragraphs that help classroom teachers determine youngsters' strengths and weaknesses in reading.

Directions for administering and scoring IRIs appear in almost every reading methods textbook, which is an indication of the widespread popularity of this diagnostic technique. Of necessity, the various textbook directions on how to administer and score an IRI are usually generic in nature and tend not to match the directions of a specific inventory that students are expected to administer in a practice or field-based setting. This mismatch between what is learned from a methods textbook and what is relevant for application in the field setting often presents a problem to preservice teachers.

The problem of inconsistency in directions was simulated in the exploratory study that formed the basis of this chapter. Specifically, preservice teacher education majors either read a generic set of directions for administering an IRI, or they read a set of directions that were matched to the specific IRI presented in the interactive video simulation. Among the advantages of interfacing a videotape player with a microcomputer in this study was the realistic effect it created for the preservice teachers who participated in the simulation. They communicated individually with the reading diagnostician on the monitor screen in a fashion that closely simulated a face-to-face interaction. In addition, students had the option of stopping the simulation and restarting it any time they were unable to keep pace with the instruction.

Before describing the simulation in detail, a brief review of previous computer simulations used with preservice and in-service teachers is presented. Following the description of the interactive video simulation, findings relevant to the mediating effect of students' thought processes are discussed. A section on future directions for studying student thinking using interactive video concludes the chapter.

PREVIOUS COMPUTER SIMULATIONS

Presenting prospective teachers with simulations of tasks they will confront in actual practice is a teaching technique that has been employed for at least a quarter of a century. (See Cruickshank, Clingan, & Peters, 1979, for a review of the use of simulations in teacher education.) Most of the early simulations used media other than computers and dealt with classroom management problems or problems created by ineffective communication between the principal and the staff, rather than with classroom instruction.

More recently, computer simulations have focused on the instructional skills that teachers need to become effective educators. Of particular interest here are those simulations that focus on teaching some aspect of reading instruction to students enrolled in preservice or in-service teacher education courses. For example, Vinsonhaler and his colleagues (chapter 8 of this volume) have developed a computer simulation for studying the decisions made by reading diagnosticians. In addition, two reports from the 1970s describe computer simulations designed to teach students about informal reading inventories. One of those studies (Roe & Aiken, 1976) used a computer-assisted instruction program called Reading Laboratory (RDLAB), which was designed to teach preservice teachers how to make their own informal reading inventory and administer it to an elementary school pupil. Results of that study showed that the use of RDLAB was at least as effective as the more traditional approaches to teaching students about informal reading inventories and, in some instances, more effective.

The other study (Henney & Boysen, 1979) used a PLATO computer simulation that presented hypothetical cases of children exhibiting reading skill deficiencies. After the preservice teachers had diagnosed the children's reading problems (and after PLATO had "remediated" the problems as specified by the teachers), they retested the children. On instruments designed to measure students' ability to administer the IRI correctly, there were no significant differences between the group that participated in the computer simulation prior to administering it to a child and the group that did not participate. However, the experimental group had significantly fewer undiagnosed weaknesses than the control group.

At present the emphasis in interactive video simulation research is not focused on determining whether computer-assisted instruction is superior to the more traditional approaches of instruction. Instead, researchers are designing studies that attempt to validate theory-based computer/video instructional materials (Henderson, Landesman, & Kachuck, 1983) or test the efficacy of interactive video for teaching problem solving (Bransford, Sherwood, Kinzer, & Hasselbring, 1985). Other computer simulation studies, such as the one presented in this chapter, are focused on determining the extent to which interactive video is useful in exploring students' cognitive and affective processing of text.

AN EXPLORATORY STUDY

Description of the Simulation

The interactive video simulation used in the present study consisted of two 30-minute programs. The first program, "Assessing Reading Problems with the Informal Reading Inventory," taught students how to administer, score, and interpret the *Contemporary Classroom Reading Inventory* (Rinsky & deFossard, 1980). The second program, "Planning for Instruction Using the Informal Reading Inventory," involved students in making instructional decisions based on their interpretation of results obtained in the first program.

Storyboard.   The script for the video scenes and the accompanying graphic displays produced by the computer formed the substance of the storyboard, a portion of which is included here to give a sense of the content and the format of one of the programs (see Figure 9.1).

Program 2 contained a variety of question-answer formats. For example, after viewing a discussion between April's third-grade teacher and the reading specialist (concerning April's dependence on the classroom teacher for the pronunciation of words during oral reading), students were asked to think of possible causes for such behavior and to use the computer keyboard to type their answers to this open-ended question. The computer would search for any phrases that included words such as "poor sight vocabulary," "lack of sight vocabulary," and so forth. If incorrect phrases were typed, the computer would cue the student until the correct response was given. The video screen would then display what the reading specialist believed to be the cause of April's dependence on the teacher, and students could compare their answers to the expert's.

Flashbacks were used to prompt students' memory of a particular scene when necessary. Also, students had the option of playing a sequence over again and then exiting from the replay at any point by pressing the < ESCAPE > key. There were built-in safeguards, however, that prevented students from exiting a sequence until the questions associated with that sequence were answered correctly.

Hardware and Software Components.   Hardware consisted of an Apple IIe with two disk drives, a Panasonic 8200 video player, a video monitor, and an interactive board from BCD Associates. In addition to the videotape, the software component consisted of two floppy diskettes programmed in Super Pilot.

Materials and Methods

Participants.   Thirty-one female and 12 male preservice teacher education students volunteered to be part of an exploratory study designed to determine how their thinking mediated the effects of instruction in the use of an informal diagnostic reading technique. None of the students had been exposed previously to information about informal reading inventories. Most of the participants had not taken any of the professional core courses in teacher education, but all were in their last quarter of a basic liberal arts program. Although 50 students volunteered initially, only the 43 with complete data sets at the end of the study were included in the analysis.

Materials.   From the pool of volunteers, students were assigned randomly to one of four groups. Group 1 participated in the simulation after reading a set of generic directions that did not match precisely the IRI presented in the videotape. That is, they were similar to explanations found in reading methods texts. This set of directions was labeled "nonrefutation text." Group 2 also participated in the simulation, but their text contrasted the directions for the *Contemporary Classroom Reading Inventory* to the generic directions. This set of directions was labeled "refutation text" because it refuted the notion that all IRIS were administered, scored, and interpreted in the same way. Groups 3 and 4 did not participate in the simulation, but they read the same sets of directions that Groups 1 and 2 read, respectively.

The two sets of directions, containing approximately 600 words each, described how to administer, score, and interpret informal reading inventories. Portions of the two text types appear below:

- *Nonrefutation text*: "Although directions for administering, scoring, and interpreting an informal reading inventory will vary from one instrument to another, a generic set of instructions is presented here. Typically, an informal reading inventory consists of a series of graded word lists and a series of fictional reading passages that become progressively more difficult as one advances through the grades. To administer an informal reading inventory. . . ."
- *Refutation text*: "Despite what many of the reading methods textbooks imply, the various informal reading inventories available today are not that similar in terms of their directions for administering, scoring, and interpreting results. The *Contemporary Classroom Reading Inventory* (CCRI), for instance, is a good example of the differences that exist among inventories. The CCRI tests children's ability to read nonfictional passages (science and social studies material) as well as fictional passages. Also, the CCRI contains cloze activities in addition to the usual graded word lists and graded passages. To administer the CCRI. . . ."

Instrumentation.   The instruments included one knowledge domain pretest, a written free-recall measure, two versions of a multiple-choice test (to accompany either the nonrefutation or refutation text), and two versions of a poststudy questionnaire (one for the group that participated in the simulation and one for the group that did not participate). The pretest contained 15 true/false items designed to test fairly detailed information about informal reading inventories (e.g., item 7: "The highest level at which a child can understand the ideas in the material that is read to him or her is called the frustration level"). The written free-recall measure was a lined sheet of paper with directions for writing down all that could be remembered from the nonref-

(*Continued on p. 148*)

Figure 9.1 Storyboard for Program 1

Scene 1
(Narrator's voice is heard as the following information appears on the video monitor screen)

You are about to use some of the latest educational technology -- a combination of computer assisted instruction and videotape.

Don't worry though; it's simple to use if you just read the instructions and follow them carefully.

If this is the first time you've worked on a computer, you'll need to get used to pressing the <RETURN> key after you type something. Right now, type your first name and then press <RETURN>.
donna

Scene 2
(Narrator's reading continues)

All right, DONNA, I'm going to show you some scenes of a reading specialist giving April, a 3rd grader, an informal reading inventory.

As April reads, you will use your copies of the pupil text to code her performance, right along with the reading specialist in the videotape. Then I'll show you how the specialist coded April's performance so you can check your understanding of how to administer and score an informal reading inventory. Press <RETURN> when you're ready.

Scene 3
April: (Reads word list)
Reading specialist: "Okay, very good."

146

P___	F___	S___
and _____	forget _____	dragon _drink_
blue _____	again _____	floor _____ _for_
did _____	game _____	nothing _____
new _____	liked _kind_	thought _threw_
soon _____	one _____	right _____
they _____	seen _____	mouse _most_
get _____	what _____	inside _____
will _____	funny _____	empty _____

Scene 4
Word list as scored by the specialist

DONNA, why did the reading specialist
stop testing April on the words in isolation?
Press the letter of your answer and
<RETURN>.
a) April is in the 3rd grade.
b) April mispronounced more than 5 words.
c) April was reluctant to proceed quickly.
d) More than 5 seconds elapsed between
   words.
Your answer?
d

Scene 5
(Narrator's reading re-sumes)

The directions for this inventory do not
specify a time limit; some inventories do,
however. Think about it and try again.

Scene 6
(Narration continues)

147

utation and refutation texts. The two versions of the multiple-choice
test contained 14 items. Each item had a stem followed by three
distractors and one correct answer. The two versions of the poststudy
questionnaire consisted of six open-ended questions.

Procedure.   At a designated time, students individually reported
to the reading center, where they were greeted by a research assistant
and informed of the purpose of the study. Prior to viewing the interactive video program, students completed a pretest to identify their
prior knowledge about an IRI. They then read one of the two texts on
how to administer an informal reading inventory and watched as the
research assistant demonstrated how to use the computer to operate
the videotape player. Time spent with the interactive video program
was limited to 20 minutes, after which a student completed the free-
recall measure, the multiple-choice test, and the poststudy questionnaire. Students in the control groups followed the same procedure
with the exception of viewing the videotape.

Scoring.   Following a parsing of the two texts that was modeled
after Johnson's (1970) procedure, a rating sheet was developed to use
in scoring the free recalls. One point was awarded for each of the 12
topics identified on the rating sheet that also appeared in a student's
free recall. Topics included items such as defining an IRI, naming its
components, identifying types of errors, and coding examples of errors. Also, each correct response on the multiple-choice test was
awarded one point. Responses to the poststudy questionnaire were
categorized according to inferences made about students' thought
processes. For example, a student's statement about the effectiveness
of interactive video was taken to reflect his or her perception of
instruction, whereas a statement that indicated confusion about administering the *Contemporary Classroom Reading Inventory* was considered to reflect the student's thinking as based on previous experience and background knowledge (especially when that student was
known to have read the generic directions).

Analysis and Results

The data were analyzed in two stages. In stage one, individuals'
raw scores on the free-recall and multiple-choice tests were analyzed
using an analysis of covariance (ANCOVA). The covariate was the pretest of prior knowledge. In stage two, data from the poststudy questionnaire were analyzed qualitatively. Students' responses to each ques-

tion were read several times. Similarities among the responses were noted and categorized according to treatment group. Finally, two or three responses from each group were designated as exemplars and were used to illustrate how students' thinking could be inferred to mediate the effects of instruction.

Tables 9.1 and 9.2 contain the means and standard deviations for text by treatment group effects on the free-recall and multiple-choice tests, respectively. With free recall as the dependent measure, there was a statistically significant main effect for text, $F(1, 36) = 32.74$, $p < .001$, but not for treatment, nor for the interaction between text and treatment. With the multiple-choice test as the dependent measure, there were statistically significant main effects for both text, $F(1, 36) = 45.31$, $p < .001$, and treatment group, $F(1, 36) = 29.01$, $p < .001$. Again, there was no significant interaction between treatment group and text.

Findings relevant to how students' cognitive and affective thought processes mediated the effects of instruction were analyzed through the inspection of their responses on the poststudy questionnaire and through a content analysis of their written free recalls. These findings are presented next, using the following framework. First, students' perceptions of instruction are discussed in terms of how they performed on the free-recall and multiple-choice tests. Next, the mediating effects of students' inferred attentional and affective thought processes on performance are examined. Finally, the role of background knowledge (as provided by the interactive video simulation) in mediating students' performance is explored.

Table 9.1 Means and Standard Deviations of Text by Treatment Group on Free-Recall Measure

	Interactive Video (N = 22)		Control (N = 21)	
Text	X̄	SD	X̄	SD
Refutation	6.73[a]	2.53	5.70	2.11
Nonrefutation	3.09	1.44	2.54	1.04

[a] Raw score correct out of a possible 12.

Table 9.2 Means and Standard Deviations of Text by Treatment Group on Multiple-Choice Measure

Text	Interactive Video (N = 22)		Control (N = 21)	
	$\overline{\mathrm{X}}$	SD	$\overline{\mathrm{X}}$	SD
Refutation	9.82[a]	1.83	7.90	1.29
Nonrefutation	7.36	1.36	5.18	1.08

[a] Raw score correct out of a possible 14.

Students' Perceptions of Instruction. Preservice teacher education majors' perceptions of how closely the different sets of IRI directions matched the directions on the videotape were assessed through Question 3 of the poststudy questionnaire (see Figure 9.2 for the complete questionnaire). In response to Question 3 ("If you had had an opportunity to ask the researcher any questions during the time you were watching the videotape, what would you have asked her?"), most of the students who read the generic set of directions expressed some type of frustration. For example, one student asked simply, "Why am I confused?"

Students who read the set of directions that matched the IRI on the videotape and refuted the notion that all IRIs are administered in the same way asked such things as, "Now that I have determined what level the child reads on, what is the method for improving that child's comprehension?" In general, students' responses reflected that they understood how to administer and score the *Contemporary Classroom Reading Inventory* and that they were ready to move on to the next step in the procedure.

According to the significant main effect found for text on both the free-recall and multiple-choice measures, the refutation version of the directions was favored over the nonrefutation version regardless of whether the students viewed the videotape. Thus, students' perceptions of the instruction they received via text type may have mediated the effects of that instruction somewhat, but not solely because the directions matched the IRI in the videotape. More likely it was the

Figure 9.2 Questionnaire

---

1. Did participating in the interactive video simulation help you to understand the written directions better?

   Yes_____   No_____   Undecided_____

2. Please give a reason why you responded as you did in Question #1 above.

3. If you had had an opportunity to ask the researcher any questions during the time you were watching the videotape, what would you have asked her?

4. If you had had an opportunity to ask the researcher any questions during the time you were reading the passage, what would you have asked her?

5. If you had had an opportunity to ask the researcher questions during the time you were completing any of the post-reading tests, what would you have asked her?

6. In your best estimate, what do you think the researcher will find out from conducting this study?

---

comparison/contrast nature of the refutation text's top-level structure that accounted for the better performance on the outcome measures (see Meyer & Freedle, 1979, for a discussion of the highly memorable aspects of comparison/contrast text structure).

Attentional and Affective Thought Processes. Whether students' attentional and affective thought processing mediated the effects of instruction was examined by inspecting the responses to Questions 1, 2, and 6. To the first question ("Did participating in the interactive video simulation help you to understand the written directions better?"), 91% of the students who read the refutation text responded affirmatively, and 9% were undecided. The same pattern of responses held for the students who read the nonrefutation text.

Question 2 asked students to give a reason why they responded as they did to Question 1. An analysis of the responses to Question 2 revealed that students generally thought the interactive video simulation held their attention and made the written sets of directions more interesting. For example, one student said, "Watching the video made me a bit more interested in what I had read. I was more attentive because of the video." Another student commented, "I was able to relate what I'd seen on the screen with the passage that was written. Also, the passage explained most of what took place in the video—like when the girl reached capacity level in her comprehension." Students' responses sometimes reflected popular conceptions of media. For example, one student observed: "With the videotape there was a visual image of the testing procedure. We are in a society that relies heavily on visuals." In fact, there is some evidence that a learner's perceptions of media interact with invested mental effort and learning (Salomon, 1984).

Question 6 asked, "In your best estimate, what do you think the researcher will find out from conducting this study?" The students' responses to this question suggest that they perceived their experience in interacting with the computer and videotape to be a rewarding and positive one. For instance, one student wrote, "I think you will find that the use of more visuals will help to guide student teachers in the understanding of testing, and that information given in more than one way is remembered better." Another student hypothesized that the researcher would find "using videotapes with a computer is a valuable adjunct to learning."

Overall, students who reported an increase in attention and interest when they were involved in the computer simulation tended to score high on the multiple-choice test. This observation, coupled with the significant main effect for the simulation group on the multiple-choice test, suggests that students' attentional and affective thought processes may have influenced the effects of instruction to some degree. Until this speculation can be tested, however, it remains just that.

Role of Background Knowledge.   The notion that an individual's available knowledge prior to reading a selection determines to a large extent what he or she will comprehend has been well documented in the literature on schema theory (e.g., Anderson, Reynolds, Schallert, & Goetz, 1977; Bransford & Johnson, 1972). Tierney and Cunningham (1984) devoted more than a third of their chapter on comprehension research to a discussion of the importance of building and activating students' background knowledge prior to reading. In the present study, the role of background knowledge (as provided by the interactive video simulation) in mediating students' performance was explored through the inspection of their responses to Question 5 on the poststudy questionnaire and through a content analysis of their written free recalls.

Question 5 posed this hypothetical situation: "If you had had an opportunity to ask the researcher questions during the time you were completing any of the post-reading tests, what would you have asked her?" Responses to this question suggest that students in the interactive video group were well aware of the computer simulation's efficiency in building background knowledge. One student asked if her ability to perform well on the multiple-choice test was related to "the additional instruction that I got on the videotape." Another student wondered why he had not been allowed to see the videotape first, since he was "a visual learner and could have benefitted from seeing how the CCRI was administered before reading about it." Not unexpectedly, students in the control group made no reference to the computer simulation's effectiveness in building background knowledge.

A content analysis of students' written free recalls revealed that, compared to members of the control group, students who had been exposed to the computer-simulated diagnostic reading technique produced more detailed descriptions of how to administer, score, and interpret an informal reading inventory. Although the mediational paradigm would suggest that the interactive video simulation may have played a role in providing students with background knowledge that was rich in memorable details, the present study's main analysis did not permit testing of that idea.

FUTURE DIRECTIONS

This exploratory study of how students' cognitive and affective thought processes may mediate the effects of computer-simulated instruction demonstrates that computer technology can be employed to examine differences in how students go about learning from text. In the future, research is needed that systematically controls for competing hypotheses about how mediated learning occurs. For example, in future studies using an interactive video simulation, members of the control group might be provided with a script of the videotape to alleviate potential differences in outcome measures due to exposure time. Or, as one student suggested in the present study, the interactive video simulation might be used prior to reading (to supply missing background information) as well as after reading (to clarify information from the text).

Finally, as the technology for interactive video simulations like the one described above undergoes continued development, it should be possible to create intelligent tutoring systems that are designed to provide information about the thought processes of the learner during a learning experience. With this advancement in technology, researchers will find themselves having to rely less on the inferences they can draw from the paper-and-pencil products of their subjects.

REFERENCES

Anderson, R. C., Reynolds, R. E., Schallert, D. L., & Goetz, E. T. (1977). Frameworks for comprehending discourse. *American Educational Research Journal, 14,* 367–381.

Bransford, J. D., & Johnson, M. K. (1972). Contextual prerequisites for understanding: Some investigations of comprehension and recall. *Journal of Verbal Learning and Verbal Behavior, 11,* 717–726.

Bransford, J. D., Sherwood, R. D., Kinzer, C. K., & Hasselbring, T. S. (1985). *Havens for learning: Toward a framework of developing effective uses of technology* (Tech. Rep. No. 85.1.1). Vanderbilt University, Learning Technology Center, Nashville, TN.

Cruickshank, D. R., Clingan, M. L., & Peters, G. (1979). The state of the art of simulation in teacher education. *Simulation/Games for Learning, 9,* 72–82.

Doyle, W. (1977). Paradigms for research on teacher effectiveness. *Review of Research in Education, 5,* 163–198.

Henderson, R. W., Landesman, E. M., & Kachuck, I. (1983, April). *Effects of interactive video/computer instruction on the performance of underachieving students in mathematics.* Paper presented at the annual meeting of the American Educational Research Association, Montreal, Canada.

Henney, M., & Boysen, V. (1979). The effect of computer simulation training on ability to administer an informal reading inventory. *Journal of Educational Research, 72,* 265–270.

Johnson, R. E. (1970). Recall of prose as a function of the structural importance of the linguistic unit. *Journal of Verbal Learning and Verbal Behavior, 9,* 12–20.

Meyer, B. J. F., & Freedle, R. O. (1979). *Effects of discourse type on recall* (Prose Learning Series Research Rep. No. 6). Tempe, AZ: Arizona State University.

Rinsky, L. A., & deFossard, E. (1980). *The contemporary classroom reading inventory.* Dubuque, IA: Gorsuch Scarisbrick.

Roe, M. H., & Aiken, R. M. (1976). A CAI simulation program for teaching IRI techniques. *Journal of Computer-Based Instruction, 2,* 52–56.

Salomon, G. (1984). Television is "easy" and print is "tough": The differential investment of mental effort in learning as a function of perceptions and attributions. *Journal of Educational Psychology, 76,* 647–658.

Tierney, R. J., & Cunningham, J. W. (1984). Research on teaching reading comprehension. In P. D. Pearson (Ed.), *The handbook of reading research* (pp. 609–655). New York: Longman.

Wittrock, M. C. (1986). Students' thought processes. In M. C. Wittrock (Ed.), *Handbook of research on teaching* (3rd ed.) (pp. 297–314). New York: Macmillan.

10
Computer Speech in Reading Instruction

Richard K. Olson and Barbara Wise

Recent technological developments in computer speech make it possible to duplicate and even improve on some aspects of reading instruction that have required the presence of a human model. Children typically learn to read by noting the relations between the teacher's speech and the relevant letter patterns or words. These relations can now be efficiently presented with computers. For example, computer speech may be paired with simple letter patterns and words on the screen to familiarize children with the basic rules of phonics. At a more advanced level, children can improve their word-decoding skills in the context of meaningful, interesting text by designating unknown words on the screen with a light pen and receiving immediate speech feedback for the highlighted word or word segment.

There are several different approaches to the production and utilization of computer speech in reading instruction. Each method of speech production has its unique advantages and disadvantages for different instructional applications. In the first section of the chapter we will briefly discuss three basic methods of producing computer speech. In the second section we will discuss the use of these different types of speech in several different instructional settings.

The third section of the chapter presents an overview of our

The research was supported by NICHD grant no. 2 P01 HD 11681-07, by grant no. RR07013-85 from the Biomedical Research Support Grant Program, Division of Research Resources, NIH, and by a Digital Equipment Corporate Contributions Grant. We thank the teachers and students from University Hill Elementary School and from Alameda Senior High School for their participation in the research. Greg Foltz developed the feedback software. Vicki Steele edited the phonetic feedback files for the stories. Communications should be addressed to the first author at the Department of Psychology, University of Colorado, Boulder, Colorado 80309.

research on computer-based reading and synthesized speech in the remediation of reading disabilities. Most children learn to read successfully during the early grades under a variety of conventional teaching methods. Unfortunately, conventional instruction does not seem to be sufficient for some normally intelligent children. The plight of these reading disabled children motivated our development of the Computer-Based Reading and Speech-Feedback System. Our initial studies suggest that the system may substantially improve the prognosis for disabled readers, but a number of important methodological issues need to be studied before the full educational potential of computer speech can be realized. We conclude the chapter with a discussion of the research opportunities introduced by computer speech and reading displays.

METHODS FOR GENERATING COMPUTER SPEECH

Computer speech production techniques range from the digital recording of a model speaker to the complete synthesis of speech by machine. Two of the most common methods used in educational settings, digitized speech and linear predictive coding, and recent developments in synthesized speech are described in this section.

Digitized Speech

Digitized speech is produced by initially recording a person's voice and then digitizing the analog signal for storage in the computer. When speech is requested from the computer, the digitized signal is converted back to an analog wave form for transmission to a loud speaker. As indicated by the current use of digital discs in the record industry, the quality of sound can be indistinguishable from the input signal.

The major limitation of digitized speech for computers is its high demand on memory (Witten, 1982). The digital signal for one second of speech may require up to 4,000 bytes of memory for a good quality sound. If the speech signal is stored in the main core memory of the computer for rapid access by a program, only a few words could be stored in the microcomputers used in most classrooms. Computers equipped with an external memory device such as a hard disk could store many more words in digital form. The high speeds of hard-disk technology allow for the rapid retrieval of this information for conversion through the computer to an analog signal. Current magnetic disks for microcomputers commonly store 20,000,000 bytes of information, or enough for roughly 5,000 words of digitized speech. The development of optical disk systems for microcomputers will support the storage of even greater amounts of digitized speech. Although most computers in the schools do not currently have access to high-speed magnetic or optical disks, this is very likely to change in the near future as costs decline.

Linear Predictive Coding

Because most microcomputers in the schools have not had access to high-speed disks, efforts have been made to reduce the storage requirements of digitized speech. One of the most common techniques for doing this is called Linear Predictive Coding (LPC). In this approach, words are recorded from a speaker and the resulting analog signal is digitized. The digital signal is then broken into 25-millisecond data frames that are reduced to twelve parameters. Ten of these parameters describe the shape of the wave form and the remaining two describe the pitch and volume. Storage requirements for the resulting encoded signal are about 5–10% of the raw digitized signal, and the speech signal produced by the computer will sound like a normal human voice if the proper voice model and encoding procedures are used. A special speech-production chip (Texas Instruments 5220) is required to translate the encoded signal back to speech.

The LPC encoding procedure requires a fair amount of interaction with an operator. Street Electronics, which produces the popular Echo II speech production board for the Apple II computer, estimates that an operator of the LPC system can encode about 40 words per day.

The main advantage of LPC over pure digitized speech is the reduced demand on memory, although a single word may still require 200 bytes of information. If a large speaking vocabulary is needed, memory limitations still pose problems for the use of LPC in microcomputers operating with floppy disks.

Synthesized Speech

The third major approach to computer speech production is through synthesized speech. Some of the more advanced systems are text-to-speech translators. Text is transmitted to the synthesizer in ASCII code, and the corresponding speech code is developed by the synthesizer through the application of complex grapheme-phoneme correspondence rules. Special pronunciations are stored in the synthesizer for most of the frequent "exception words" in English. The synthesizer responds to punctuation in continuous text by including the appropriate pauses between words and inflections. The technical details of one of the most powerful systems (DECtalk) are described by Klatt (1980).

The use of a text-to-speech synthesizer places minimal demands on computer memory because the only signal that must be stored in the main computer is the spelling and punctuation for the words to be spoken. A further advantage is that the potential vocabulary is unlimited. Any word or nonword that can be spelled can be spoken by the synthesizer. Whenever a unique pronunciation is associated with a particular spelling, it is possible to bypass the internal grapheme-phoneme correspondence rules and present the appropriate pronunciation using phonemic code.

Although the sounds produced by speech synthesizers are based on an analysis of the critical components of human speech, they do not depend on the initial recording of human speech that is required for digitized speech and linear predictive coding. As a result, synthesized speech often does not sound natural. However, the technology of speech synthesis has advanced rapidly over the past few years. Several of the newer systems are capable of producing synthesized speech that approaches the intelligibility levels of natural speech (Greene & Pisoni, in press).

The most common source of text-to-speech synthesis in educational settings has been the Echo II synthesizer produced by Street Electronics for the Apple IIe. The Echo II is a remarkable speech production device for the price and it can produce good-quality speech in the LPC mode described above. However, its intelligibility in the text-to-speech mode is not good for most words. In our research (Olson, Foltz, & Wise, 1986) and that of others (Greene & Pisoni, in press), as few as 40% of the words presented in isolation by the Echo II could be correctly identified. When words are directly encoded in an optional phonemic mode, their intelligibility is improved in some cases, but it is still far below that of natural speech. As a result, the educational application of the Echo II text-to-speech processor has been limited.

Some of the newer and more expensive text-to-speech synthesizers for microcomputers have far surpassed the intelligibility level of the Echo II. We are using a text-to-speech synthesizer produced by Digital Equipment Corp. called "DECtalk" that was first marketed in 1984. In one intelligibility study with college sophomores, 96% of a set of words presented out of context by DECtalk's "Perfect Paul" voice were correctly identified. The correct identification rate for the same words recorded in natural speech was also 96% (Olson et al., 1986). A second study used the same set of words with a group of nine disabled readers between 8 and 12 years of age. This group's recognition of DECtalk words was 95% correct, compared to 98% correct for the same words in normal speech. The difference was statistically significant ($p < .05$), but it was clear that disabled readers were also able to recognize words spoken by DECtalk at an impressively high rate. When the words were spoken in context, the disabled readers recognized over 99% of the words from DECtalk. Further discussion of the disabled readers responses to DECtalk is presented in the third section of the chapter.

In addition to DECtalk, the 3.0 version of the Prose 2000 text-to-speech synthesizer produced by Speech Plus also has a nearly normal intelligibility level. The disadvantage of DECtalk and the Prose 2000 is that they are at present much more expensive than the Echo II. The primary use of the higher-priced text-to-speech synthesizers is currently in the business world, where they are used to answer phones and provide information. These systems may be too expensive for many schools, but it is likely that prices will decline in the near future, and systems will be available without the hardware for telephone communications. Based on our research with the DECtalk synthesizer, we anticipate that the application of highly intelligible text-to-speech systems will rapidly expand into the area of reading instruction.

APPLICATIONS OF COMPUTER SPEECH TO READING INSTRUCTION

The three types of computer speech described in the previous section have been applied to reading instruction in a variety of ways. The different approaches can be grouped into two major categories. The first category includes the use of a relatively small amount of computer speech while the reader interacts with the computer through the keyboard. A variety of teaching packages currently on the market use this approach. The second category includes screen-interaction and speech-production techniques that allow the reader to obtain unlimited speech feedback for text.

Current Commercially Developed Systems with Limited Speech

Most of the currently available software packages using speech for reading instruction concentrate on the development of basic phonics skills in the initial stage of reading. A limited amount of speech is used to instruct the subjects to respond to information on the screen by using the computer keyboard, and to reward them for making the correct responses (e.g., "Very good, that is correct"). Additional speech is used to orient the beginning reader to the component sounds of words or pictures on the screen. For example, *cat, hat,* and *rat* might be pronounced by the computer while the corresponding words are presented on the screen. The general goal is to develop the child's understanding of the most common grapheme-phoneme correspondence generalizations. Any given program typically uses no more than a few hundred words, phrases, or component word sounds.

Because the amount of speech in current reading instruction programs is limited, it is possible to use digitized speech or linear predictive coding. One program using digitized speech is marketed by the WICAT Corporation in Provo, Utah. The program is run on WICAT's mainframe Hydra computer, which controls up to 30 instructional terminals. The Hydra computer has access to a large hard disk that allows for the efficient storage of digitized words and phrases. When speech is required in the program, the digitized information is accessed from the system disk and converted to an analog signal for the subject.

Linear predictive coding and related methods are used in most systems based on microcomputers, such as the Apple or IBM PC, because few of these systems in the schools have had hard disks for the storage of digitized speech. The number of companies offering LPC speech with reading-instruction software has grown rapidly over the past two years. A partial list includes IBM, Houghton-Mifflin, Scholastic Software, Chatterbox Voice Learning Systems, Laureate Learning Systems, and Early Learning.

The most popular instructional package with speech is produced by IBM under the title, Writing to Read. The package was first marketed in 1984. The corporate weight and marketing power of IBM has led to the widespread use of the Writing to Read program in a very short time. Computer speech for Writing to Read is produced from an IBM PCjr with a voice attachment. The primary purpose of the speech component is to teach the children basic phonics rules. Other components of the package include the typing of words in a phonetic alphabet and reading while listening to tape-recorded stories.

At present, it is not clear that computer-speech training of phonics skills has any unique advantages for beginning readers. There has been little published experimental data comparing the efficacy of computer-speech training with other methods. One exception is a study by the Educational Testing Service of IBM's Writing to Read package

(Murphy & Appel, 1984). The study appears to have been quite thorough in its evaluation of thousands of children before and after participation in the training program. In comparison to control groups that were not trained in the program, Writing to Read students showed significant advantages in several reading and writing skills. One problem with the study was that children trained in the Writing to Read program spent more time in reading instruction than the control groups. The control groups would have provided a more valid comparison if they had spent an equal amount of time with other methods of reading instruction. Also, it is difficult to know the specific contribution of computer speech to the childrens' success with the program. It is possible that the writing component was the major factor leading to improved reading and spelling skills. The efficacy of computer speech in the teaching of basic phonics skills needs to be demonstrated in more carefully controlled experiments.

Screen-Interactive Systems with Large Vocabularies

A novel approach to the use of computer speech in reading instruction is based on the combination of a large speech data base or speech synthesizer with a screen-interaction device. In these systems, children read normal text from the display screen of a microcomputer. When they encounter a word that they are uncertain how to read, they can target the word with a mouse, touch screen, or light pen for immediate speech feedback (McConkie & Zola, chapter 6 of this volume; Olson et al., 1986).

McConkie and Zola used a unique method of storing speech to support their screen-interactive system. The analog signal for about 2,500 words was directly recorded on the magnetic media of a hard disk. When a word was targeted on the screen by the subject, the computer accessed the location for the analog recording of the word on the disk and this was played back to the subject while the targeted word was highlighted on the screen in reverse video. Technically, the computer is involved only in accessing the analog speech signal rather than producing it from a digital record or synthesizer. The quality of the speech signal is essentially the same as from a digital recording.

McConkie and Zola noted that their feedback system enables poor readers to read more difficult and interesting material than would otherwise be possible. The system was employed with a group of prisoners who were poor readers. Extensive practice with the system led to significant gains in their reading skills. The reader is referred to the chapter by McConkie and Zola in this volume for further details.

The Computer-Based Reading and Speech-Feedback system developed in our laboratory uses a DECtalk text-to-speech synthesizer (Olson et al., 1986). The DECtalk synthesizer was adopted because we needed a much larger vocabulary than 2,500 words, and we wanted to segment the feedback for words both phonetically and orthographically. The text-to-speech synthesizer supports an infinite vocabulary and can conveniently present the component sounds of words in different temporal relations. In this system, when readers target words on the screen, different feedback conditions are possible. The whole word may be highlighted on the screen as a unit while it is spoken in the normal way, or it may be orthographically and phonetically segmented to help build the reader's phonetic coding skills. Our research efforts with the system are concentrating on the optimal way of segmenting the orthographic and speech feedback for different reading-disabled children. The background for this research and some results of a pilot study are presented in the following section.

COMPUTER-BASED READING AND SPEECH-FEEDBACK FOR DISABLED READERS

Background

A substantial number of children have unusual difficulty learning to read, despite their normal intelligence and educational opportunities. Our earlier research with these disabled readers has shown that, as a group, they may be able to read a number of familiar printed words, primarily through orthographic coding or "sight reading," but that most disabled readers are uniquely deficient in their abilities to phonetically decode or "sound out" unfamiliar printed words and in related analytic language skills (Olson, Kliegl, Davidson, & Foltz, 1985; Olson, 1985). Consequently, the development of their reading vocabularies lags substantially behind their oral vocabularies.

Longitudinal analyses have shown that most disabled readers who were identified in the early grades retain their reading deficit into the later grades and adulthood, relative to the performance of their normal controls (Olson, 1985). However, there are some significant and encouraging exceptions to this group trend. A few children who demonstrate reading difficulties in the early grades eventually achieve normal reading levels.

One factor contributing to the ultimate success of some disabled readers is their continued instructional support in reading through the later grades. Unfortunately, most schools do not have the resources to

provide the intense individualized instruction that is needed to motivate and train disabled readers. Many disabled readers become dis-
couraged by their early failures and avoid reading. Others are motivated to continue reading on their own, and they show greater
improvement; but they are often hampered by their weak phonetic
coding skills. Disabled readers may correctly guess unfamiliar words
in context in association with their limited alphabetic skills, but this
approach often leads to decoding errors because context is not a very
reliable predictor for words in continuous text (Gough, 1983). In the
absence of feedback for their frequent decoding errors in silent reading, the development of better decoding skills is actively retarded by
incorrect learning trials (Jorm & Share, 1983), comprehension suffers,
and the pleasures of reading are diminished.

It seemed to us that computer-based reading and speech feedback could help disabled readers acquire decoding skills. They could
read text for meaning and pleasure while conveniently and privately
obtaining the decoding help they needed. The learning of word-
decoding skills while reading continuous text for meaning embodies
the ideal goal for reading instruction stated by Singer (1981, p. 295):
"Use a method of instruction that teaches students how to identify
printed words, and at the same time use their language ability while
reading."

A major advantage of computer-based instruction over the typical
group instruction in classrooms is the ability to present a highly individualized training program (Moskowitz & Birman, 1985). With the
Computer-Based Reading and Speech-Feedback System, reading
material can be selected to fit the child's interests and general level of
reading ability. It is also possible to vary the type of orthographic and
speech feedback for targeted words to match each child's unique
profile of reading and language skills. Our research has shown that
there are substantial individual differences in these profiles for disabled subjects at a given level of reading ability as well as across
different levels of reading ability and age (Olson et al., 1985; Olson,
1985).

A central hypothesis of our current research with the Computer-
Based Reading and Speech-Feedback System is that the optimal level
of segmentation in orthographic and speech feedback will depend on
the child's profile of reading and language skills. The different levels
of segmentation provided by the Computer-Based Reading and
Speech-Feedback System are described below.

Units of Processing in Speech and Reading:
Instructional Implications

The units of processing in skilled reading and in reading development have been a fundamental issue in the different models considered by psychologists and educators (see LaBerge & Samuels, 1974). The hypothesized processing units range in size from grapheme-phoneme relations to whole words and phrases. Current models often include provisions for the parallel representation and activation of different-sized processing units in word recognition (see Humphreys & Evett, 1985; Stanovich, 1982). Processing units in word recognition have also been an important issue in different approaches to reading instruction. Training programs with a "sight-reading" emphasis consider the whole word to be the most appropriate unit for instruction. Programs with a "phonics" emphasis concentrate on grapheme-phoneme correspondence. Other programs attempt to represent both approaches or some intermediate-sized processing unit such as the syllable (Rozin & Gleitman, 1977).

There has been a substantial amount of research on the efficacy of different training programs for beginning readers. The consensus seems to be that there are significant advantages through the first and second grades for most children in programs that emphasize phonics training (Beck, 1981; Chall, 1967; Perfetti, 1985; see also National Institute of Education, 1984; see Miller & Burnett, chapter 11 of this volume for a different point of view). Unfortunately, there is much less evidence or consensus on how to instruct children who are having unusual difficulties learning to read. The answer to this question is complicated by the significant individual differences among disabled readers in their component reading and language processes (Olson, 1985). It is possible that different instructional approaches are needed for disabled readers depending on their unique profile of reading and language skills. In training with the Computer-Based Reading and Speech-Feedback System, one child might show the greatest benefit from small-unit segmentation while another would do better with larger units.

The different orthographic and speech segmentation conditions used in our research represent different positions on the processing-unit dimension. We will consider four processing units below and justify our selection of three of these. We will then turn to the results of a pilot study that included the three segmentation conditions.

Graphemes and Phonemes

The smallest possible unit of orthographic and speech segmentation would be individual graphemes and their corresponding phonemes. There are several reasons for our decision not to present this level of segmentation. First, grapheme-phoneme correspondences in English are not one-to-one or consistent with respect to the acoustic quality of phonemes in different contexts (Vellutino, 1980). Second, phonemes within syllables tend to be "shingled" together and co-articulated in speech (Liberman, Liberman, Mattingly, & Shankweiler, 1980). Although single grapheme-phoneme segmentation and blending is a common educational practice for beginning readers, Liberman (1983) has pointed out that it may be counterproductive to try to isolate many phonemes in this way, especially the stop consonants *p*, *b*, *t*, *d*, *g*, and *k*, which require the addition of a schwa sound when pronounced in isolation. For example, pronouncing the isolated phonemes for a word such as *pat* results in "puh," "ah," "tuh." Liberman believes that children need to be made aware of the different phoneme segments in speech and reading, but this awareness can be produced in other ways.

The third reason we did not segment each phoneme is that it would be too disruptive to the normal course of reading. It would take too much time, and it would distract the reader from the general goal of reading for meaning and pleasure.

Subsyllable Segmentation: Onset and Rime

Our smallest unit of orthographic and speech segmentation is based on linguistic and psycholinguistic research showing that there is a structure within syllables above the single phoneme level. Treiman's (1985) review of a number of studies, including her own work on "pig latin" type word games, led her to conclude that it is easier for both adults and children to segment syllables in certain places in spoken language. For example, she found that it was easier for both adults and children to break the syllable between the initial consonant cluster and the vowel than within the consonant cluster or between the vowel and the final consonant cluster. Treiman's work supports previous claims of linguists that phonemes in a syllable are grouped into two major constituents (Fudge, 1969). The first is an optional "onset" consisting of a consonant or consonant cluster. The second is an obligatory "rime" that consists of a vowel, which may or may not be followed by up to four consonants. All of the experiments on onset-rime segmentation have been done using oral, rather than written language. In collaboration with Becky Treiman, we have designed experiments to confirm whether the onset/rime c/vcc division is easier than the cv/cc division for learning printed words.

The subsyllable segments based on the onset-rime division will usually avoid the "puh ah tuh" problem of sounding out phonemes that should not be phonetically isolated (Liberman, 1983), although initial stop consonants will require the addition of a schwa to make them pronounceable (e.g., "puh" "at" for *pat*). These subsyllable segments will often be similar to the larger ones that are trained in some phonics programs. It is hypothesized that while some disabled readers may show limited benefits from dealing with these segments in traditional phonics training programs, they might be more motivated and able to learn the segments while reading and obtaining feedback in normal text from the computer.

In the orthographic and speech-feedback training for subsyllable segments, the letters relating to the onset are separately highlighted in reverse video while they are spoken. Following a brief delay, the orthographic pattern for the rime is highlighted as its speech sound is spoken. The simultaneous presentation of the appropriate orthographic segments by eye, and speech segments by ear, should make their relation particularly salient to the reader.

Syllables

Rozin and Gleitman (1977) suggested that it might be best to acknowledge the syllabic nature of English writing and speech explicitly in children's reading instruction, particularly for poor readers. Beginning normal readers may have sufficient ability to analyze language into its phonemes and benefit from phonics instruction, but beginning poor readers are often hampered by their more limited ability in phonemic analysis. They can, however, analyze the speech stream at the syllable level. Rozin and Gleitman reasoned that instruction with an emphasis on syllabic units would give beginning readers a more linguistically accessible unit to work with in their word decoding. Moreover, syllables provide a unit wherein grapheme-phoneme correspondences would be more consistent in their acoustic quality, and they avoid the awkward exercise of attempting to isolate and then blend phonemes in sounding out a word like *pat* (e.g., "puh ah tuh" in phonics training, or "puh at" in the onset-rime segmentation condition).

Recent work by Taft (1979) on the Basic Orthographic Syllabic

Structure (BOSS) has generated much research about what kind of syllabic structure adult readers actually use. Researchers have tried to determine whether adult readers use a Vocalic Center Group (VCG) unit, which is based on phonological considerations, or the BOSS unit, based on orthographic and morphologic considerations. For instance, *reading* and *actor* are divided by VCG as *rea/ding* and *ac/tor*, but are divided by BOSS as *read/ing* and *act/or*. Taft found that BOSS units aided lexical access more than VCG units did. Lima and Pollatsek (1983) found that any syllabic unit, defined either phonologically or orthographically, was more helpful in lexical decision and priming tasks than nonsyllabic units. However, with their expanded stimulus set, neither syllabic unit held any significant advantage over the other, but with inflected words, the meaningful root morpheme proved the best prime of all, whether it conformed to VCG or BOSS rules. Other research indicates that morphemic units are used by readers (Murrell & Morton, 1974; Taft & Forster, 1976), but how to divide single morpheme words is still ambiguous.

We are planning experiments to clarify whether the type of syllabic boundary used makes the learning of new words easier for children. For this original study and because of Lima and Pollatsek's (1983) results, syllable boundaries were used as defined by *Webster's Dictionary*. These boundaries tend to preserve root morphemes and prefixes and suffixes as units, and they were used except when a grapheme/phoneme correspondence (GPC) for consonants would have been violated by such divisions: for example, *in-dig-e-nous* was divided instead as *in-di-ge-nous*, because the pronunciation of the *g* as /j/ depends on the following *e*. In the second syllabification, a short *i* is needed in an open syllable, contrary to a frequently taught phonics rule. However, GPC generalizations are much less consistent and predictable for vowels than for consonants (Venezky, 1970), and the information content for consonants is higher than of vowels. Therefore, we have chosen to honor GPC generalizations for consonants over those for vowels when they conflict at syllable boundaries.

Whole Words

On the large side of the segment dimension, we have included a whole-word feedback condition. The potential advantages of whole-word feedback are that it is least disruptive to the normal flow of reading, and it eliminates mistakes arising from improper blending of the segments. The potential disadvantage is that the subjects may not learn as much about phonological word-decoding skills with whole-word feedback. For younger beginning readers, there is evidence that the whole-word method of reading instruction may yield a slightly larger reading vocabulary at the beginning of instruction, but studies have shown that phonics decoding approaches are superior by the end of the first year of instruction (see Perfetti, 1985, for a review).

A Pilot Study with the Computer-Based Reading and Speech-Feedback System

Our first study was designed to provide data on several issues that needed to be resolved before embarking on a long-term study of the relative benefits of the different feedback conditions. The pilot study included a test of DECtalk's intelligibility that has already been discussed in an earlier section. The results of that experiment showed that DECtalk's intelligibility was very close to normal speech for both normal and disabled readers.

The primary questions addressed by the pilot study were: (1) whether disabled readers would be sensitive to their decoding errors and target the problem words during the normal course of reading stories; (2) whether the targeted words would be subsequently recognized in posttraining tests; and (3) whether speech feedback would improve text comprehension. Additional questions concerned the subjects' relative ability to use a mouse and light pen as targeting devices, responses to reading text at different difficulty levels, and the relative benefits of segmenting the orthographic and speech feedback at different levels. Finally, we wished to determine whether disabled readers would enjoy reading with the system and whether they would be motivated to continue using it in a long-term study of reading with the different segmentation conditions.

Fifteen reading-disabled children between 8 and 12 years of age were selected from elementary schools in Boulder, Colorado. An additional group of eleven disabled readers between 15 and 18 years of age was selected from a local high school. The subjects were referred to the study by their reading teachers on the basis of their meeting two criteria: a normal-range IQ, and a reading performance that was substantially below what was expected for their grade level. The children varied widely both in their absolute reading level and in the severity of their reading disability. We wished to determine the usefulness of the system for disabled readers at different levels of reading proficiency and age.

Two different computers and targeting systems were used in the study: An Apple II+ was interfaced with a mouse, and an IBM PC was interfaced with a light pen. Both systems were connected through a serial line to a DECtalk speech synthesizer. Speech stimuli were presented in DECtalk's "Perfect Paul" male voice. Reading material and comprehension questions for the study were drawn from the Spache Diagnostic Reading Scales (Spache, 1963). Text displays were white-on-black, upper and lower case, in 40-column format.

The subjects were given a word-recognition test to determine their reading grade-level and a brief practice session in targeting numbers on the screen with either the Apple/mouse system or the PC/light-pen system. Then they listened to DECtalk present instructions for reading and targeting words in the stories. The subjects were told to read the stories for meaning and to target each word that they could not decode or were uncertain of, in order to obtain orthographic and speech feedback. They were told that they would later be tested on the words they targeted, along with other difficult words in the text, and that they would be asked four comprehension questions at the end of each story. The instructions emphasized that subjects should attempt to decode difficult words *before* targeting them for feedback. In the oral reading conditions, they had to actually attempt an oral reading of each word before targeting it. This allowed us to evaluate the benefits of targeting for words that were read incorrectly prior to targeting. Few correct words were targeted by the subjects.

Six stories, each approximately 200 words in length, were read during the test session. The first two stories were presented at a difficulty level appropriate for their reading grade level, where the subjects would be expected to make relatively few decoding errors. Difficulty levels for the next two stories were one grade level above their reading grade, and the last two stories were two grade levels above their reading grade. After each story, the subjects were asked four comprehension questions by the experimenter. Then a word recognition test was presented on the computer that included a randomized list of all of the words that were targeted plus six of the most difficult words in the text that were determined from a previous study. The subject's oral response to each word in the recognition tests was recorded as correct or incorrect on the computer by the experimenter, and then the next word was presented. No feedback was given about the accuracy of their responses. A final recognition test was presented after all of the stories had been read. This test included all of the words that had been targeted in the six stories.

The first two stories in the training session were read aloud with speech feedback. The second pair of stories, which were at the next higher grade level, included one that was read aloud with speech feedback and one that was read aloud without speech feedback in counterbalanced order across subjects. In the control condition without feedback, the synthesizer was simply turned off and the subjects were asked to continue targeting words they were uncertain how to read. The highlighting pattern that was appropriate for the subject's assigned segmentation condition was continued for each targeting response in the no-feedback condition. The subjects were asked to study and try to decode the targeted words while they were highlighted on the screen. The last two stories at the highest difficulty level were both read with speech feedback, but one was read aloud and the other silently in counterbalanced order. All of the oral reading was tape-recorded for later analyses of reading errors. Most subjects completed the entire session within one and a half hours, including breaks. A questionnaire was administered at the end of the session to determine the subjects' reactions to different aspects of the system and their interest in participating in a long-term training study.

The pattern of results with the Apple/mouse and PC/light-pen systems were similar, although subjects seemed to find the light pen easier to use. We are using the light-pen system in our long-term training studies.

The results presented in Table 10.1 are based on nine subjects who had at least 4% but not more than 24% oral reading errors and who targeted at least 47% of their oral errors. Some subjects made too many or too few oral reading errors due to the limited range of the text materials. Two of the younger and most severely affected disabled readers made over 50% oral reading errors because our first-, second-,

Table 10.1 Percentages for Selected Disabled Readers

Mean Percentages	All Oral Feedback Stories (4)	Feedback vs. No Feedback		Oral vs. Silent	
		F	NF	Oral	Silent
Oral Errors	15.5	16.5	18.5	22.9	_ _ _
Targeted Oral Errors	65.7	58.9	29.0*	68.1	a
Recognized Test 1	74.7	89.6	15.9**	58.7	55.7
Recognized Test 2	55.8	67.5	26.6	52.4	46.6
Correct Comprehension	_ _ _	88.9	63.0*	75.0	65.8

*$p < .05$ **$p < .01$ a = 18.8% words targeted.

and third-grade stories were too difficult for them. These two subjects said they liked "reading" with the system. It markedly aided their comprehension and they recognized an average of 43% of targeted oral errors on the first test and about 20% on the second test. Because they were overwhelmed by the number of unfamiliar words they had to learn and remember for the recognition tests, however, their recognition performance was not as good as that of the subjects whose data are included in Table 10.1. Some of the older high school subjects made fewer than 3% oral reading errors, and their individual story data were too unstable for the analyses. Finally, several subjects were excluded who targeted a very low percentage of their oral reading errors. These disabled readers had been told by their teachers to rely heavily on context in their reading of unfamiliar words, which may aid comprehension but detract from word recognition skills (Jorm & Share, 1983). We found in postexperimental training with these subjects that their sensitivity to decoding errors could be improved by pointing them out as they read. It was clear from these results that pretraining in sensitivity to decoding errors is needed for some children to take full advantage of the feedback.

The first column in Table 10.1 contains the mean results for the four stories that were read aloud with feedback (two stories at reading grade level and one each from the higher grade levels). Over the four stories, the subjects averaged 15.5% oral errors, of which they targeted 65.7% for feedback. This demonstrates a reasonable amount of sensitivity to their decoding difficulties. Of the words that were initially read incorrectly in the oral stories and targeted, 74.7% were recognized in the tests that followed the comprehension questions after each story, and 55.8% were correctly recognized in the final recognition test for all targeted words at the end of the session. Both tests showed an impressive gain in word recognition over the duration of the test session. It should be noted that the recognition scores were for words taken out of context and presented in isolation. It is likely that recognition scores would be even higher if the words were read again in context.

The results presented in the second and third columns of Table 10.1 are for the speech-feedback and no-speech-feedback conditions presented in the third and fourth stories of the test session. For both the recognition test that followed each story and the final recognition test, the percentage of targeted oral errors was significantly higher in the speech-feedback condition. It was apparent from the results that speech feedback was the primary factor that improved word recognition. The bottom row in columns 2 and 3 of Table 10.1 shows that the benefits of speech feedback were also reflected in the subjects' comprehension scores.

Columns 4 and 5 in Table 10.1 present means for the oral and silent reading conditions in the last two stories of the series. The targeting frequencies, performance in the recognition tests, and comprehension scores were not significantly different in the two conditions, although there was a trend toward better performance in the oral reading condition. The silent condition was included in this study because we plan to have children read silently in a long-term study with feedback systems set up in the schools. It was necessary to show that children would also target words and benefit from speech feedback in silent reading.

It can be seen that the percentage of oral errors is higher and the recognition rates are lower for the most difficult stories represented in column 4, when compared to rates for feedback stories that were one grade level lower in column 2, and the difference was greater for stories at the lowest difficulty level. The declining trend in percent recognition across difficulty level is confounded by presentation order in the series of stories, but a similar trend was observed across subjects when those with many oral errors were compared with those with fewer errors. It seems that when the error rates get too high because of text difficulty, subjects become overwhelmed and show less benefit from their feedback. Of course the natural flow of reading is disrupted when there is a high frequency of decoding errors and targeting.

The final issue addressed by the study was the effects of the whole-word, syllable, and subsyllable feedback conditions. Of the nine subjects whose data were included in Table 10.1, two had subsyllable feedback, five had syllable feedback, and two had whole-word feedback. The mean targeted word recognition scores for the immediate and final tests were 70.5% and 35.8% for subsyllable, 76.5% and 54% for syllable, and 77.6% and 61.5% for whole-word conditions. Of course the samples in the feedback conditions are too small for any of these differences to be significant.

Two of the youngest and most severely affected disabled readers assigned to the subsyllable feedback condition did not finish the session. These children had great difficulty blending the subsyllable segments and failed to recognize many of the words after speech feedback. The children were better able to recognize words from feedback when they were segmented syllabically. Thus, the results from these subjects suggest that subsyllable segmentation may not be an effective form of feedback to aid in word recognition for some severely disabled readers, at least over the brief training period of this study.

Of course it is the long-term consequences of extended training with the different feedback conditions that are most important for the remediation of reading disabilities and for teaching beginning readers. The type of feedback that provides the greatest short-term gains in recognizing targeted words may or may not be the best way to build a child's phonological decoding skills, which can be applied to successfully decode new words without feedback.

One very encouraging result from the present study was the unanimously enthusiastic responses of the subjects and their parents to the Computer-Based Reading and Speech-Feedback System. Their responses to the questionnaire showed that they would like to have the system available at home or school so they could read interesting materials that would otherwise be too difficult for them. All of the subjects said they would be interested in participating in future studies with the system.

CONCLUSIONS AND NEW DIRECTIONS IN RESEARCH

Computer speech is playing an increasing role in reading instruction. Software that uses a limited amount of digitized speech or linear predictive coding for the development of basic phonics skills has been available for several years. Some of these programs seem to be quite well designed, and user reports are enthusiastic. However, there has been little empirical research comparing the use of computer speech with other methods of phonics instruction.

A second generation of computer-speech systems is now being developed that includes screen-interaction capabilities and speech support with large or even unlimited vocabularies. These systems open new possibilities for the instruction of word-decoding skills during the course of normal reading. Our Computer-Based Reading and Speech-Feedback System allows children to read stories from the computer and obtain synthesized speech feedback for unknown words. The synthesized speech used in the system (DECtalk) was shown to have good intelligibility for both normal and disabled readers. Its unlimited vocabulary and flexibility in speech segmentation are significant advantages over other methods of computer-speech production for reading instruction.

While our system should be helpful for normal beginning readers, we believe that it will be particularly valuable for disabled readers whose reading vocabularies continue to lag significantly behind their oral vocabularies. A pilot study demonstrated that disabled readers enjoy using the system and they showed significant short-term gains in word recognition and comprehension when speech feedback was available.

The central research issue we are pursuing is the optimal level of orthographic and speech segmentation for disabled readers with different reading and language profiles. Long-term training studies in the schools have been designed with the different segmentation conditions to determine their influence on specific reading and language skills. A major advantage for computer-based instruction in these studies is that the training conditions can be precisely defined so we will know exactly how each subject has been treated. This level of control is very difficult to attain in studies of different training programs administered by teachers (see Rozin & Gleitman, 1977).

In conclusion, the recently developed speech capabilities of microcomputers open up some new and efficient ways for instructing disabled and beginning readers. Our research is designed to provide a sound empirical base for applying this new technology.

REFERENCES

Beck, I. L. (1981). Reading problems and instructional practices. In G. E. Mackinnin & T. G. Waller (Eds.), *Reading research: Advances in theory and practice* (Vol. 2, pp. 53–94). New York: Academic Press.

Chall, J. A. (1967). *Learning to read: The great debate.* New York: McGraw-Hill.

Fudge, E. C. (1969). Syllables. *Journal of Linguistics, 5,* 253–286.

Gough, P. B. (1983). Context, form, and interaction. In K. Rayner (Ed.), *Eye movements in reading: Perceptual and language processes* (pp. 203–211). New York: Academic Press.

Greene, B. G., & Pisoni, D. B. (in press). Perception of synthetic speech by adults and children: Research on processing voice output from text-to-speech systems. In L. E. Bernstein (Ed.), *The vocally impaired* (Vol. 2). New York: Academic Press.

Humphreys, G. W., & Evett, L. J. (1985). Are there independent lexical and nonlexical routes in word processing? An evaluation of the dual-route theory of reading. *The Behavioral and Brain Sciences, 8,* 689–740.

Jorm, A. F., & Share, D. L. (1983). Phonological recoding and reading acquisition. *Applied Psycholinguistics, 4,* 103–147.

Klatt, D. H. (1980). Software for a cascade/parallel formant synthesizer. *Journal of the Acoustical Society of America, 67,* 971–995.

LaBerge, D., & Samuels, S. J. (1974). Toward a theory of automatic information processing in reading. *Cognitive Psychology, 6,* 293–323.

Liberman, I. Y. (1983). A language-oriented view of reading and its disabilities. In H. Myklebust (Ed.), *Progress in learning disabilities* (Vol. 5, pp. 81–101). New York: Grune & Stratton.

Liberman, I. Y., Liberman, A. M., Mattingly, I., & Shankweiler, D. (1980). Orthographic and the beginning reader. In J. F. Kavanagh & R. L.

Venezky (Eds.), *Orthography, reading, and dyslexia* (pp. 137–153). Baltimore: University Park Press.

Lima, S. D., & Pollatsek, A. (1983). Lexical access via an orthographic code? The Basic Orthographic Syllable Structure (BOSS) reconsidered. *Journal of Verbal Learning and Verbal Behavior, 22,* 310–332.

Moskowitz, J., & Birman, B. (1985). Computers in the schools: Implications of change. *Educational Technology, 25*(1), 7–14.

Murphy, R. T., & Appel, L. R. (1984). *Evaluation of the Writing to Read instructional system 1982–1984* (Educational Testing Service report). Princeton, NJ: Educational Testing Service.

Murrell, G. A., & Morton, J. (1974). Word recognition and morpheme structure. *Journal of Experimental Psychology, 102,* 963–968.

National Institute of Education. (1984). *Becoming a nation of readers* (Contract No. 400-83-0057). Washington, DC: U.S. Department of Education.

Olson, R. K. (1985). Disabled reading processes and cognitive profiles. In D. Gray & J. Kavanagh (Eds.), *Biobehavioral measures of dyslexia* (pp. 215–243). Parkton, MD: York Press.

Olson, R. K., Foltz, G., & Wise, B. (1986). Reading instruction and remediation with the aid of computer speech. *Behavior Research Methods, Instruments, and Computers, 18,* 93–99.

Olson, R. K., Kliegl, R., Davidson, B. J., & Foltz, G. (1985). Individual and developmental differences in reading disabilities. In G. E. MacKinnon & T. G. Waller (Eds.), *Reading research: Advances in theory and practice* (Vol. 4, pp. 1–64). New York: Academic Press.

Perfetti, C. A. (1985). *Reading ability.* New York: Oxford University Press.

Rozin, P., & Gleitman, L. R. (1977). The structure and acquisition of reading II: The reading process and the acquisition of the alphabetic principle. In A. S. Reber & D. L. Scarborough (Eds.), *Toward a psychology of reading: The proceedings of the CUNY conference* (pp. 55–141). Hillsdale, NJ: Lawrence Erlbaum.

Singer, H. (1981). Instruction in reading acquisition. In O. J. L. Tzeng & H. Singer (Eds.), *Perception of print: Reading research in experimental psychology* (pp. 291–311). Hillsdale, NJ: Lawrence Erlbaum.

Spache, G. D. (1963). *Diagnostic reading scales.* Monterey, CA: McGraw-Hill.

Stanovich, K. E. (1982). Individual differences in the cognitive processes of reading I: Word decoding. *Journal of Learning Disabilities, 15,* 485–493.

Taft, M. (1979). Lexical access via an orthographic code: The Basic Orthographic Syllabic Structure (BOSS). *Journal of Verbal Learning and Verbal Behavior, 18,* 21–39.

Taft, M., & Forster, K. (1976). Lexical storage and retrieval of polymorphemic and polysyllabic words. *Journal of Verbal Learning and Verbal Behavior, 15,* 607–620.

Treiman, R. (1985). Phonemic analysis in spelling and reading. In T. H. Carr (Ed.), *The development of reading skills* (pp. 5–18). New Directions for Child Development, No. 27. San Francisco: Jossey-Bass.

Vellutino, F. (1980). Perceptual deficiency or perceptual inefficiency. In J. F.

Kavanagh & R. L. Venezky (Eds.), *Orthography, reading and dyslexia* (pp. 251–270). Baltimore: University Park Press.

Venezky, R. L. (1970). *The structure of English orthography*. Paris: Moulton.

Witten, I. H. (1982). *Principles of computer speech*. New York: Academic Press.

11

Using Computers as an Integral Aspect of Elementary Language Arts Instruction: Paradoxes, Problems, and Promise

Larry Miller and J. Dale Burnett

The role of computers in education may be approaching an important crossroads as unqualified support for their use begins to erode. Seymour Papert's vision of creative computer use, which he described in *Mindstorms* (1980), has become a focal point for critics skeptical of technology's impact and usefulness in education (Sloan, 1984). Paradoxically, the use of drill and practice programs, considered by many writers, including Papert, to be one of the reasons the potential of computers in education has not been realized fully, now attracts defenders (Marsh, 1985–86; Siegel & Davis, chapter 7 of this volume). Naive optimism is predictable whenever innovation is introduced into schools, as attested by the initial claims of an earlier era concerning the impact of typewriters in improving the quality of children's writing. Today, there continues to be confusion about the place of computer technology in education and how it can be used best, if at all.

Many of the controversies surrounding the use of microcomputers in education are similar to those debated currently in the area of language arts such as whether reading should be taught as series of subskills, with an initial emphasis on decoding, or fostered as a holistic process, with an early and continuing focus on meaning. However, technology also has spawned several unique issues. Spache and Spache (1986), for example, raised an argument against using computers in reading instruction by citing cost considerations. Authors such as Ohanian (1984) acknowledge the potential motivating power of the computer but worry that poorly designed software may stifle rather than enhance children's interest in reading. Balajthy (1986) described many technical and educational issues that require consideration as to technology's place in language arts education. For example, Balajthy noticed that print legibility once again has become an important issue for publishers and educators.

The goal of this chapter is to illustrate how two opposing views of reading instruction raise different issues and suggest different viewpoints concerning classroom computer use. For this purpose we will portray two teachers, one espousing a subskill perspective in reading instruction and the other a holistic orientation, as they attempt to use technology productively in their classrooms. Our descriptions of the existing problems and paradoxes facing these teachers may seem that we are portraying a bleak picture of computer use, but this is not the case: Solutions exist for many of these quandaries. Although there are difficulties in integrating computers into language arts instruction, we contend that knowledgeable teachers can overcome many of them. However, if teachers do not see the computer as an integral component of schooling that occupies a natural place in their instructional approach, then some of the predictions concerning technology's failures may be realized.

A SUBSKILL PERSPECTIVE

Many of the contentious issues concerning computer use in education have their roots in learning theory, and in one's understanding of how language is acquired and processed (Pearson, 1984), rather than in technology itself. Samuels (1980) noted that reductionist and holistic views of language processing and instruction have existed for centuries, and although he attempted to reconcile many of the differences between the two positions, the debate concerning the value of these views, which endures generally, has specifically spilled over into technology's role in fostering literacy.

A classic example of this situation is the ongoing controversy over the value and use of subskill-oriented drill and practice programs. Early critics contended that drill and practice failed to tap the potential of the computer's power and versatility, but Roblyer (1982) defended their use by pointing out that some courseware does not need the full capabilities of the computer. He argued that as long as the educational goal is clear, and the computer can carry out the task, it presents a worthy application. Grabe (1986) defended computerized drill and practice when he observed that children often complete stacks of dittoed worksheets, and that they may as well carry out these low-level, frequently boring activities on computers.

Few authors base their attacks on, or defense of, drill and practice programs on theories of learning, yet logically this is the key to their use. An exception is Lesgold (1983) who, focusing on the area of reading, contended that microcomputers can be used best to provide pleasant practice in developing automatic word recognition skills rather than to teach higher level activities. His view did not emanate from technological considerations; instead, he based his ideas on research showing a positive relationship between decoding speed and comprehension (Perfetti & Lesgold, 1979; Lesgold & Perfetti, 1978). High correlations between reading speed and comprehension prompted Lesgold to consider rapid decoding the key to efficient reading. This view concerning the importance of automaticity in decoding also is supported by the research of LaBerge and Samuels (1974).

Although we do not accept Lesgold's vision of computer use in teaching reading, there is a congruency between his ideas of how print is processed and how one should use computer-based instruction. Lesgold put aside arguments based on graphics, memory capacity, and data collection, concentrating instead on a theoretical view of language processing and learning, and his technological applications are consonant with his notion of where the important issues reside. His beliefs about applications of computer technology and how language is processed are congruent, and although simply developing a theoretically consistent stance in applying computers to language arts instruction does not eliminate debate, it does focus discussion on critical issues.

The issue whether subskill-oriented approaches have a place in language arts instruction does not end with a theoretical justification of their general use. Accepting this position means that significant questions proceeding from it will surface. How many subskills are there in reading? Is there a justifiable hierarchy of these skills? Is it possible to measure mastery of these skills? Can subskills be taught? These are just four of the perennial questions facing anyone attempting to develop a reductionist approach in reading instruction, and these issues extend to attempts to apply this orientation to computer assisted instruction.

Rebecca's Quandary

To illustrate the paradoxes, problems, and promise of computer use in an elementary school setting, consider the situation of Rebecca, a second-grade teacher with 10 years' experience who uses a subskill approach to language arts instruction, in this instance reading. She has worked through many of the general problems mentioned above by adopting Otto's notions on the value and application of subskills (Otto, 1977). Thus, she does not adhere to a strict hierarchy of subskills but instead uses them to focus instruction, and she provides ample follow-up opportunities for students to integrate the subskills using realistic print situations.

Introducing computers into this context would appear to be easy and natural, as there are numerous computer programs available that use a reductionist approach, whether by design or serendipity (Rubin, 1983; Reinking, Kling, & Harper, in press). However, close examination of these programs presents Rebecca with her first problem because frequently exercises present print only at the letter or word level. Her attempts to use computer-based activities to help her students develop vocabulary and comprehension skills are frustrated by a lack of software in these areas. Moreover, she notices that most programs provide little or no opportunity for students to use the skills taught or to practice them in any meaningful way.

A second problem is encountered when Rebecca observes that computer programs often use methods of instruction or provide practice in a manner different from those typically used in regular classroom situations. For example, she uses an analytic approach in teaching decoding skills; however, when she examines one program, she discovers that its format follows a synthetic approach. Other programs, using computers equipped with voice synthesizers, also employ a synthetic approach to decoding, and although the technology is advanced, the use of such programs might confuse rather than enlighten her students. Thus, Rebecca must seek out programs that are congruent with her usual approach to instruction.

Because Rebecca uses a modified basal approach in teaching reading, it makes sense to use computer-assisted instruction that complements her particular series. Unfortunately, the company that publishes her basal series has not produced a matching computer courseware package, and she must therefore examine programs that claim to be compatible with any textbook approach. Such a claim is easy to make, but close examination of one package reveals several incongruencies between the computer-based lessons and her approach to reading instruction. Rebecca does stress decoding in her class, but with the emphasis placed on initial consonants and consonant clusters; in one computer package, many of the exercises focus on single vowels, vowel clusters, and vowels followed by *r* or *l*. Having these additional activities available may appear to be an advantage, but if

Rebecca does not use them she is purchasing software with a limited value. Although the program permits the selection of only those activities relevant to her approach, Rebecca discovers much of the computer-based program to be inconsistent with the emphasis in her teaching.

Rebecca is aware of the frequent complaint of critics that many computer-based reading activities resemble those found in existing basal workbooks, providing practice but little or no instruction (Balajthy, chapter 3 of this volume; Wheeler, 1983). With this caveat in mind, she examines a variety of programs, seeking those that offer useful instruction along with practice and opportunities for integrating the skills. Because she teaches second grade, Rebecca is especially concerned about the language used to instruct the learner. This facet of instruction is especially important in computer-based learning because the teacher may be unavailable to assist the student having difficulty. The computer, however, may offer unique advantages for assisting students during independent reading (Reinking, chapter 1 of this volume).

After previewing several computer-assisted instruction programs, Rebecca discovers two negative traits compounding her difficulties in finding useful software that provides both instruction and practice. First, what many publishers call instruction she thinks is only practice. For example, in one program students are required to select the main idea of a passage from among four choices. If the response is incorrect, the computer gives "immediate feedback" as to the correctness of the answer, requesting another choice or directing the student to similar but supposedly easier passages requiring the same skill. In Rebecca's mind, this does not qualify as instruction. In another instance, she discovers that the language of instruction is complex and difficult for the students to understand. She believes that anyone who can read and comprehend the instructions probably doesn't need the skill exercise itself. This problem is similar to the one raised by Osborn's (1984) evaluation of workbooks that accompany basal reading series.

Automatic record keeping is cited frequently as one of computer-assisted instruction's prime qualities, so Rebecca wants to select programs that allow her to monitor students' abilities and their progress toward learning goals. She finds no shortage of such programs. Because many software evaluation schemes consider record keeping an important factor, publishers frequently include a record-keeping component in their software. By creating graphs of each student's performance and using the printout capabilities of the computer program, she can make hard copies for permanent records as well as for parent/teacher conferences. However, upon close inspection of several programs having a record-keeping component, Rebecca discovers an important limitation. Performance is often measured in a gross manner; specific weaknesses are not recorded. Thus, in a word identification program, the only information available is that Kevin missed 8 out of 20 words. This information provides Rebecca little useful information to guide instruction.

Rebecca's Solution

So what happens to Rebecca's quest to use computers as a natural aspect of her language arts program? A pessimist might contend that the obstacles outweigh the virtues, and when pragmatic factors such as time and expense are included, perhaps Rebecca should be content with her conventional options for instruction. Rebecca, however, takes several positive steps to select and integrate into the classroom software that is compatible with her espoused theory. The key to her use of computers and selection of software is the decision to consider learning first and technology second (Miller & Burnett, 1986). There are many confounding factors in making computers an integral aspect of learning, but informed decisions can be made in this instance because Rebecca has analyzed her needs. When quality software, congruent with her theoretical stance, is available, Rebecca can make technology one component of instruction; when it does not meet her criteria, she can use other methods.

Rebecca need not be limited to software that focuses on the instruction and practice of skills. If she wishes to provide opportunities to integrate the use of various subskills, she may follow up instruction and practice with programs that focus on more integrative responses to text. Interestingly, these programs may be similar to those selected by teachers with a more holistic view of reading, although key differences may be found in how and why they are used.

In addition to making careful software selections, there are other teaching decisions facing Rebecca in her quest to use computers productively. For example, should students be encouraged to work in groups at computer stations? If the development of automaticity in decoding skills through computer-based practice is an objective, individuals must have time to use the computer privately. When comprehension skill development is the goal, she may decide that it is more productive for her students to complete an activity in small groups, capitalizing on the interaction of their thinking in joint problem solving and diminishing the impact of complex exercises or tutorials on less-able readers. Thus, there are practical considerations that interact with Rebecca's beliefs about how reading should be taught.

A WHOLE-LANGUAGE PERSPECTIVE

When one considers approaches to teaching the language arts, holistic and subskill orientations have frequently been viewed as opposite ends of a continuum. Although they represent two different beliefs about language processing and learning to read and write, Samuels (1980) contended that some common ground is shared. In addition, those who subscribe to either point of view have a variety of instructional options. Just as there are many variations of the subskill approach (cf. Distar's emphasis on a linear hierarchy of skills with Otto's notions of focused reading instruction), whole-language approaches also take different forms. Newman (1986), for example, has argued that whole language is not a method but rather a way of thinking about language and language learning. Instead of a set curriculum of objectives or prescribed teaching methods, she has argued that general principles of instruction guide the teacher who accepts a whole-language orientation.

Like teachers employing a subskill orientation, those who advocate a whole-language position also must answer difficult questions. Although some are theory related, others focus more on the realities of how schooling is conducted. How do process strategies differ from skills? How does one evaluate the reading and writing processes? What evidence is there that writing really fosters reading, and vice versa? Does the whole-language advocate believe in a curriculum? If so, what would compose that curriculum? What is the alternative to writing behavioral objectives? These are just a few of the general questions one can pose.

Narrowly constrained computer programs that focus on skills in isolation are unacceptable to teachers who believe in a whole-language approach because such teachers see language systems as interactive and supportive. For example, Langer (1982), operating from a whole-language or total communication orientation, criticized early software development and use in the language arts and contended that most programs violated her beliefs about both how language processes operate and how children learn. Edelsky (1984) pointed out that nearly all subskill-oriented programs are based on principles contradicted by current knowledge on language processing and language learning. Rubin and Bruce (1984) found that only about 10% of language arts software dealt with language at the sentence or text level, a statistic indicating a problem for teachers seeking software containing discourse.

Harste, Woodward, and Burke (1984) recently presented a rationale for a whole-language perspective and offered some instructional ramifications of this orientation. They argued that the heart of all language activities—reading, speaking, writing, listening—is meaning, and meaning is contextual. Thus, a whole-language classroom must provide opportunities for all language systems to be used interactively. Language learning is not a matter of concrete skill development in their view; instead, it is seen as the integration of complex language processes. And learning does not occur as a series of specific steps but rather as a series of successive approximations. The classroom conditions required to implement this perspective include ample opportunities for students to engage in functional and natural uses of written text. Reading and writing are thought of as tools instead of subjects to be studied.

Unlike Lesgold, who presented suggestions for translating his theoretical notions into practice, Harste, Woodward, and Burke (1984) did not address the issue of how computers fit into their perspective. However, other writers, working from a similar perspective, have described how computers may contribute in fostering the language arts (Collins, 1983; Liebling, 1984; Rubin & Bruce, 1984). Word processing, writing coaches, message systems, simulations, data bases, and interactive texts are applications consistent with a whole-language orientation. However, computer software based on whole-language principles may also present hidden problems and paradoxes. Some of these issues are highlighted below.

Gayle's Quandary

Consider another teacher, Gayle, whose language arts instruction is based on a whole-language perspective. Gayle teaches in a self-contained fourth-grade classroom. Like Rebecca, she wishes to use computers in a manner consistent with her espoused theory of language learning, and she wants to integrate computers into her teaching. On one hand, her decisions are easier than Rebecca's because many of the available subskill-oriented drill and practice programs can be rejected easily. These programs are obviously inconsistent with her notions concerning literacy development and learning. Unfortunately, eliminating this pool of software restricts considerably the software she can select. Further, by automatically rejecting all subskill-oriented programs, Gayle may miss creative opportunities to adapt software to her purposes.

Some of the programs Gayle examines seem to fit her perspective. For example, a recent computer program purporting to teach reading through children's writing appears to take advantage of the connection between reading and writing (Tierney & Leys, 1984). However, close examination of the program reveals one of the major problems facing the teacher who sees language holistically: partial theoretical congruency. While the program fosters writing by encouraging the use of invented spelling and permitting students choice in selecting topics, it also includes numerous phonic drills where phoneme/grapheme relationships are presented in isolation. Gayle's quandry is whether or not to use a program only partially congruent with her beliefs about teaching the language arts.

Another promising writing program allows children to create pictures prior to composing a story. She is aware of the research that suggests pictures aid in the composing process (Graves, 1981). Unfortunately, close examination of the program discloses two important flaws that conflict with Gayle's notions about fostering the writing process. First, pictures can be created only from a finite set of previously stored figures (trees, animals, people, vehicles, houses, etc.), and there is thus less of a feeling of ownership of the text. A second problem is the program's inability to print out the story and pictures. Stories can be stored but not printed, which denies authors the opportunity to publish their stories. Again, an important aspect of the composing process, one normally present in Gayle's classroom, is missing.

While the programs described in the previous paragraphs do not satisfy Gayle, some computer-assisted writing software does match her needs. This software allows students to select most of their own topics, progress through various stages of the writing process, use invented spelling in initial drafts, and publish their final drafts. For example, one program guides students through a series of questions designed to stimulate prewriting, while another assists writers in revision. Here, Gayle runs into a problem similar to the one encountered by Rebecca—directions and explanations often are too difficult for her students to read independently. Some of her less-able readers may not be able to profit from the questions and tutorials found in current computer-guided writing programs. Many of the available programs seem to be designed for high school and university students. Despite this limitation she does find some programs designed specifically for elementary-level children (Tchudi, 1983).

Shell programs—those facilitating the entry of original work into the computer—offer promise to Gayle because they allow children the possibility of creation as well as ownership; moreover, some instructional packages permit students to use the concept or strategy being taught in a personal, meaningful way. Gayle believes that the consummate shell program is one that permits word processing (Daiute, 1983; Schwartz, 1985). And she is aware of new programs that combine prewriting outlines with word processing. Gayle shares the enthusiasm of many of her peers concerning the potential of word processing applications in reading and writing instruction (Bradley, 1982; Miller, 1985). The features available in word-processing packages should allow her to continue the positive aspects of her normal writing approach while taking advantage of the special features offered by the computer. However, Gayle discovers that she must choose carefully because many word-processing programs designed for elementary students restrict the revision and editing options available (Newman, 1984).

Gayle is also interested in interactive texts, a label that has been used to describe two different applications of the computer to language arts. In one instance, interactive text is a narrative that enables the student to manipulate the events of a story. This type of interactive text may develop awareness of the choices authors make in writing stories and may also foster the development of story schema. Moreover, this kind of interactive text can provide an opportunity for multiple readings with a meaning emphasis, a technique consistent with a whole-language perspective. Notwithstanding the apparent promise of interactive narratives, Gayle discovers she agrees with Dillon's (1985) criticism of computer software that presents stories: Many stories in existing programs have little literary merit.

The second instance of interactive text also intrigues Gayle because it is congruent with her beliefs that reading and writing should be an integral part of content area instruction (Moffett & Wagner, 1976). One program presents expository text accompanied by an automated table of contents, presentation of key words in context, electronic index, and a concept mastery test. If certain concepts are not understood, the reader may request that they be presented in alternative ways, which may include a graphic representation of the content (see Reinking, chapter 1 of this volume). Although she saw this type of program demonstrated by a researcher at a conference, Gayle has discovered that this type of software is not yet widely available commercially.

The use of simulation programs makes sense to Gayle because they take advantage of unique computer capabilities and blend naturally with her ideas about using content as a normal part of language arts instruction. A simulation of Halley's Comet fits well into her current science teaching, while another simulation requiring children to run a store is useful for teaching mathematics, and Gayle finds in this instance that the computer is a reliable tool for integrating language arts into the teaching of content. Some simulations, however, unnecessarily limit her students' creativity by forcing them to answer low-level questions. Gayle also discovers that some simulations have game formats that are fun for students but can distract them from the purposes of the simulation. For example, one program takes students on a simulated trip across America in pioneer times, and this matches a topic discussed in her social studies class; unfortunately, some of her students are distracted by a "hunt" option in the program, spending most of their time shooting at a deer running across the screen.

Gayle's Solution

Despite the limited amount of software congruent with her perspective, Gayle does find ways for the computer to contribute to language instruction. She decides that a data base is useful because it can be manipulated to serve the subject under study. It fosters the learning of classification and retrieval strategies, and it allows students to enter personal information (Bell, 1985). For example, in a mathematics activity, children might use data about their tastes in clothes, food, music, and so forth to learn about graphing, ratios, and percentages. At the same time they can communicate their results in writing.

She also decides to use several other shell programs that prove useful. Word processing becomes an integral tool in her composition program. She finds that children have a propensity to write longer stories using word processors, and these become useful vehicles for teaching revision and editing skills (Daiute, 1983). A shell program that allows her students to create a newspaper provides the impetus for her students to begin publishing their own newspaper. In each instance the computer program complements and facilitates activities normally seen in Gayle's classroom.

Other programs present opportunities for computer use as well. Although interactive stories may not be great literature, the decisions required to construct a story allow her students to engage in repeated readings for meaning. Other programs match the reading strategies she is attempting to foster by encouraging prediction and confirmation. Notwithstanding their weaknesses, some simulations add variety and active involvement to her teaching units. Finally, computer-guided writing programs, despite some drawbacks, provide many of the supports normally given students in a conference with a teacher.

CONCLUSIONS

We have illustrated some of the issues facing teachers in their quest to move technology into the classroom. The paradoxes and problems are sometimes frustrating, but many successful teachers seem to be able to navigate their way through these difficulties. Given an awareness of the issues, teachers can make informed choices concerning technology and how it can be applied to language arts instruction. Teachers will benefit from an examination of their beliefs about language arts instruction. As Schön (1983) contended, they need to become reflective practitioners. Clearly, this type of thinking will lead to different perspectives as the two examples in this chapter have shown, and thus use of technology will vary, but, as Olson (1984) argued, whether the computer becomes a Trojan Horse or a teacher's pet is dependent not on technology alone but on teachers' perception of technology as an integral component of teaching and learning. In one of the early books on the use of computer technology in education, Ellis (1974) commented, "thinking about the computer's role in education does not mean thinking about computers, it means thinking about education."

REFERENCES

Balajthy, E. (1986). *Microcomputers in reading and the language arts*. Englewood Cliffs, NJ: Prentice Hall.

Bell, S. (1985). Data bases in the primary school. *Classroom Computing, 5*, 9–12.

Bradley, V. N. (1982). Improving students' writing with microcomputers. *Language Arts, 59*, 732–743.

Collins, A. (1983). *Learning to read and write with personal computers* (Reading Education Report No. 42). Champaign, IL: The Center for the Study of Reading.

Daiute, C. (1984). *Computers and writing*. Reading, MA: Addison-Wesley.

Dillon, D. (1985). Who's in charge here? In D. Chandler & S. Marcus (Eds.), *Computers and literacy* (pp. 86–107). Milton Keynes, England: Open University Press.

Edelsky, C. (1984). The content of language arts software: A criticism. *Computers, Reading, and Language Arts, 1*(4), 8–11.

Ellis, A. B. (1974). *The use and misuse of computers in education*. New York: McGraw-Hill.

Grabe, M. (1986). Drill and practice's bad rap. *Electronic Learning, 5*, 22–23.

Graves, D. (1981). *A case study observing the development of primary chil-*

dren's composing, spelling, and motor behaviors during the writing process (NIE Grant No. G-78-0174). Washington, DC: National Institute of Education.

Harste, J., Woodward, V., & Burke, C. (1984). *Language stories and literacy lessons.* Portsmouth, NH: Heinemann.

LaBerge, D., & Samuels, S. J. (1974). Toward a theory of automatic information processing in reading. *Cognitive Psychology, 8,* 292–323.

Langer, J. (1982). *Computer technology and reading instruction: Perspectives and directions.* (ERIC Document Reproduction Service No. ED 214 131)

Lesgold, A. (1983). A rationale for computer-based reading instruction. In A. C. Wilkinson (Ed.), *Classroom computers and cognitive science* (pp. 167–181). New York: Academic Press.

Lesgold, A., & Perfetti, C. (1978). Interactive processes in reading comprehension. *Discourse Processes, 1,* 323–336.

Liebling, C. (1984). *Creating the classroom's communicative context: How parents, teachers, and microcomputers can help* (Reading Education Rep. No. 47). Champaign, IL: The Center for the Study of Reading.

Marsh, M. (1985-1986). The great computer drill and practice put-down. *The Computing Teacher, 13,* 4–5.

Miller, L. (1985). Computers and writing: A theoretical perspective. *The McGill Journal of Education, 20,* 19–28.

Miller, L., & Burnett, J. D. (1986). Theoretical considerations in selecting language arts software. *Computers and Education, 10,* 159–165.

Moffett, J., & Wagner, B. J. (1976). *Student-centered language arts and reading, K-13: A handbook for teachers* (2nd ed.). Boston: Houghton Mifflin.

Newman, J. (1986). *Whole language: Theory and practice.* Portsmouth, NH: Heinemann.

Newman, J. (1984, May). *What are we trying to teach?* Paper presented at the colloquium for Canadian Research in Reading and Language Arts, Lethbridge, Alberta.

Ohanian, S. (1984). Watch out! Some reading software can destroy kids' desire to read. *Classroom Computer Learning, 4,* 27–31.

Olson, J. K. (1984, June). Microcomputers in the classroom: Trojan horse or teacher's pet? Paper presented at the annual meeting of the Canadian Society for the Study of Education, Guelph, Ontario.

Osborn, J. (1984). The purposes, uses, and contents of workbooks and some guidelines for publishers. In R. C. Anderson, J. Osborn, & R. J. Tierney (Eds.), *Learning to read in American schools* (pp. 45–112). Hillsdale, NJ: Lawrence Erlbaum.

Otto, W. (1977). Design for developing comprehension skills. In J. Guthrie (Ed.), *Cognition, curriculum, and comprehension* (pp. 193–232). Newark, NJ: International Reading Association.

Papert, S. (1980). *Mindstorms: Children, computers, and powerful ideas.* New York: Basic Books.

Pearson, P. D. (Ed.). (1984). *Handbook of reading research.* New York: Longman.

Perfetti, C., & Lesgold, A. (1979). Coding and comprehension in skilled reading. In L. Resnick & P. Weaver (Eds.), *Theory and practice in early reading*. Hillsdale, NJ: Lawrence Erlbaum.

Reinking, D., Kling, M., & Harper, M. (in press). Characteristics of computer software in reading: An empirical investigation. *Computers, Reading, & Language Arts*.

Roblyer, M. D. (1982). Courseware: A critical look at "making best use of the medium." *Educational Technology, 22*, 29–30.

Rubin, A. (1983). The computer confronts language arts: Cans and shoulds for education. In A. C. Wilkinson (Ed.), *Classroom computers and cognitive science* (pp. 201–217). New York: Academic Press.

Rubin, A., & Bruce, B. (1984). *Quill: Reading and writing with a microcomputer* (Reading Education Rep. No. 48). Champaign, IL: The Center for the Study of Reading.

Samuels, S. J. (1980). The age-old controversy between holistic and subskill approaches to beginning reading instruction revisited. In C. M. McCullough (Ed.), *Inchworm, inchworm: Persistent problems in reading education* (pp. 202–221). Newark, DE: International Reading Association.

Schön, D. A. (1983). *The reflective practitioner*. New York: Basic Books.

Schwartz, H. J. (1985). *Interactive writing*. New York: Holt, Rinehart & Winston.

Sloan, D. (Ed.). (1984). *The computer in education: A critical perspective*. New York: Teachers College Press.

Spache, G. D., & Spache, E. B. (1986). *Reading in the elementary school*. Boston: Allyn & Bacon.

Tchudi, S. (1983). The write idea: Computer assisted invention. *Focus, 9*, 10–16.

Tierney, R., & Leys, M. (1984). *What is the value of connecting reading and writing* (Reading Education Rep. No. 55). Champaign, IL: The Center for the Study of Reading.

Wheeler, F. (1983). The puzzler: An answer to the reading riddle? *Classroom Computer Learning, 3*, 46–51.

About the Contributors

DONNA E. ALVERMANN holds a joint appointment as an associate professor of Reading Education and a fellow in the Institute for Behavioral Research at the University of Georgia. Alvermann conducts research into the effects of varying instructional approaches on comprehension. She has written three interactive video programs and is presently one of five authors for a basal reading program to be published by D. C. Heath.

ERNEST BALAJTHY is an assistant professor of Education at the State University of New York at Geneseo. He has published numerous articles about computers and reading and has also written a text entitled *Microcomputers in Reading and Language Arts*.

DALE BURNETT is an associate professor in the Faculty of Education at The University of Lethbridge in Lethbridge, Alberta. His primary responsibility is in the area of instructional uses of computer technology. Other interests include cognitive approaches to thinking and problem solving, mathematics education, and research methodology.

DAN B. DANIEL is the director of technology with the Houston Independent School District, Houston, Texas. He is coauthor of a widely used reference text on computers and reading. His professional activities have included investigating the effects of reading text on a computer screen, serving as a consultant to international agencies, and supervising the development of courseware.

DENNIS M. DAVIS, a specialist in computer-based education, is a member of the PLATO Education Group of the Computer-based Education Research Laboratory, University of Illinois at Urbana-Champaign. He is also a consultant for firms designing computer-based instructional materials and has written a number of computer books and lessons.

LAWRENCE T. FRASE has published approximately 70 papers on human learning, reasoning, instruction, writing, text design, and computer applications. His current work is on psychological processes in software development. In addition to being a member of ACM and IEEE, he is also a Fellow of APA and a recipient of the AT&T Bell Laboratories Distinguished Technical Staff Award for outstanding accomplishments.

MICHAEL L. KAMIL is an associate professor of Education at the University of Illinois at Chicago. He received his Ph.D. in experimental psychology from the University of Wisconsin—Madison. His research interests are in the application of computer technology to instruction, theories and models of the reading process, and teacher decision-making behavior.

GEORGE W. MCCONKIE received his Ph.D. in experimental psychology from Stanford University in 1966. He was on the faculty at Cornell University until 1978, and is currently a professor of Educational Psychology at the University of Illinois at Urbana-Champaign, and senior researcher at the Center for the Study of Reading.

LARRY MILLER is an associate professor at the Faculty of Education, Queen's University, Kingston, Ontario. His current interests include studying children who read and write prior to school entrance, translating reading theory to practice, and investigating how teachers use computers in schools.

RICHARD K. OLSON is professor of Psychology at the University of Colorado, Boulder, Colorado. Dr. Olson received his Ph.D. in psychology from the University of Oregon in 1970. He is co-investigator and project coordinator for a program project titled Differential Diagnosis in Reading Disability that is funded by NICHD. Dr. Olson is principal investigator on another NICHD project titled Computer-Speech Feedback in Text for Dyslexic Children.

RUTH POLIN was a researcher in reading with the Institute for Research on Teaching at Michigan State University and is currently engaged in research and evaluation in teacher education.

DAVID REINKING received his Ph.D. from the University of Minnesota. After serving on the faculty of Rutgers University, he moved to the University of Georgia, where he is currently an assistant professor of

Reading and associate director of the Reading/Language Arts Computer Resource Center. His experiences with computers and reading include conducting research on computer-mediated text and developing instructional software.

MARTIN A. SIEGEL, a University of Illinois professor of Educational Psychology, is an international lecturer and consultant in the instructional design of computer-based educational courseware. He is assistant director of the Computer-based Education Research Laboratory, University of Illinois at Urbana-Champaign, and has written numerous computer-based lessons for the PLATO system.

JOHN F. VINSONHALER received his Ph.D. at the University of California, Berkeley. A professor at the College of Education at Michigan State University, he has directed research and published on computers in education, computers in medicine, computers in reading, computer education, expert systems, and cognition.

CHRISTIAN WAGNER received his Ph.D. from Michigan State University. Currently an assistant professor in the School of Engineering and Computer Science at Oakland University, he has researched and published articles in the area of computer science, computer education, robotics, expert systems, and artificial intelligence.

ANNETTE B. WEINSHANK began her career as a classroom teacher. She went on to receive a Ph.D. in educational psychology from Michigan State University. She has published articles in the areas of evaluation, accountability, and diagnostic and remedial reliability in reading.

BARBARA WISE has master's degrees in Special Education (with emphases in reading and in learning disabilities) and in Developmental Psychology. She has taught children with learning and reading problems for seven years and is currently completing a Ph.D. in Developmental Psychology at the University of Colorado.

DAVID ZOLA received his Ph.D. in educational psychology from Cornell University in 1982. He is currently an assistant professor of Educational Psychology at the University of Illinois at Urbana-Champaign, and a senior researcher at the Center for the Study of Reading.

Index